SUSTAIN//DECAY

A PHILOSOPHICAL INVESTIGATION OF
DRONE MUSIC AND MYSTICISM

OWEN COGGINS//JAMES HARRIS

EDITORS

CONTENTS

INTRODUCTION : A CIRCULAR SCAFFOLD

Owen Coggins//James Harris

//Sssssssssssssssssssssssssssssssssssssss.........
            Mmmmmmmmmmmmmmmmmmm.........
                        Ngngngngngngngngngngngngngn.........   //

Charlie Blake, Dronoclasm //

//I draw circles and sacred boundaries about me; fewer and fewer climb
    with me up higher and higher mountains—I am building a mountain
    chain out of ever-holier mountains //

Friedrich Nietzsche, Thus Spoke Zarathustra //

//And what defines the scale of the ultimate symbolic mountain is its inac-
    cessibility to ordinary human approaches. [...] The door to the invisible
    must be visible //

René Daumal, Mount Analogue //

//Before time… before even the gods… there was only…//

Bong, "The Dreams of Mana-Yood-Sushai" //

...Drone is the beginning and was before the beginning // Drone was the Nothing // Nothing Droned // The droning of Nothing was the Nothing from which Drone is self-created...

...Om // the first sound, the cause of the universe, itself a drone // an empty signifier swells to overfull // evolves, fragments, ramifies into a constellation of meaning the way a solid droning tone may begin to wobble, vibrate, oscillate // mutating, expanding, infecting // spreading, branching, self-intersecting, self-interweaving, self-absorbing, self-annihilating, becoming different through manifesting the same // "The empty set is the set with nothing in it. The number 1 is the set with only the empty set in it. And so on…"

...the End of Drone, already contained within the drone, is the End of Everything // Drone is the End which outlasts itself...

...from near-silent single tone pure ambient minimalism to crushing oceanic hyper-amplified metallic maximalism // from trance-like repetition of sameness to explicit experimentation with the radical question of what it can mean for a sound to be different from or the same as another sound // drone rotates or fades or spirals away from linear historical/genealogical genre conventions toward a meta-foundational sonic arsenal // drone is capable of infecting all genres as it is itself composed of ontologically primary techniques for sound generation and modulation, realized in extreme extension toward outer- or inner-most depths, boundaries, limits, frontiers, horizons // different variants of drone select different techniques to maximalize or minimalise, whether hijacking and mutating source material or inaugurating original tonal topologies // all genres (all life, all differentiation) can be imagined as mere clusters of patterns of iterations of momentary deviations from the drone...

...elements, both sonic and metaphorical, of drone exist in natural and artificial worlds, in geometries of plant and water, architecture, even space, underground, mind // the Universe breathes - the physical expands and contracts // the Socius hums incessantly in communal conversation // the ceaseless oscillatory dynamics of the Brain silently howl...

//For we know that all creation keeps on groaning together //

St. Paul, Romans 8:18-22 //

...this book is a call to approach composition and attentive listening as ritual practice // to approach drone music as a training ground for the attention, for *cognitive endurance*, for a *weird absorption* from which hidden transformations might flower // to approach the melodic and rhythmic movement toward and away from central harmonic figures, the manipulation of the "tension between background and foreground" as ritually patterned upon the mystics' tuning of the tension between subject and object, between inner and outer worlds // listening to the spark of impenetrable darkness, in contemplation of the shadow paradoxes of language, mysticism and death...

...the spectral spectacle of drone's all-devouring taste mirrors the range of this book // intensive studies of emptiness, inaccessibility, and eternity // death, death of god, death of death // forest, mountain // infection, parasite, swarm: disparate mind in shattered multiplicity // sine waves between ascetic austerity and wild excess, at either pole confessing the violence of the sacrifice, of the sacred // insane or becalmed transformations of perception, infinitesimal time-slices and isoluminant eidolons // all contained within the elastic-walled labyrinth of this new spacetime, our non-terminating Cymatic Church...

...drone casts paradoxes into perception // sounds heard as light, metaphorical and alchemical, offer the transmutative properties of mystical shimmer //Wolfe// in 'resonance subordinated to redundancy' //Freeman// spatial sense is transformed, illusioned, bewitched, the drone 'echoing off an invisible realm' //Wolfe// drone foregrounds the difference and connection between sound and hearing //Kang// 'the possibility of stasis and the sprawling occupation of its power' //Drone Box// levitation //Attila// 'It escapes itself in a perspectival "experience" of time not tethered to the specific form of the human subject, to be integrated into an exceeding and not-necessarily human - an alien or machinic-transcendent subjectivity' //Caron// drone is excess and/or asceticism //MOUTH// honey and tar // Strickland/////

...drone invokes antinomies and contortions in language too, which, 'alienated, orbits around a central absence' //Coggins// words dancing in rituals of forgotten purpose around the chalk circle which it is not forbidden but rather impossible to enter // in the language spat from drone's black centrifuge, there is again and again repetition and repetition and yet transcendence of sameness // the intuition of the death of intuition //Shakespeare// the absolute emptiness of emptiness //Absentology// drone is ambient, atmosphere, a hum behind the world, but it is also metal... that pagan resonant interval //Drone Box// riffs beyond riffs, metal about metal, a meditative treatment of heavy metal's symbolic codes so radical it may not be recognised as such //Coggins// this Möbius strip, this snake which eats itself yet is still nourished, yet is still consumed, this convulsion, infects and is infected, is the infection // is the ashy pest // 'is legion, yet imperceptible, neither faith nor reason can fathom their presence or the principles that pertain to them except through their manifestation in distress, agony and death throes' // MOUTH/////

...drone is death and drone is immortality, which is death // endless life is 'an increasingly pestilential drone', a background before which our deaths become relief //Shipley// it all starts with the signal path //Newstead// we 'send a signal and let it die' //Hissen// the signal, channel, noise all at once introducing 'a silent mode of communication that is directed towards nothing other, the No-Other, which is death' // Absentology// silent but communicative, towards death yet from death, expression through mortal silence // the gift of the skull of a fox //Legard// 'Everything that is dead quivers' //Cascone// 'not rhythm at all but merely a near endless ripple of vibration stretched across expanses of time...' // Norman/////

...drone ruins // is found in ruins // decays, sustains // witnesses decay // drone is 'eternity's future burden' //Shipley// that term, burden, bourdon, an archaic term for drone, the memory of the word ruined by time // monoliths, pyramids, stone circles, temples //Attila// 'the subject sinks into the labyrinth of the ear...' //Freeman/////

...drone is the life which grows through the ruins, testifies to ruin, is agent of ruin // creeper // root // undergrowth, overgrown // to the palace of birds, to a shallow garden // Legard// a 'monstrous aspect' of Nature 'seeks to annihilate everything individual' //Shakespeare// a 'whole forest is heard in each sound...' //Cascone/////

...drone is the absolute // it is 'the infinitely dense form of silence, the recollection without object' //Absentology// the sound of 'a god pulling gravity's strings...' //Norman/////

...drone is finally a portal //*Cascone*// a mountain, liquefied // the listener 'must conceptually climb untold numbers of unholy mountains to see the surface again' //*Harris*// the pieces included here departing from each other and returning, requiring a re-reading of an earlier segment, a tumbler falls into place, the lockpicking continues, repeat ad infinitum, ad nauseam // an incessant, droning, re-volving system of holy mountains // each climb faltering, failing, exhausting, "coming up against an insuperable object", rotating into a new mountain with its own failures // each failure driving a new mountain range, each new range innovating its own apparatus for climbing from out of the experience or the text, for *climbing out of experience or out of text*, for *climbing out of climbing itself* // written in the textual body of the climber, the history or memory or output of the climber, each climb demands tools from the other climbs, each apparatus applied to old mountains makes new challenges makes new failures, growth comes to be measured in cycles of failure, "progress" measured only by the uninitiated // for Wittgenstein, language was a ladder to be climbed up, and then discarded // for Daumal, the base of the mountain must be accessible while the summit inaccessible (as outlined in a book which stops, mid-sentence, unfinished at his death) // this book too, then, is one to be climbed out of // drone sound at the end of sound // 'record needle gently click-flapping' //*Norman*// 'Listen to all at once if possible. Join' //*His-sen*/////

//For what is God but the index that pointed to the failure of all signs?//

Michel de Certeau, The Mystic Fable //

//For what is drone but the unending echo of generational potential?//

Aliza Shvarts, "Troubled Air" //

In addition to the text and art presented herein, we have gathered a small archive of links, audio, video, art, inter-views, and words from friends, contributors, collaborators, and co-conspirators at voidfrontpress.org. Contributor Kim Cascone has also curated a compilation entitled 'Transcendigitalism.' A track listing and credits appear at the end of his essay.

OC/JH

Void Front Press

DRONOCLASM
OR THE SWARMING OF ANGELS IN LIMITLESS NIGHT

Notes towards a series of inhuman meditations on the emergent sub-disciplinary fields of Necrophonics, Xenosonics[1], Melismatics and Pleromatics, as well as the ancient arts of Kleptomancy, Nyxosophy, and Seidre, as these fields pertain, both collectively and in isolation from one another, to the question of the drone.

Charlie Blake

[A FRAGMENT]

The laws of physics are like music notation—things that are real and important provided that we do not take them too seriously.[2]

The drone (bourdon) effect refers to the presence of a constant layer of stable pitch in a sound ensemble with no noticeable variation in intensity. Linked to music in its designation … the drone effect can also be observed in urban and industrial soundscapes.[3]

Start with a sound made up of many particles, then see how you can make it change imperceptibly, growing and developing, until an entirely new sound results.[4]

… to go down to the cellar is to dream it is losing oneself in the distant corridors of an obscure etymology, looking for treasures that cannot be found in words. (Bachelard 343)[5]

The following fragment was discovered under full moonlight and between six parallel mirrors as per instructions in the ruins of the central square of La Defense in Paris in the summer of 2052. It had been partially ravaged by a combination of acid rain and granular decay, and showed signs of the beginnings of gross syntactical deterioration—a side-effect, no doubt, of the Dreamcancer[6] which had become increasingly virulent in that area in the previous two months. It has since been reconstructed as carefully as possible by your field agent and is hereby presented along with this typescript to the curator of the Charles Kinbote Fellowship collection at the Museum of Lost Objects, Miskatonic University, Arkham, Rhode Island, USA. Whether or not this text is an 'enchantment' has yet to be determined, but until such time as this has been clarified, readers are advised to avoid reading any of this text aloud or in the presence of parallel mirrors, direct moonlight, phenomenophagic agents or—and especially—phonoegregores.[7] In addition, be aware that

10

any attempt at a melismatic recovery of the text in live space will immediately alert the Central Committee as to its existence and whereabouts.

LS ¥ 09. XI. 2052

prologue

Kleptomancy—divination by theft, whether from oneself or another. Self-quotation to the point of infinite regress, either through pure spatial or linear repetition or temporal transection of that repetition. A divinatory fugue said to be induced by standing between two or more parallel mirrors illuminated from above by an all too pellucid moon. A symptom of certain forms of chronic neologophilia in cases of transmodal anxiety syndrome. Sometimes a synonym for a déjà vu within a déjà vu (archaic).[8]

part one—necrophonics

How does sense emerge from its opposite? And is there a sound that extends beyond death? Or rather (and to qualify my second question before my first), is there a sound that reaches back into life from death? Is there a sound that can be said to emerge swiftly and then draw back sharply into the deep granular abyss of that oh so intimate darkness—a murmuring, humming melismaticum, perhaps, a sonic shapeshifting organ of sense or a *vagrant* phonoegregore that darts synaesthetically back and forth through the twisted, anachronic veil—first like a vaporous net or spectral reticulum—next like a pure absence of form, (albeit and paradoxically both firm and penetrating and soft and envaginating)—and then finally, as a viscous serpentilian or slippery reptilian tongue, retracting with our vital and sonorous attention curled tightly into its forked embrace? Picture this event sonically as well as haptically and visually for a moment. Picture this event as an erotic confusion, a metaphysical tangle, all mixed together and then all mixed up in various arbitrary scales, epiphanies, and velocities of presentation and apprehension, shimmering and spinning elliptically in the *chora*. Picture this synaesthetically and cryptoaesthetically in your mind's eye as something distinctly serpentine, or neo-Platonic even, or even as a form of *vagrant* materialism. Then remind yourself that this process is to be understood in the first instance as a spiritual exercise in the manner of my one time colleague and once trusted friend Ignatius Loyola and his followers, but in this case an exercise for audiovagrants and cybervores in which the friction between diverse concepts, arguments, affects, flows and percepts in imaginal space—objects and events and images unexpectedly encountered at various speeds and accelerations and from various directions in irregular and non-linear patterns and then clashed together, generates an array of sounds that reverberate and resonate in stages into some kind of universal pattern, and thus and thereby into some hidden and yet over-arching consonance or dissonance or cloud of consonances or dissonances. Imagine this, perhaps as a diagram or map of three roads meeting at a crossing, distinct and yet entangled at an opening or clearing, (Heidegger's *lichtung*, the murderer's glance, the glint of a knife in a velvet glove, a single pink rose, the missing heart of a travelling funfair).

Remind yourself, however, that this is a process that might seem to begin with a kind of hylomorphic resonance, superficially or even trivially (in the sense of three roads meeting at a crossroads or a clearing) reminiscent of the reassuring star-demon magic of the

Renaissance magus Marsilio Ficino, but which tends in due course towards the creation, rather, of the chaosomorphic conditions of spatial resonance and temporal reverberation required to enable the substantiation, manifestation and enunciation of the Dronoclasm.

Reverberation—A propagation effect in which a sound continues after the cessation of its emission. Reflections of the sound on surfaces in the surrounding space are added to the direct signal. The longer these reflections conserve their energy, the greater the reverberation time. In everyday language, reverberation is often referred to as the "cathedral" effect, or by extension, as echo. (111)[9]

> (Flakes of music falling now like
>
> snow onto the vitrified earth,
>
> settling on the withered branches,
>
> scattering across the glassy waters,
>
> forming membranes—extending …

> Ssssssssssssssssssssssssssssssssssss………
>
> Mmmmmmmmmmmmmmmmmm………
>
> Ngngngngngngngngngngngngngn………)

Now, imagine this sonic spectralism as an image or a scent or a taste or a sensation of speed or acceleration, or indeed as a Luciferean sleight if you so wish, or even if you don't, or as a triangulation of where I am now as I speak to you now, a locational picture, that is, as I write to you now. For you now. In this moment. At this moment. Now. As you listen in the limitless night, as you watch the angels as they swarm and swoop. As you send your hungry tendrils out into this intimate darkness. Sensing this palpable darkness in this room here below ground. Below you. Where you are. Here with me now. Below zero. Absolute zero. Deep below ground. In the icy oblivion. Imagine this as a story unfolding in scalar leaps, a story that will become a sound and then a profound and resonating repetition of many near identical sounds enveloping our world, our universe or even the metaverse itself. Phenomenophagism. A hum, A drone. A murmur. A melisma. Imagine that. And then imagine the same in terms of noise and feedback and the intimate circuitries of response and repetition. For this is raw and revisionist cybernetics as hierophantic spectacle, entropic thermodynamics as a mode and a modality of the informatrix, as conatus redux and reversed, synaesthetic code and hieroglyphic density, revealing in its intensity, in its base materialism, in its seemingly nebulous lines of flight, in its hyper-pixelated flurries of colour, line, perspective, movement, depth, text, voice, sonics, haptics and olfaction, revealing.…

Revealing the elements of the drone itself as a cloud effect of resonance.

Note in everyday language the term "resonance" includes any acoustically observable sonic effect, particularly reverberation. Resonance is a general physical phenomenon found in all periodic sinusoidal movements, particularly in mechanics, acoustics, optics, and electricity. The identity of the role of certain elements make it possible to perform studies by analogy, referring to a general system that includes the actual case of resonance at the sonic level.[10]

In its most overt form at this stage it is, however, the lizard and the bell and the darkness first of all. A curious melange—a chimera even, perhaps, a congeries of forms confusing sense and conceptual taxonomy, undulating beneath sense, even, to feed on intuition, to feed on affect. Phenomenophagism against the grain. A figure echoed in silver tracery and thus and thereby traced and beaten into the soft metal alloy of its own containment, woven into the fabric of its own demise. An invagination of form in a kind of sonic froth, at least in one sense of invagination. Yes. Though perhaps this is not it at all. Or at least not most of it anyway. For we must return to the sonic and the necrophonics to give this sense and dimension in the phenomenal world so that it may be consumed.

Perhaps in that case it might be a sound more like the reverberations of a deeper and more resonant casing, a bell of metallic and parabolic design, perhaps, or even of a pure and crystalline tone isolated from its form entirely—a sonic spectrality—barely substantiating as yet from its pleromatic origins—barely present in our phenomenal universe at all—xenosonically emanating through inverse vibration from the great outdoors that half-anti-correlationist Quentin Meillassoux once dreamed of and merely ghosted as yet here and now, now and here, traced on the aether, scratched and scraped across quantum vacuoles, that is, or subatomic particles, and then necrophonically absorbed, like the bell that the theosophists would one day fabricate under the careful scrutiny of great Russian witch Madame Blavatsky in one of those hot Indian Victorian summers, so as to signal the irruption of an apport into our gross, mechanical realm, so as to herald a shower of rose petals appearing from thin air and scattering over perfumed hair and powdered flesh and patterned silk and that polished mahogany table we would sit at and the fans and sherry glasses of our formerly garrulous now mouths-agaping guests—tada!— and thus and thereby astonishing the credulous and irritating the sceptical in more or less equal measure. The bell and the lizard. Or perhaps it was the dragon

and the bell and the darkness. It hardly bears thinking about now. But I will because I must. For it is here in this akashic cellar, now exiled and abandoned, that I must recall these exoteric and esoteric factors and variables so that I can begin now the composition of my greatest work, of our greatest work:

the Dronoclasm.

Zeno closed the connection for a moment. The screen flickered and settled to the monochrome white noise ambience of an old analogue television caught between channels. He listened to the buzzing in the sky. It grew in amplitude for a minute or two and then declined to a distant, collective hum. He heard a long sigh and looked round to see Mêtis regarding him coolly from their bed by the bookcase. Long obsidian hair streaked, sapphire, silver and scarlet, ebony skin, piercing sapphire eyes too, their pupils narrowed to panther slits in the strong sunlight. She raised a single eyebrow and pursed her lips, the hint of a smile. He smiled back, turned back. Reopened the channel. Resumed. He could see only vague and shifting shapes across time moving in front of the ruined hall's jagged teeth.[11]

[end of fragment]

NOTES

1. On the sonic spectralism of the sub-disciplinary fields of xenosonics and necrophonics, see my 'Sonic Spectralities: Sketches towards a Prolegomena to any Future Xenosonics' in AUDINT (Toby Heys, Steve Goodman, Eleni Ikonaidou) (eds) *Unsound/Undead* (Minneapolis: Univocal, forthcoming, 2017).

2. Norbert Weiner, cited in Curtis Roads, *Microsound* (Cambridge, Mass: MIT Press, 2001) 64.

3. Jean-Francois Augoyard and Henry Torgue, *Sonic Experience: A Guide to Everyday Sounds* (Montreal and Ithica: McGill-Queens UP, 2008) 40.

4. Iannis Xenakis , cited by Curtis Roads, *Microsound*,64.

5. Gaston Bachelard, cited by Brandon LaBelle in his *Background Noise: Perspectives on Sound Art* (London: Bloomsbury, 2015) 343.

6. On the so-called "Dreamcancer" of 2047-2049 and its implications for the initially rapid and then more gradual deterioration of conventional syntax, orthographics, the consistency of scholarly referencing and quotation and the erstwhile stability of diacritical marks amongst editors, as well as for its role as a precursor for cosmically scaled phenomenophagism, see Charlie Blake, "The Animal that Therefore I am Not: Inhuman Meditations on the Ultimate Degeneration of Bios and Zoe via the Inevitable Process of Phenomenophagism" in Patricia MacCormack (ed) *The Animal Catalyst: Towards Ahuman Theory* (London: Bloomsbury, 2014) 91-110; and 'A Thousand Chateaus: On Time, Topology and the Seriality of Serial Killing' in Edia Connole & Gary J. Shipley (eds) Serial Killing: A Philosophical Anthology (London: Schism Press, 2105) 369-389.

7. The most fully developed analysis of the phonoegregore to date may be found in Mark Couroux, "Xenochronic Dispatches from the Domain of the Phonoegregore" in Baylee Britts, Prudence Gibson & Amy Ireland (eds) *Aesthetics After Finitude* (Melbourne: RePress, 2016)) 29-34.

8. On the promise and perils of "kleptomancy" as enchantment, repetition and conceptual incantation in relation to the philosophy and practice of temporal warping and spatial dislocation, see Charlie Blake, "The Shattered Muse: Metis, Melismatics & the Catastrophical Imagination," in eds. Colin Gardner and Patricia MacCormack, Ecosophical Aesthetics (London: Bloomsbury, forthcoming 2017). On the potential consequences within the practice of kleptomancy as divination of potentially infinitely recursive self-quotation to the point of autopoetic implosion and schizotopian non-presence, see Charlie Blake, "The Animal that Therefore I am Not..," passim.

9. Augoyard & Torgue 111.

10. Augoyard & Torgue 99.

11. Blake, *The Shattered Muse*, (forthcoming. no.pag).

Unstable Metaphors for the Inaccessible

Mysticism, Blackletter, Drone Metal

Owen Coggins

Three obliquely related traditions of the inscription of sound or speech; they follow interconnected and wayward trails between texts and experiences. Wandering, excavating cryptic roots beneath ruined cathedrals and halls, they approach old doors with strange keys. Whatever weird paths their shadowed histories follow, all three evoke auras of ambivalent suspicion and opaque, extra-rational power. Mysticism, blackletter, drone metal.

The first emerged from traditions of spiritual contemplation founded on intensely charged, always intertextual experiences of reading and writing. From the start considered illegitimate, mysticism yet constituted an uneasy counterpart to the orthodox theology from which it was both distanced and inextricable. At once fundamentalist and heretical, it meditated upon, examined, and interrogated the foundations of that discourse on God. Appearing as an absent, imagined, illusory centre to comparative projects of scholarship on religion in the 20th Century, the idea of mysticism was thereby transformed and perpetuated, in a body of literature which became a part of that extraordinary tradition that it proposed to observe from without. Now, this odd name 'mysticism' hints vaguely at a range of beclouded concepts and occluded phenomena, introduced evocatively and ambivalently, just as it may signify evocation and ambivalence.

The second: a style of typographical letterform used since the earliest beginnings of printing, modelled on earlier manuscript handwriting used across Europe, though even by the early 20th Century a locus of paradoxical connotations. Named 'Old English' or 'altdeutsch,' the supposed national character of blackletter is evidently contradictory; its association with age also contested by the naming of roman letterforms 'Antiqua' since they derived from classical monumental style. Named 'gothic' lettering by Italian humanists who considered it barbaric, and associated with the broken arches and vertical dynamics of Gothic architecture, blackletter in fact had no connection to the Goths: the term 'gothic' as barbarian was also applied to the pagan runes, though later the same name was attached to 20th Century roman designs. After a debate in Germany reaching back many decades, the National Socialists in 1941 banned blackletter (though, in a further paradox, on blackletter-headed notepaper). Regardless, such letters retain a heavy charge of violence and extremity.

The third: a form of sonic practice at the margins of the already, proudly, marginal world of metal. Described as riffs beyond riffs, metal about metal, drone metal is at once extreme and ambient, a meditative treatment of heavy metal's symbolic codes so radical it may not be recognised as such.

As metal it is peculiarly disreputable. Out of proportion, one would think, with its fairly insignificant global profile, it appears to cause great concern to those provoked by its unhidden secret. In deep exploration of the very ground of metal through amplification, repetition, and extension, it questions metal, in a radical heresy and fundamentalist restatement of orthodoxy. Aliza Shvarts describes it, as 'interrogating what it is to be metal [...] at the esoteric fringe or innovative core of the discipline's canonical works' (2014, p204).

Three traditions of inextricably textual experiences, experiential texts. A marginal current in religious history; a distinctive class of typography; a contemporary extreme metal subgenre. Unlike, improperly grouped together, within while excluded from the settings which produced them. They share an atmosphere of impropriety, an adamant, straightforward, but somehow subversive insistence on the basic materials of their own transmission. Held responsible for excitations of poorly evidenced but genuinely inflamed responses, the uncertain outrages elicited by mysticism, blackletter, and drone metal can be understood together: they each inherit a symbolic order which they transform from within. Mysticism, religious discourse which interrogates theology's foundation. Blackletter, a way of writing which resists reading. Drone metal, metal which eternally returns to the riff in extension or repetition rather than in musical semantics of structure and change. The three traditions not only stand together in an ominous shadow of ambivalent power, but they also turn from transparency or meaning, towards bodily engagement with distorted, amplified signs.

It spoke less and less. It was written in unreadable messages on the body transformed into an emblem or a memorial engraved with the sufferings of love.

This chapter, then, extends, amplifies, repeats and distorts the suggestion that drone metal sound, blackletter text and mystical manners of speaking share characteristics that Michel de Certeau identifies as particular ways of operating on codes (1992, p113). Tracing practices through which symbolic systems can be turned within and against themselves, Certeau understands 'mystics' as a collection of textual operations in which the focus, the practice, even the 'experience' of a discourse is reoriented towards the material substance of the symbols through which it is made manifest; the physical, dirty, noisy edges that are both condition and boundary of any channel of communication.

Drone metal, blackletter, and the mystical commentary on reading and writing that includes the texts of John of the Cross, Teresa of Avila and also of Michel de Certeau; these traditions witness and represent a mystic turn towards the materiality of opaque signs. They inhabit the ruins of language, in thick, distorted, material noise. By sounding the physical boundaries and presenting the fragments of such institutions of meaning, they gesture towards while turning away from the lost or absent whole which is the impossible limit of their textual pilgrimages. The dense, blackened, repetitive, monotonous texts of drone metal; the heavy, thick, distorted amplification of blackletter pages: like mysticism, alienated they orbit a central absence. Turning apophatically from a lost faith in language, they deny false clarity in favour of physical, vibrating encounters with the darkness of signs. They echo down obscure paths of history and myth.

So, idiosyncratically following a tradition of mysticism as experience between reading and writing, with that reading slowed by its crystallisation in the fractured density of blackletter, and amidst the vibrations of drone metal's extended, meditative repetitions, I examine the resonances of these three themes through a contemplative reading of and commentary upon a fragment of Michel de Certeau's beautiful and incomplete *Mystic Fable* (two volumes, 1992; 2015). This quotation, found in the first volume of his work on the traces of 16th and 17th Century mystics, I have over years repeatedly read, weighed, at times inaccurately remembered, reread, and rewritten; recognising in it something that speaks profoundly but obliquely, that 'overflows it's designated space' (1992, p3).

Through constant repetitions, these lines have become engraved, speaking more and more, and less and less, unreadable on the writing body of this reader. Here then is presented neither an analysis of procedures within the inner world of an imagined text; nor an imagined text of an inner world of any supposed central author. Instead, an interlocution between. As with the active resonance between 'text' and 'experience' (the division that has so perplexed the 20th Century students of mysticism who created and insisted upon such partition), this mystical symbolic practice can be heard anew in the spinning revolutions of drone metal's leaden prayer wheels; and it can be felt in a perception that might just outrun reading, among the mute and solid anchors of those heaviest of metal letters. It: a one which already, therefore, suggests another. 'It' is itself and not itself, a counterpart and a recognition of a distance or an absence.

And then, Michel Serres comments, 'as soon as we are two, we are already three or four (2007, p59). Certeau's 'it' is a temporary, conditional index denoting mystical discourse, a discourse of mysticism. The I of the it, evidently, inevitably, is writ large and ornate; it is amplified and distorted, embellished and decorated in curves, points and thorns. 'I' in roman text is the simplest stroke of the pen, a straight and vertical line, inscribing as the foundation of written discourse a supposedly stable individual I: 'The stroke is the fundamental artefact. Nothing goes back farther than the stroke' writes Gerrit Noordzij, whose theory of writing is indeed founded on the stroke (2005, p10). Yet the gothic mystery of blackletter subverts that ideological figure of simplicity which subtly (surreptitiously. even) equates the stroke with the writing subject. Blackletter's I instead hints at heavier loads borne by that construction of identity, and yet also opens curved spaces at the centre of that intense gravity of self. After all, as Noordzij reminds us, 'a letter is two shapes, one light, one dark' (p13). What appears to be one is two. And as soon as we are two...

The subject I is, for Certeau, under question; no simple site or receptor for common experience, but a partially decipherable pattern of traces. In *The Mystic Fable*, Certeau the mystic reader, writes of reading that it is 'innumerable ways of deciphering, in texts, what has already written us' (1992, p9). No stable subject for experience, then, the I of the It remains a function of (always prior) readings and writings. And so, this I/t, this result of beginningless textualising, this 'experience' melted into the body's apprehension of texts, is not sufficient unto itself but a result of a gesture which pushes this raft of signs out onto discursive oceans vast and uncharted.

The section in Certeau's introduction to *The Mystic Fable*, from which the fragment is quoted, discusses the transformations and orientations of mystic discourse throughout the sixteenth and seventeenth centuries amidst shifting theological tides. Successive sentences discuss 'it;' that discourse is their temporary subject. But what does it mean for the discourse itself to speak? Rather than the reverse, the subject is instituted by its speech. Yet, 'it spoke.'

Yet, 'it spoke less and less.' The subject which can only instantiate and constitute itself to itself through speech, speaks. Though it speaks less and less. Written. But unreadable. A frayed edge, acknowledged, between the great ideologies of vision and understanding, of comprehension and knowledge. The body is, here already, the place where the transfer between meaning and interpretation is by turns halted and recreated.

Here also can be found drone metal, the listening body becoming text through experience, vibrated by sound which, listeners repeat, 'is to be experienced not understood,' with the latter, negative aspect emphasised as much as the former. Drone metal speaks; it speaks less and less; both facts are as essential and inextricable as they are undeniable. Description abandons or ignores any hold on the 'messages' of verbal narrative or musical structure.

And blackletter, beloved by metal culture for both tradition and transgression, as Vitus Vestergaard has outlined (2016). But above all, for distorting and amplifying the written sign. Blackletter too, speaks, and speaks less and less.

spoke less and less

Representative of archaism, that which is already lost to time, words in blackletter resemble ruins, plants growing between the monoliths and broken stone curves: known also as frakturschrift, fractured script. For Lawrence Mirsky, it resembles a 'crystalline plant' (1998, p6-8), visually representative of the ruins and trees that appear, for example, in the paintings of Caspar David Friedrich, themselves meditatively repeated in the imagery of metal's shipwrecked ruined religion, its roaring heathen storms, its wild and holy mountains.

Another riddle; classical feature of mystic writings where the oxymoron, Certeau notes, is the 'smallest mystic unit' 1996, p143. Blackletter in contemporary times is used less and less to record our verbal messages in writing; yet it is called upon, exactly because of this evocation of faded pasts, of craft or hospitality or tradition, its unavailability to unthinking transparency, to perform ambivalent works of communication at the perceptual margins of what can be understood as 'reading'. Not in its capacity for linguistic communication: the words signified become secondary, 'meaning' demoted or exiled. But in its form: a 'beautiful but illegible handwriting' like the opaque turns of phrase Certeau finds in the 16th century mystic texts (1992, p70), describing a musicality of forms which derives from the darkness of their figures. Beautiful and illegible like the sigil logos that identify and obscure extreme metal musicians, in visual figures of their distorted, indecipherable mystic voices.

The discourse of mysticism emerged in a period when the authorising power of the church was ebbing, the mystics left stranded on the shore by a receding tide, the old established institutions emptied of their ability to guarantee the foundation of experience and truth in the Word. So the mystic writings, in search of an absent foundation, speak of and with their bodies. Mystic discourse becomes a peregrination, a pilgrimage tracing the circuitous paths of a language which points away from language, which presents merely its own broken forms in order to silently imply their ruination. Deliberately contorted, contradictory, obstinate and obtuse, the mystics 'operated' upon language, forcing it into weird shapes so as to orient perception towards its contingent and material basis, pressing it or trapping it into confessing the limitations of its own substance and the ellipses of its patterns. Via indecipherability, hinting at the body's implication in communication or communion. Reaching ecstatically, empty-handedly, outside itself.

What better description of the intense power of music, imprinting its strange codes upon physical and animated flesh? Especially apt for those massive waves of drone metal vibration, enveloping bodies in profound and sustained resonance. Not in its visual or verbal appellations but in its sound and noise, when it enters the body, drone metal is unreadable, in experience that turns away from understanding. Yet it is certainly felt as message, beyond language but site of its own implacable production.

It was written in unreadable messages on the body

It is often claimed that drone metal is ineffable, completely eluding the domain of language. Yet such disclaimers preface elaborate, articulate, extended, creative discourses, again echoing Certeau's practices of linguistic contortion. Metal and blackletter meet in the arcane letter magick of tattoos, embodied more than written or read.

Blackletter is known for slowing the reader (at least, the reader who is unfamiliar with blackletter, a foreigner walking amongst broken statues). As in drone metal, a slowness, superficially about perceived speed or tempo, can be an opportunity; a dragging on the rush of cognition, an obstacle to interpretation, a weighty reminder that signs are, above or below all, things. Things in front of or even inside the body, for the body to apprehend as things, before ever they are representations of messages to be deciphered, decoded or delivered. Mysticism, blackletter and drone metal present tangled thickets of signification, respectively: a practice of theological language turned against itself in interrogation of newly uncertain foundations; a previously functioning and legible form of script which now reads as archaic and obscure, thereby presenting itself as resistant to reading through its difference; and an enforced, embodied meditation on the infinite, chaotic intricacies of vast distortion in sound as sound.

Yet, in a crisis of meaning, this is the gesture that fractured signs offer: there are symbols with no message but that their broken symbols fail to relate a message. The mystic, occult, esoteric secret is that there is no secret. Blackletter is written language to be looked at and not read. What is amplified in drone metal is amplification itself.

This amplification transforms the body. For Certeau, mystic discourse in its curiously playful and destructive treatment of language, 'transforms the detail into myth; it catches hold of it, blows it out of proportion, multiplies it, divinizes it' (1992, p10). Amplification and distortion for their own sake, conjuring mystical contemplation of the gravity of material signs.

As well as distortion transforming the body of the sound into a figure of its own excess, the sounding of the limitations of its own channel of transmission, the body of the listener is changed. Emblems and memorials: more ruins? At least, markers of a fragile hold on a past that has slipped away, markers—yet not words—which may indicate a symbolic system but remain marginal to it. Certeau's epitaphs and tombstones are 'statues erected to mark the boundaries of an "elsewhere" that is not remote, a place they both produce and guard' (1992, p2). In addition to its connection to Gothick architecture, blackletter 're-mains a monument,' according to historian of typography Stanley Morison, 'witnessing to the creative ability of medieval craftsmen' (1981, p196).

That the body is transformed by drone metal is unmistakable. Transformed into an emblem or memorial? The transformation is easily discernible at least in reverse for blackletter; words as emblem-memorials carry or accrete the crystallizations of identity and memory, revealing the oblique traces of inescapably material bodies.

Transformations and the memory of transformations; change and silent consciousness of change; functions or at least patterns which it is impossible to disentangle from the machinery or magick of time. Bodies become slowly their own memorials, illegible histories written in marks, scars, the irrevocable passing of the passage of age.

transformed into an emblem or memorial

And this lettering therefore is emblem and memorial without narrative or authority. Memorial for memory, for the drifting instantiation of time itself. Though roman letters may have been first to be inscribed in stone, blackletter is the script more often written as memorial in skin, metal needles inking emblems of less readable transformations wrought by the resonating weight of sonic metal drones operating on consciousnesses emanating within weighted bodies.

For Cristina Paoli, blackletter 'imparts a sense of lasting for a long time, or even being eternal;' it 'possesses the quality of being, above and beyond the normal' (2006, p5). Mysticism, too, always in its historical specificity, nevertheless carries with it a glamorous effect of eternity, an unmistakable, even irrational appeal to an archaic universality that resurfaces in forsaken sidetracks and extraordinary margins. There are serious dangers to these bewitching essentialisms, and (extreme) caution should be exercised of any unitary worlding theory, of the violence it threatens toward the awkward noises of difference. Yet distorted drones may offer a better pathway into eternal return, as figures of infinity inside and outside time. In Joanna Demers' hearing, 'drone music is a music for when the markers of time such as clocks, metronomes, alarms have stopped. It is an acoustic foundation from which other sounds emerged, and to which all sounds will eventually return' (2015, p17).

Drone, mysticism and blackletter, are not impositions of a limitless and fascist unity of violently erased difference, though that is indeed for each a risk and temptation. They are instead quixotic, revolving evolutions of difference and sameness. Repetition and unique extension, timelessness and endurance. The body and engraved desire. Suffering and love.

This tortured amorous erotics in the words of the 16th Century mystics, for Certeau is a symptom (again a metaphor of the body and its alteration) of a search for grounding after faith in the church as guarantor of meaning had dispersed. Elaine Scarry notes the emergence of torture at those moments where power has slipped from legitimacy in a 'crisis of belief' (1985, p14). Mysticism and torture, then, may arise concurrently at moments of rupture in authority and meaning, as ways of seeking to produce apparent certainty from the body as a last resort for certainty. And because a confession is sought, it is already under question, engraved but unreadable.

For Yvonne Schwemer-Scheddin, blackletter also appears when 'the foundations of faith were eroded. Values became flimsy, and in the face of the apocalyptic Thirty Years' War, reality took refuge in theatrical illusions. Artists reacted by embellishing the alphabet with ornamental and exaggerated mannerist forms Style drowned out the message' (1998, p53). An association endures, staining this letterform with transgressive violence.

The most pointed connotation is, despite the 1941 decree, of the Third Reich, together with a more general frisson of nationalism, though roman lettering is equally implicated in formations of national identity. But emotional association needs no assurance from historical evidence; looming ambiguities will persist. Judith Schalansky senses this shadow, writing that 'while objectionable usages roll off the abstract forms of Futura like water off a duck's back, messages seem to cling much more easily to Blackletter's differentiated letter-forms' (2008, p17-8).

engraved with the sufferings of love.

These lines appropriately associate an unkempt, dirty materiality with the dark associations of blackletter that cause it to be, in Paoli's words, 'stained with brutality and the irrational use of power' (2006, p17).

Abstract violence appears in drone metal, attacking the notes, patterns, and conventions of music, distorting limits in structure as well as sound. Aggression, suffering, pain, physically damaging volume, exhaustion: these are reported by listeners as crucial elements of drone metal's ritual transcendent immanence. Noise is violence, as well as abstract representation of violence, done to music, to sound, to order, to meaning. A mystical catharsis may be experienced in this shattering split: drone metal noise is alienating, while also therapeutically, honestly evocative of alienation. Drone metal resonates with sorrow and the ending of sorrow.

Again it is the body which bears these illegible engravings of violence and transgression. Sheila Whiteley considers Jimi Hendrix; powerful influence on drone metal (see, for instance, Earth's cover of 'Peace in Mississippi') and great pioneer of feedback, distortion, and the use of the amplifier as an instrument with which to play with power and excess. Of Hendrix's 'Purple Haze,' Whiteley writes; 'the sheer volume of noise works towards the drowning of personal consciousness,' while repetition leads to absorption in an otherworldly loss of time, and the levels of distortion are such that pitch cannot be easily determined (2000, p241-5). Both personal subjectivity and the notes played (which might stand as an index for the persona of a player) are drowned in amplified distortion; the individual is rendered illegible within their own embodied text, lost in joyous, violent, sublime noise.

The Word itself had to be born in the void that awaited it. That had been the theology of the Rhenish in the thirteenth and fourteenth centuries. It survived still in the works of John of the Cross, an intellectual who remained very scholastic. But already in his works or in those of Teresa of Avila -more modern than he- and after him, the approach took physical forms, more concerned with a symbolic capacity of the body than with an incarnation of the Verb. It was an approach that caressed, wounded, ascended the scale of perceptions, attained the ultimate point, which it transcended. It spoke less and less. It was written in unreadable messages on the body transformed into an emblem or a memorial engraved with the sufferings of love. The spoken word remained outside of this body, written but indecipherable, for which an erotic discourse would henceforth be in search of words and images. (1992, p5).

The body of this text is, I remind myself, already transformed in translation, in how it speaks (less and less?) in the translation, by Michael B. Smith, from the original French, *La Fable mystique* (1982). Looking at this text (not quite reading, not quite not reading) prompts further reflections on its distance (temporal, linguistic, cultural, mystic). The Elle, escaping entirely my eisegesis on the I of the It, instead presents, to a reader unused to the attribution of gendered pronouns to inanimate abstractions, a hint of the implications of exactly which bodies and voices were imprinted with the love and suffering that wrote that circuitous history of 16th and 17th century mysticism.

Traces, corpses, and dolorous amour echo productively between two languages, one to me partly opaque, the other seeking to return to opacity in poetically ruined typography. Most resonant, however, in the light of its begotten descendant, is 'grabé.' Like 'corps' for body, it whispers of death, but also of writing; and slowness; and weight. Grabé is at once tomb, inscription, time, and death of time. Eugene Thacker notes this connection for doom and drone: 'Doom metal presents a music of tempo that is so *grabé* that it negates tempo. Finally, drone metal with its minimalist dissipation of all music into a monolithic, dense line of sound, presents us with the whittling away of all harmony into a single, thick, absolute tone, collapsing the musical spectrum into a dense black hole' (2014, p184).

Elle parle de moins en moins. Elle se trace en messages illisibles sur un corps transformé en emblème ou en memorial grabé par les douleurs d'amour.

Estranged from language, wandering among the gravestones, occult emblems of black letters, engulfed by the noise of extreme distortion where initial signal or message is lost, silenced by the world-collapsing black hole of tone where structure is lost to timbre, texture and volume: we turn toward the opaque materiality of mystic signs.

For Barry Shank, 'the drone commands that we pay attention to the materiality of all sound, to sound's existence as a set of repeating and different vibrations' (2014, p109). Similarly, for Schwemer-Scheddin, blackletter is 'the transformation of script into image,' an image 'cut adrift from language' (1998, p53, p66). And for Simon Reynolds, traversing both sound and word, 'noise is like an eruption within the material out of which language is shaped' (1990, p60).

But it is a strange opacity, which points away from and towards itself as material mystic sign; the object of mystic discourse 'never anything than the unstable metaphor for what is inaccessible' (Certeau 1992, p77). For Paoli, the diamond ends at the top and bottom of verticals 'simultaneously project towards the heavens and towards the ground' in an 'impossible integration,' a visual, sonic paradox in perception before signification.

If, for the mystics, reading and writing became boundaries to tread but also routes beyond those limits, then drone metal, blackletter and mysticism present inextricable circumscription, wandering excess. Pathways, gates, and boundary stones. Walls, and also ruins. Doors, but also keys.

It spoke
less and less.
It was written
in unreadable
messages
on the body
transformed
into an emblem
or a memorial
engraved with the
sufferings of love.

Certeau, Michel de, 1982
La Fable mystique, I
Paris: Editions Gallimard.

Certeau, Michel de, 1992
The Mystic Fable Volume 1
trans. Michael B. Smith
Chicago: University
of Chicago Press.

Certeau, Michel de, 2015
The Mystic Fable Volume 2
trans. Michael B. Smith
Chicago: University
of Chicago Press.

Demers, Joanna, 2015
Drone and Apocalypse
Winchester & Washington:
Zero Books.

Mirsky, Lawrence, 1998
'The Crystalline Plant' in
Peter Bain and Paul Shaw, eds.
*Blackletter: Type
and National Identity*
New York: Princeton
Architectural Press, p6-9

Morison, Stanley, 1981
'Black-Letter Text' in
*Selected Essays on the History of
Letterforms in Manuscript and Print*
Cambridge: University
of Cambridge Press.

Noordzij, Gerrit, 2005
The Stroke: Theory of Writing
trans. Peter Enneson
London: Hyphen Press.

Paoli, Cristina, 2006
Mexican Blackletter
New York: Mark Batty LLC.

Reynolds, Simon, 1990
Blissed Out: The Raptures of Rock
London: Serpent's Tail.

Scarry, Elaine, 1985
The Body in Pain
New York & Oxford:
Oxford University Press.

Schalansky, Judith, 2008
Fraktur Mon Amour
New York: Princeton
Architectural Press.

Schwemer-Scheddin, Yvonne, 1998
'Broken Images: Blackletter
between Faith and Mysticism' in
Peter Bain and Paul Shaw, eds.
*Blackletter: Type
and National Identity*
New York: Princeton
Architectural Press, p50-67.

Serres, Michel, 2007
The Parasite
trans. Lawrence Schehr
Minneapolis: University
of Minnesota Press.

Shank, Barry, 2014
*The Political Force of
Musical Beauty*
Durham & London:
Duke University Press.

Shvarts, Aliza, 2014
'Troubled Air: The Drone
and Doom of Reproduction in
SunnO)))'s Metal Maieutic'
Women and Performance
4: 2/3, p203–19.

Thacker, Eugene, 2014
'Sound of the Abyss'
in Wilson, Scott ed.
*Melancology: Black Metal
Theory and Ecology*
Winchester & Washington:
Zero Books, p182-194.

Vestergaard, Vitus, 2016
'Blackletter logotypes
and metal music'
Metal Music Studies
2: 1, p109-124.

Whiteley, Sheila, 2000
'Progressive Rock and Psychedelic
Coding in the work of Jimi Hendrix'
in Middleton, Richard ed.
*Reading Pop: Approaches to
Textual Analysis in Music*
Oxford & New York: Oxford
University Press, p235-261.
---

text/experience/text;
listening while writing:

Bong
Untitled (Mongolith)

Acid Mothers Temple
& the Melting Paraiso U.F.O.
New Geocentric World of...

Sunn O)))
Domkirke

Earth
Angels of Darkness,
Demons of Light II

Kevin Drumm
Tannenbaum

Aidan Baker/N/Dirk Serries
Enomeni

Corrupted
Garten der Unbewusstheit

Menace Ruine
Union of Irreconcilables

Orthodox
Amanecer en Puerta Oscura

Sleep
Jerusalem

William Basinski
Disintegration Loops dlp 1.1
Water Music II

27

TRANSCENDIGITAL IMAGINATION
DEVELOPING ORGANS of SUBTLE PERCEPTION

Kim Cascone reproduced from www.InterferenceJournal.com with permission

The illusion of life was absolute: mobility of expression, the continual working of the lungs, speech, various actions, walking—nothing was missing. —Raymond Roussel (2011)

Resurrectine

Martial Canterel, the proprietor of the surreal compound featured in Raymond Roussel's (2011) surrealist novel Locus Solus leans over a corpse laying on a hospital gurney inside a glass-walled refrigerated building. With careful precision he drills a hole in the corpse's skull just above one ear, then injects a syringe of Resurrectine into the cranial cavity. After the liquid floods the corpse's skull, he slides a small bar of Vitalium into the hole and the corpse jolts to life.

The corpse shifts off the gurney and begins to reenact a random scene from its life. Canterel and his assistants have provided props and extra actors to complete the ghoulish tableau as the family of the deceased watch in delight while their reanimated loved-one plods through its one-act play.

The theme of reanimation, or resurrection, of the dead is not new; it is resurrected time and again in fiction, films and television. And many of our spiritual mythologies and religious stories are also built upon the theme of death and resurrection of a spiritual leader or prophet. Even the culture of sound art unknowingly participates in this act of reanimation. Sound recording—in particular field recording and sampling—can be likened to storing sound in a digital mausoleum, later to be reanimated via playback.

Searching for the Soul

In a forest, a figure trudges along a path, apparently carrying some sort of electronic equipment. The figure comes to a stop and begins recording sounds with a microphone. A whistle of wind in the pine needles above, bird songs embroider the distant waves of highway traffic, a jet noisily clambers its flight path to cruising altitude. The figure remains motionless, microphone outstretched, eyes closed, immersed in the ambiance of the forest. After collecting some sound, the figure scrambles back on to the trail, twigs and leaves crunching underfoot and gradually passes from view. Cut to: a bedroom sound studio. The figure from the forest is now seated behind a laptop. A small mixing board sits off to one side and two loudspeakers loom in front. The figure taps the space bar on a laptop and suddenly, like the corpse in Locus Solus, the forest sounds jump to life: birds, wind, distant traffic, the distant jet plane—the sound of the forest is reanimated and dances in the speakers. While listening to the recording, a puzzled expression flashes over the face of the recordist. The sound of the forest now seems two-dimensional, flat, lifeless, corpse-like. Although the sound is technically perfect, it lacks the enchantment experienced in the forest. Baffled, the recordist twists at some knobs on the mixing board searching for something missing in the sound—the soul of the forest.

This is a common experience for many new recordists. They have yet to learn that the microphone collapses sound into a flat aural plane, then stores it in the recorder as a granulated stream of quantized data. It can be confusing at first, but recording removes the soul from a sonic landscape. Audio-visual technology, by virtue of its nature, collapses the dimensionality of sound and light phenomena while transforming it for electro-mechanical storage. What is returned from storage is a corpse-like version of what went in. But we've learned to suspend our disbelief and unconsciously adjust for it. For example, we know full well that a movie is not real, but our brain activity reflects that we are experiencing a real event. A warning label should come affixed to all audio recording equipment: 'sensation does not equal experience'.

The Desouling of the World

Everything that is dead quivers. Not only the things of poetry, stars, moon, wood, flowers, but even a white trouser button glittering out of a puddle in the street…

Everything has a secret soul, which is silent more often than it speaks. Wassily Kandinsky (1977)

Our technologically-oriented society is heavily invested in maintaining a reductionist-materialist world-view. We see the world as objects to be consumed, controlled or transformed to suit our needs. Only the data or phenomenon that can be measured, analysed and explained according to the laws of physics is sanctioned as being real. Other 'ways of knowing' the world, e.g., the spiritual, mystical or poetic—knowledge which is unable to be validated by science—have become devalued or even taboo in many cases.

As a result, we have come to see ourselves as separate from nature. Even language upholds a rigid subject/object distinction; we learn to trust only what we experience with our physical senses as being real and even then only if it can be scientifically validated. This materialist world-view has supplanted the spiritual and some feel that our dismissal of spiritual experience helps explain the state of our world: rampant consumerism, selfishness and greed, exploitation of fellow humans and animals, depletion and pollution of natural resources, a populace fuelled by an insatiable desire for material wealth—all of which reflects the atrophying of our spiritual knowledge. It is our materialist consciousness that blinds us to nature's holistic web of energy, that ephemeral energy, or soul, missing from the forest recording.

Technology reduces the creative process to a set of primitive actions, a series of functional modules that, when patched together, form a workflow which produces a cultural artifact. In writing about the philosophy of Marshall McLuhan, author J.M. Culkin states: "We become what we behold. We shape our tools and then our tools shape us" (1967). In our conflation of tool and message, imagination ceases to express itself through technology; rather it is technology that funnels and shapes our imagination and expresses itself through the artwork.

Resurrecting World-Building

Other forms of awareness and connections to other, more subtle and fleeting forms are available to us through epiphanies, synchronicities, mystical experiences, and other special moments when individual human consciousness merges into something much greater. Our minds and bodies all have access to the same creative source that animates every atom and star. The world is created in unitary thought is only the smallest fragment of a much greater reality, for we can live and have direct awareness of the universe that is beyond all forms, images, and theories. F. David Peat (1991)

Philosopher Owen Barfield proposes in his book Saving the Appearances: A Study in Idolatry (1988) that reality, i.e., everything that exists 'out there' is merely a sub-atomic world of potential that our sense-perception encapsulates into an outer layer or a shell that we organise into physical objects reposing in an externalized field that we call reality. With the discovery of quantum mechanics we now know that our perception of the phenomenal world is largely dependent upon the perceiver's organising mode of consciousness, and that the perceiver and the observed phenomenon form a single seamless whole. Knowing this, it becomes evident that our perceptual awareness, based in a materialist consciousness, is rooted in a false duality, one that limits our ability to fully experience the world as artists.

But there is a state of awareness that we all have access to if we so choose, one that is in need of being resurrected.

Throughout history, philosophers have called this perceptual state of awareness by various names: the su-

persensible, mundus imaginalis, imaginal perception, active imagination, subtle realm, participatory consciousness—each term points to a heightened state of perceptual awareness—perhaps better explained as feeling the "presence in which the essence of a thing is fully manifested in its existence" (Avens 1988 p. 385). Holistic physicist and author F. David Peat writes, "once the barriers between inner and outer, inscape and landscape, are dissolved, and fixed responses give way to fluid and complex actions, then a new form of active perception can be practiced" (1991 p. 217). It is my belief that this state of 'imaginative-perception' is missing in sound art today, and that in order to revive the project of world-building in art, it is first necessary to resurrect this state of awareness.

New Organs of Perception

The human being knows himself only insofar as he knows the world; he perceives the world only in himself, and himself only in the world. Every new object, clearly seen, opens up a new organ of perception in us. Johann Wolfgang von Goethe (Mueller 1952 p. 235)

Many listening workshops—albeit well-intentioned—make a fundamental mistake: they unwittingly perpetuate a materialist world-view by focusing on the sensory-perception of sound while neglecting imaginative-perception. The mode of sense perception is one that we use on a daily basis: we modulate our perceptual scope and focus in order to selectively attend to event-objects occurring in the outer world. The listener (in here) hears a sonic event-object (out there). The listener remains separate from the environment.

In his book The Wholeness of Nature, psychologist and philosopher Henri Bortoft describes these two modes of awareness as "onlooker consciousness" and "participatory consciousness" (1996). Onlooker consciousness, or sensory-perception, maintains a subject/object duality, while participatory consciousness, or imaginative-perception, transcends this dualism by merging subject and object into a holistic continuum of consciousness. Again, quantum physics tells us the same thing: the observer affects the observed reality. Or in the context of sound art: the listener becomes the listening and the listening becomes the sound.

Psychologist and writer John Welwood describes this imaginative mode of awareness as one in which the listener: "feels out and integrates whole textures and networks of relationships, in ways that are impossible for the serial method of focal attention" (1977 p. 15). Welwood further suggests that imaginative-perception "allows us to recast the inner/outer duality in a different way. Inner truth, inner reality does not refer to a realm of the psyche inside the organism, but rather to the living, dynamic, holistic process that shapes and structures the outer reality of constituent parts" (1977 p. 20). In other words, the listener experiences sound as a continuous holistic field of relations, rather than separate, discrete, sonic event-objects.

By constantly funnelling our attention through the lens of duality, we rob ourselves of the capacity to experience the world in a deeper, more direct way. By opening oneself to experiencing the world as a continuum as opposed to a duality, the artist can resume the task of world-building. In order for sound artists to resurrect and develop their imaginative-perception, they need a different approach to a purely sensory-based mode of listening.

Binary/Dualism Transcended

If we wish to awaken in mankind the true artistic mood, we must, to a certain degree, transport ourselves back into those ancient times when the celestial, the poetic mood, lived in the human soul. Rudolf Steiner (1964 p. 62)

Creating new circuits in art means creating them in the brain. Gilles Deleuze (1997 p. 26)

When we shift from our materialist-only consciousness towards a holistic one, we will no longer experience the world as 'inner' or 'outer'. As this distinction disappears we are less dominated by sensory awareness as our imaginative awareness becomes heightened, non-local, fluidic and malleable. John Welwood better explains this state of imaginative awareness, "From a Buddhist perspective this pure awareness is our original nature, and meditation is the major way to let it emerge from its normally submerged background role" (1977 p. 19). I will save enumerating the various techniques that can help artists develop their imaginative-perception for another time, but I will briefly mention here that daily meditation is the most effective means for accomplishing any inner work.

In a piece I wrote for a magazine (Cascone 2012), I describe my experience with meditation while studying music in college and how I began to sense the world in a very different way. This enabled me to tap into the rich world of my unconscious, which led me down a very different artistic path than what my music school was pointing to. My imaginative-perception had become so heightened that I was compelled to translate what I heard in my 'mind's ear' into the world through electronic music. This technique of quieting the mind and allowing the unconscious to come to the surface is the most powerful tool for any artist wanting to develop 'new organs of perception'.

Being Transcendigital

All the arts concerned with things in accordance with nature are contained within Man himself. Plotinus (Ennead III viii) (Katz 1950 p. 41)

Cut to: We are back in our forest scenario. Again, we see the sound recordist with their microphone and recorder, but rather than perceiving sonic event-objects as existing in the outer world, they are perceived as contiguous with the imagination. In this heightened state of imaginative awareness one becomes open to the myriad narratives that surround oneself. Transcending the technology, one becomes attuned to the subtle synchronicities in the fabric of sound flows.

In the forest, not only are the patterns heard, and the meaning contained in the whole understood, but the whole forest is heard in each sound as well. A fabric of sonic synchronicities permeates the forest, the mundus imaginalis unfolds, the veil is lifted and the continuity of nature is revealed.

Back in the studio, the narrative re-emerges from a palimpsest of synchronicities hidden in the recordings. Technology recedes into the background as imagination becomes foregrounded. A spark of life is imbued in the corpse of sound extracted from the digital realm, not as an act of reanimation from without, but as resurrection from within. A transcendigitalism occurs, allowing the mundus imaginalis to flow through a circuit completed by technology and into the materialist world of atoms and bits. By developing new organs of perception we can let art flow through technology rather than from it.

NOTES

Ressurectine and Vitalium are fictional substances invented by the protagonist Martial Canterel in 'Locus Solus' []

"What we observe is not nature herself, but nature exposed to our method of questioning." Werner Heisenberg

References

Avens, R., 1988. The Subtle Realm: Corbin, Sufism & Swedenborg, In: Emanuel Swedenborg: A Continuing Vision : A Pictorial Biography & Anthology of Essays & Poetry. Swedenborg Foundation, New York, pp. 382–391.

Barfield, O., 1988. Saving the Appearances: A Study in Idolatry, 2nd edition. Wesleyan, Middletown, Conn.

Berman, M., 1981. The Reenchantment of the World.. Cornell University Press, Ithaca.

Bortoft, H., 1996. The Wholeness of Nature : Goethe's Way Toward a Science of Conscious Participation in Nature, 1st edition. . Lindisfarne Press, Hudson, N.Y.

Cascone, K., 2012. Sense Around Sound: Tune in to deeper awareness through the art of subtle listening. Conscious Dancer 20

Culkin, J.M., 1967. A Schoolman's Guide to Marshall McLuhan.. The Saturday Review 51–53, 71–72.

Deleuze, G., 1997. Negotiations 1972-1990.. New York.

Gebser, J., 1987. The Ever-Present Origin.Ohio University Press.

Goodman, N., 1978. Ways of Worldmaking: blueprints for a word-house refuge. Hackett Publishing.

Kandinsky, W., 1977. Concerning the Spiritual in Art. Revised edition. Dover Publications, New York.

Katz, J., 1950. The Philosophy of Plotinus. Appleton-Century-Crofts, New York.

Lubicz, R.A.S. de, 1985. Nature Word Reissue edition. ed. Inner Traditions, Rochester, Vt.

Mueller, B., 1952. Goethe's Botanical Writings.. Ox Bow Press, USA.

Peat, D., 1991. The Philosopher's Stone : Chaos, Synchronicity and the Hidden Order of the World.Bantam, New York, N.Y.

Roussel, R., 2011.Locus Solus..Oneworld Classics: Richmond.

Steiner, R., 1964. The Arts and Their Mission.. The Anthroposophic Press: Spring Valley.

Welwood, J., 1977. Meditation and the Unconscious: A New Perspective. The Journal of Transpersonal Psychology 9, 1–26.

Response Article

For interested readers, Philip Legard has composed an article in response to the above.

Kim Cascone: Curator

There's a spectre haunting music — the spectre of materialism.

In a book titled "Sound Between Matter and Spirit" Frits Julius, a student of Rudolf Steiner, suggests that the color of a blue flower is not really part of the flower itself, but rather that it emanates from another plane through the form of the flower and that one's imagination can travel into that realm through the blueness of the form.

Likewise, sound can serve as a portal through which psychic events, occurring in the subtle realm, can manifest on the material plane. Those who can hear into these radiated sound shapes interpret them as psychic "gestures" or events.

We come into this world with this psychic ability undamaged but gradually lose it as we grow older and materialism tightens its grip on our consciousness. Those who are unable to hear through these portals can only sense the material properties of sound, e.g, pitch, loudness, timbre, location, acoustics, etc. The non-material or spiritual aspect of sound is lost because we allow these organs of perception to atrophy. There are ways to keep these organs of spiritual perception nourished and healthy but I have written about this elsewhere.

Our current state of digital narcosis reinforces a materialist world-view through a reductionist lens, which is why most people involved in electronic music can only perceive the materiality of sound and not its spiritual aspect.

Both sound art and electronic music seem to be stuck in this mode of materialist perception, and the musicians who are unable to see this continually recycle the past into artifacts served to a culturally amnesiac public.

The Transcendigital compilation you hold in your hands is an attempt to resurrect the spiritual in music. Although created and recorded with digital, as well as analog, technology the source comes from a different space. The music here was conjured via a temporally dilated portal: the drone.

The musical drone, used in many spiritual practices, dilates time for both performer and listener, allowing them to temporarily exist outside of time. It is possible while in this state to renew our organs of spiritual perception and to not only experience but also to channel the enchantment in the world around us.

I hope the listener can find those organs of perception and let this collection serve as nourishment for them. When the soul is deaf the ears can't hear.

Transcendigitalism

track listings & credits

track 1
>project name: Lucid Nation
>title: Effaced
>composed by: Maldonado, Pontiac, Spivey
>© Lucid Nation 2016

track 2
>project name: Martijn Comes
>title: Specular Light, Diffused Light
>© 2016 Martijn Comes

track 3
>project name: Rag Dun
>title: Taktsang Palphug at Night
>© 2015 W. David Oliphant

track 4
>project name: Ethernet
>title: Sigils
>© 2016, Tim Gray

track 5
>project name: Deeper Than Space
>title: Izanagi
>© 2016 Adam Douglas / Dope Computer Music

track 6
>project name: Kristina Wolfe
>title: Somewhere in the Past
>© 2016 Kristina Wolfe

track 7
>project name: Hawthonn:
>title: Cave-Witch, Grass-Witch, Star-Witch
>Music by Layla & Phil Legard
>Vocals, grass reeds and electronics
>© 2016 Hawthonn

track 8
>project name: Michael Northam
>title: Solar Throat
>© 2016 orogenetics

track 9
>project name: Kris Force
>title: The Mirror
>© 2016 Kris Force
>created with Max msp, Buchla 100 and Moog 3P
>additional Buchla and Moog performance by
>Kevin McKereghan

track 10
>project name: Chasny/Metcalfe
>title: Quarternary
>© 2016 Chasny/Metcalfe

https://silentrecords.bandcamp.com/album/transcendigitalism-a-compilation-of-esoteric-drones

THE BOUNCING WALL

Lamar Freeman

$$f = \frac{v}{2}\sqrt{\left(\frac{\ell}{L_x}\right)^2 + \left(\frac{m}{L_y}\right)^2 + \left(\frac{n}{L_z}\right)^2}$$

Drone, or the communication occurring between two orders that amplify structuration (I = I), is a system amplifying frequencies that match its own vibration. It is resonance subordinated to redundancy. There are many structures that resonate. The State is a resonance chamber, a closed-vessel that couples resonance with forced movement;[1] a resonant chamber whose center is everywhere and circumference nowhere. Through mediation and remediation—recording and rerecording—images and words are rendered unintelligible, nothing more than the operators of resonance (artifact drones, codec[2] drones). Alvin Lucier's I Am Sitting In A Room[3] is one such example of this phenomenon: the subject, hidden behind a device, vanishes into artifacts of resonance. Lucier makes it clear that he is not performing an experiment to demonstrate a physical fact, but rather to demonstrate how the resonant frequencies of the room "destroy" his voice[1] until it becomes nothing more than an articulation of the resonance chamber. The "irregularities" of his voice are "smoothed" in the process. Drone wrests the ironic dimension and conceptual distance from words, it becomes more important than what the words originally signify,[2] and what the words speak of. All structures have resonant frequencies, and all mediated and remediated words exhibit artifacts of resonance.

For Flusser, mediated resonance is the byproduct of an historically emergent triple abstraction: from world

---

1   Deleuze, G., & Guattari, F. (1987). A thousand plateaus: Capitalism and schizophrenia. Minneapolis: University of Minnesota Press.

2   A codec encodes a data stream or signal for transmission, storage or encryption, or decodes it for playback or editing. Codecs are used in videoconferencing, streaming media, and video editing applications. Resonance is a lossy codec. This is evident in the homage to Alvin Lucier's I Am Sitting In a Room "VIDEO ROOM 1000", in which the subject uploads a video of himself reciting Lucier's instructions, then downloading and uploading the recording 1,000 times, in order demonstrate the digital artifacting of audio and video. The subject becomes artifact in the white, cubic space of the resonance chamber.

3   The text spoke by Lucier: "I am sitting in a room different from the one you are in now. I am recording the sound of my speaking voice and I am going to play it back into the room again and again until the resonant frequencies of the room reinforce themselves so that any semblance of my speech, with perhaps

---

the exception of rhythm, is destroyed. What you will hear, then, are the natural resonant frequencies of the room articulated by speech. I regard this activity not so much as a demonstration of a physical fact, but more as a way to smooth out any irregularities my speech might have."

1   With the exception of rhythm.

2   Baudrillard, J. Violence of the Image. Lecture.

to primitive mediation, from primitive mediation to linear and scientific reification, from linear and scientific reification to digital media.[3] Mediated resonance traverses all three layers of abstraction. Flusser argues that mediating devices have organized the world through this abstraction process such that an ever-increasing number of media devices are produced.[4] For him, media platforms (resonance chambers) reduce subjects who do not understand the logistics of digital media to mere functionaries within the devices' ever widening and inescapable domain.[5] There are always chambers of resonance, walls upon which drones muster.[6] Stupidity's never blind or mute.[7] Expressive freedom is not liberatory in a world saturated with and programmed by digital media.[8]

Drone is the redundancy of interpellation. In recording voice, words, and images to digital media the subject concedes something, gives up resistance and confirms

authority of the one who commands that they are subjectified in the terms of Flusser's triple abstraction. In this way, the subject becomes a figure in the discourse, a functionary who's lost their ironic and conceptual dimension. "Every milieu is vibratory, in other words, a block of space-time constituted by the periodic repetition of the component."[9]

The terms of identity are crystalized through publicly repudiated heterogeneity. To say that "I am sitting in a room" the "I" must be a part of a social discourse, and to be addressed by another, the subject must be heard. The subject must therefore enter visible and audible fields, or resonance chambers. Resonance occurs when a system is able to store and easily transfer energy between two or more different storage modes (such as kinetic energy and potential energy in the case of a pendulum). Resonant chambers are structured by what can be seen and what can be heard. The field of audibility must be structured in such a way that we can hear what we say. Anechoic chambers, for instance, do not possess this capacity. Anechoic chambers can be so quiet that the absence of background noise can make the subject aware of sounds they've never been conscious of, like the sound of blood flowing in their head, and their sense of space can be distorted. In order for drone to occur, the air must resonate with the emission of a wave without harmonics. A sober gesture, such as voicing instructions into a recording device and replaying and rerecording, palpitates the walls and air of the resonance chamber in a fashion that is prodigiously simple, creatively limited, and selective. The signifying or "communicational" values of the voiced instructions indicate only the road of no return.

3   Flusser, V. (2000) Towards a Philosophy of Photography. Trans. A. Matthews. London: Reaktion Books.

4   Think of the runaway oscillation of Soundcloud, Instagram, Tumblr, Youtube, etc.

5   Bowman, M. 2016. "Technology doesn't understand us, and we don't understand technology despite the fact that it is a constant presence in our lives…"

6   Lucier specified that performances of I Am Sitting in A Room need not use his text, and the performance may be recorded in any room.

7   Deleuze, G. Negotiations 1972-1990. pp. 129-130.

8   "…it's not a problem of getting people to express themselves but of providing little gaps of solitude and silence in which they might eventually find something to say. Repressive forces don't stop people expressing themselves but rather force them to express themselves; What a relief to have nothing to say, the right to say nothing, because only then is there a chance of framing the rare, and ever rarer, thing that might be worth saying. What we're plagued by these days isn't any blocking of communication, but pointless statements. But what we call the meaning of a statement is its point. That's the only definition of meaning, and it comes to the same thing as a statement's novelty. You can listen to people for hours, but what's the point?" Deleuze, G. Negotiations 1972-1990. pp. 129-130.

9   Deleuze, G., & Guattari, F. (1987). A thousand plateaus: Capitalism and schizophrenia. Minneapolis: University of Minnesota Press.

The subjective element of the voice has a different role depending on whether it confronts nonsubjectified power structures or nonsubjectified group individuation.[10] Lucier's instructions individualize, not according to the relation of the subject and the resonance chamber, but according to the affects experienced. The mediatization of the subject may produce the effect of drone, as if the subject had fallen into and continues to spin in a kind of black hole (the drone of the resonance chamber (ear = labyrinth)). This creates an impoverishment and fixation leading to a black hole[11] that can (potentially) form an échappatoire (for example, the "flutter" or dynamic instability of an elastic structure in a fluid flow, caused by positive feedback between the body's deflection and the force exerted by the fluid flow).[12] The white cubic walls of the resonance chamber may begin to bounce under such conditions.

To escape the drone of resonance chambers, the mediatized subject must flutter an échappatoire into existence. The labyrinth of the ear offers an escape route. It is possible to mine the depths of the digital media through which the subject is mediatized, and through which they become inherently of the mode of mediatization. It is necessary to tap into the device's labyrinth to capture the artifacts therein, to exploit the sounds that are not made by, but occur in between, the device; the whirring of the circuit boards, the molecular vibrations and white-noise elements, the wires and cables. The voice of the subject must be transfigured, made alien, but remain a stable entity. The substratum of the mediatized subject must be unearthed.

Anechoic chambers siphon drone off into razorback staggerings, and are antithetical to resonance chambers. Giuseppe Pinot Gallizio's Cavern of Anti Matter is also antithetical to the resonance chamber, and is suited to unearth the sonic substratum of the mediatized subject.[13] The dissolution of the resonance chamber is necessary to create an échappatoire. Vast, phantom terrains must be traversed wherein the subject reflexively articulates fundamental exploitations of drone. The sonic must reshape the resonant chamber, to the extent that the sonic representation of the environment reaches a saturation or flutter point. Thomas Nagel[14] and Florian Hecker[15] both address the potential echolocational escape of resonance chambers.[16]

---

10   "...the relations of the universal or the relations of the 'dividual.'" Ibid.

11   Ibid.

12   In a linear system, 'flutter point' is the point at which the structure is undergoing simple harmonic motion - zero net damping - and so any further decrease in net damping will result in a self-oscillation and eventual failure. The dramatically visible, rhythmic twisting that resulted in the 1940 collapse of "Galloping Gertie", the original Tacoma Narrows Bridge, is commonly misunderstood as resonance phenomenon. The catastrophic vibrations that destroyed the bridge were not due to simple mechanical resonance, but to a more complicated interaction between the bridge and the winds passing through it—a phenomenon known as aeroelastic flutter, which is a kind of "self-sustaining vibration" as referred to in the nonlinear theory of vibrations. K. Yusuf Billah and Robert H. Scanlan (1991). "Resonance, Tacoma Narrows Bridge Failure, and Undergraduate Physics Textbooks". American Journal of Physics 59 (2): 118–124.

13   Giuseppe Pinot Gallizio was a founding member of the Situationist International and was captivated by how encounters with resonance chambers might create tension with the drone of infinite reproducibility and distribution.

14   Nagel, Thomas (1974). "What Is It Like to Be a Bat?". The Philosophical Review 83 (4): 435–450.

15   Hecker, Florian. Chimerization. 2011.

16   "For Plato, truth is an activity of mind and speech, relegating the body and writing (and, by extension, poetry and art) to the realms of shadows and images." Gardener, Colin, "Let it Bleed: The Sublime and Plato's Cave, Rothko's Chapel, Lincoln's Profile," Mike Kelley: Catholic Tastes, exh. cat., Whitney Abrams (New York: 1993), 123-124.

Hecker's Chimerization is antithetical to Lucier's I Am Sitting in A Room. Both are recitations of texts or rules in a room, but the former is recorded in an anechoic chamber[17] and processed through chain-linked, hyper-chaotic algorithms; the latter is recorded and rerecorded in a resonance chamber, slipstreamed on the runaway oscillation of drone. The absolute difference of Hecker's algorithms dissolve the drone of the resonance chamber. Somewhere from deep within the inner sanctum of the resonance chamber the voice of the subject musters on the bouncing wall. Faintly, attenuated by the increasingly complex network of walls between the subject and the recording device, the drone is grafted into a complexly spatialized environment. A spectrum of electronic treatments of varying timbres distort the subject's voice, threading it through a mélange of sounds, arranged in repetitive forms, and processing it with interference. Despite this the voice of the subject is stable, though alien.

What is achieved is a functional échappatoire, a process focusing on the decomposition of sound and synthesizing incompatible modalities without fusing them in order to obtain a narration beyond immediate comprehension, an almost indecipherable hieroglyphic of acoustic artifacts. The subject sinks into the labyrinth of the ear. They sit in a white, empty cube where two small speakers descend from the ceiling on long, metal arms (in contrast to the single, supine recording device in Lucier's room). It is an austere, sterile, almost clinical space. There are only the speakers and the floor and the walls. A perfectly ordinary room. But the subject's voice seems to mine the depths of the media through which it is heard. An invisible, sonic substratum within the room is unearthed. The microscopic deconstructed-and-then-reconstructed aural impressions are siphoned off from an infinitely complex web of machanic activity. The subject's voice—conventionally connected with individual subjectivity, or communication—appears as just another element of sound, with emerging and receding clarity, amongst other textures of sound surfaces and signals.

It is impossible not to have a physical reaction to the complexly spatialized listening environment. After the drone of the resonance chamber is thoroughly dissolved, the shifting of the subject's internal compass intensifies, rearranging the coordinates of their mind, discombobulating them.[18] The space and materiality of available sensory data is at odds with what they are hearing. When they close their eyes they can picture a hyper-convoluted honeycomb labyrinth branching out around them, the voice reaching out across insuperable, inane voids; through rips in the fabric of reality itself. And then they open their eyes and they are back in the perfectly ordinary, empty, cubic resonance chamber with the two black speakers descending from the ceiling like surgical instruments. Hecker's prioritization of the sonic above the visual comes at the subject sideways. The object-shape of the media device—a set of plain speakers, cables, and sound production ephemera—is quite ordinary and minimal, but the voice's impact as invisible sound and frequency effects the subject in untimely, complex ways.

Hecker also exploits the "Haas" or "Precedence Effect" to dissolve the drone of the resonance chamber.[19] He

17   Recorded in an echo-less space, the subject's voice is superimposed back against itself – reduced, then reconstituted in a process Hecker terms "decomposition", to be blurred and dissolved, the processing shifting slightly between each superimposition.

18   As in an anechoic chamber.

19   The precedence effect or law of the first wavefront is a binaural psychoacoustic effect. When a sound is followed by another sound separated by a sufficiently

incorporates a delay between one speaker and another, adjusted to the degree that the subject cannot identify which they are hearing first.[20] Hecker also creates special sound installations which transmit a subject's voice as they speak instructions to a group of individuals lying on the floor with their eyes closed. The subject's voice is both diverted and amplified through a form of spatial distortion effected by the installation, making it impossible to know where the speaker is in relation to the individuals' static locations. The space thus becomes a gyrating vector in stark opposition to the experience of gravity and the sensation of lying on the floor.

Hecker has done many experiments with bouncing sound off the walls of resonance chambers. His experiments have created flutter points within the white cubic walls of the resonance chamber, with its drone logic and its suspension of the subject within neutral territory. His coupling of sound and space into a singular event creates phantom terrains, new topographies not delimited by the logic of drone. The sterile, cubic, white space of the resonance chamber is perceptually dissected, contorted, twisted, alternatively cordoned and filled as the subject re-enters it via the alien sound compositions. The white cube stretches into a minaret, fluttering the ceiling into a towering honeycombed pinnacle. It becomes hard for the subject to get a grasp on their spatial orientation, despite the fact that the resonance chamber is illuminated beneath unforgiving, constant, artificial light.

The subject must create events in which the prioritization of mediatized drone is destabilized; where echoes, bouncing and shattering off and against the walls, heighten their sense of topographical fictions. Through these events, they may inhabit "real" space in a new way which forces them to reimagine it, even to visualize it differently.

When the walls begin to bounce, and the subject sinks into the ear's labyrinth—an échappatoire where alien sonic territories spread maps across their mind—a blackness, a quantum wave function fluctuates before them. Geo- metric space warps into hyper-Penrosian dimensions. Cave systems spread through the walls as if mammoth worms have devoured the resonance chamber around them.

The subject's voice tries to reach them, to make itself intelligible, but is perpetually stifled by the machinations of the void. It sounds like a poltergeist speaking in tongues. The voice comes from the extreme limits of phantom terrains. There is an almost chemical processing of the subject's voice, distorting its message and its locality. But when the subject opens their eyes the wave function collapses; the limitless possibilities stretching before their imagination fold back into the cubic sterility of the resonance chamber. Then the subject's interpretation of the resonance chamber begins to change, as if they are inside a gigantic, fluctuating Necker Cube: when they close their eyes the walls are concave, but when they open them again they are convex. A sort of multi-stability oscillates back and forth so rapidly that eventually it congeals into a quantum jelly. The flutter point recedes, and the bouncing wall resumes its perfect ordinariness.

The opposition between Hecker and Lucier is clear: a re-

_____

short time delay (below the listener's echo threshold), listeners perceive a single fused auditory image; its perceived spatial location is dominated by the location of the first-arriving sound (the first wave front). The lagging sound also affects the perceived location. However, its effect is suppressed by the first-arriving sound.

20   The Bouncing Wall.

shaping of the resonance chamber (a static frame that is crucial to drone's reality) can recalibrate subjectivity. Nagel poses the question: what might the "inner life" of the bat be like?[21] He wonders how the bat perceives the topography of the resonance chamber with its high-frequency echolocation. It is clear that sonic, topographical fictions must be machinically actuated to counteract the dominant spectacle of drone's reality. Plato's Cave[22] describes how the human mind conjures a fixed version of the world based on available sensory data. Hecker's Chimerization can be thought of as an inversion of this. By refusing the drone of the resonance chamber and reversing and processing it into "virtual" echoes siphoned off from phantom terrains—a super-complicated system of subterranean tunnels that can be described only through the sound signals that guide and work against available sensory data—reality, in the form of the everyday drone of the resonance chamber, is dissolved.

Chimerization causes the subject to realize that the invisible, sonic architecture existing within the neutral zone of the resonance chamber is a mysteriously different space. The topographical fictions created by Hecker's composition press the subject, moving them, and alternately thrilling and jarring their senses in unfamiliar ways. The electronic blips and bleeps in the work—noises that the subject normally recognizes as signals reminding him of banal tasks: to check his e-mail, cross the road, or turn the oven off[23]—carry for them this signaling association, embedded semaphores pointing them this way and that, almost absurdly, without purpose, dragging them into an involuntary choreography of action. There are other, darker, low-frequency sounds that make the subject realize a deeply static sense of the center of their body. The alien voice communicates ideas of logic or conversational exchange, detourned to outlandish ends. These elements draw the subject further and further into the ear's labyrinth, guiding them like sentient insects. These sounds which ordinarily imply for the subject logic, transparency, and communication are turned around to describe other, unfamiliar places—subterranean catacombs with stalactites and stalagmites obscured by darkness. From the counterpoint space of the resonance chamber's curious, fluorescent cube, Chimerization conjures new imaginings within the subject, deconstructing familiar patterns and registers of drone logic to expose other realities.

In the midst of all this the subject has a sonic epiphany. They feel the hair on their arms stand on end; goosebumps spreading across their skin, turning their hair follicles to feathers, then scales, and then porcelain which shatters against a concrete barrier of air. They hover at the zenith of an anti-gravity parabola. They are pressed with an alternate destiny. A flutter point is reached, and the bouncing wall bounces ever further into the void.

---

21   Nagel, Thomas (1974). "What Is It Like to Be a Bat?". The Philosophical Review 83 (4): 435–450.

22   In the allegory, Plato likens people untutored in the Theory of Forms to prisoners chained in a cave, unable to turn their heads. All they can see is the wall of the cave. Behind them burns a fire. Between the fire and the prisoners there is a parapet, along which puppeteers can walk. The puppeteers, who are behind the prisoners, hold up puppets that cast shadows on the wall of the cave. The prisoners are unable to see these puppets, the real objects, that pass behind them. What the prisoners see and hear are shadows and echoes cast by objects that they do not see.

23   Resonance phenomena occur with all types of vibrations or waves: there is mechanical resonance, acoustic resonance, electromagnetic resonance, nuclear magnetic resonance (NMR), electron spin resonance (ESR) and resonance of quantum wave functions. Resonant systems can be used to generate vibrations of a specific frequency (e.g., musical instruments).

INNER-SENSE and EXPERIENCE:
DRONE MUSIC, ESOTERICISM and the HIEROEIDETIC FIELD

Phil Legard

The Field of Imagination: Art, Esotericism and Hieroeidetic Knowledge

As a musical genre that has blossomed alongside the development of the 'post-secular' sensibility, drone music invariably attracts mystically-loaded hyperboles such as 'transcendent', 'ecstatic'—even 'tantric'.[1] But, moving beyond journalistic cliché, to what extent do philosophies or practices that we might categorise as mystical or 'esoteric' actually shape the experience of creating and listening to drone music?

Arthur Versluis has proposed that the term hieroeidetic may be invoked as a descriptor of esoteric art.[2] A compound of two Greek terms, Versluis describes the eidetic as pertaining to a particular form of imagination—one that possesses a certain intensity, such as the "particularly luminous and vivid imagery found among young children and in dreams."[3] He does not

---

1   These adjectives all occur in a recent précis by Danny Riley, Northern Noise: Looking for the Perfect Drone with Northern England's DIY Transcendentalists (Bandcamp Daily). Despite this, many of the bands in the article do not hold explicitly occult or esoteric attitudes, with the exception of Matthew Bower (of Skullflower, Sunroof!) who has a long involvement with occultism beginning in the 1980s, and collaborated during that period with Alex Binnie (later of Zos Kia). Guttersnipe's Xylocopa Violacea has also expressed her relationship with the imagination in terms complementary to the hieroeidetic approach discussed in this chapter (Xylocopa Violacea, personal communication).

2   Arthur Versluis. Restoring Paradise: Western Esotericism, Literature, Art, and Consciousness. (New York: SUNY Press, 2004), 22-26. Although Versluis has been criticised by some continental scholars of esotericism for a 'religionist' view of esotericism as a monolithic tradition (vide Wouter J. Hanegraaf. "Textbooks and Introductions to Western Esotericism", Religion, 43:2, 178-200), I suggest that a number of his positions are insightful, and worthy of re-evaluation: as the academic field of Western Esotericism enters its third generation, a turn toward historiographically-informed cognitive and sociological approaches may invite new perspectives to positions like Versluis 'sympathetic empiricism'.

3   Restoring Paradise, 22.

qualify his use of the hiero- prefix, although it suggests that such vivid imagery as previously described is set apart from mundane reality in some way, as 'sacred' or 'initiatory'. Hieroeidetic knowledge is described as being encountered "in the field of imagination midway between the mundane and the transcendent".[4] When presented to an audience of what Versluis calls 'sympathetic' and 'initiatory' percipients, such a work may also serve as a preparatory for their own gnostic experiences: it leads them away from phenomenal reality to an intermediate, mesoteric, world, and possibly, through an imaginative engagement with the images therein, to an experience of a transpersonal or transcendent world.[5] It is the possibility of a work to manifest a mysterious, hieroeidetic knowledge, or gnosis, that can be perceived as a distinguishing feature of art that is considered esoteric—Versluis' interpretation of the 'esoteric' signifying an encounter with inner, rather than outer (exoteric), phenomena.[6]

Versluis primarily points toward reading as being an activity which is primed for being hieroeidetically charged, since the immersed reader fluidly dispenses with barriers of self and other, subject and object.[7] This emphasises that hieroeidetic engagement is not passive, but born from active interior responses to a work, which can only be realised with a measure of commitment, concentration and insularity.

Given that Versluis' primary concerns are visual art and literature, how does the concept of hieroeideticacy extend to non-visually mediated art forms? The area that Katharine Norman has described as 'real world music'—that is, experimental music that emerges from the use of field recordings—may suggest one solution, since field recordings often evoke strong 'sound images' in the minds of listeners.[8] But what of the more abstracted textures of drone music?

To explore this question, we will further develop the concept of hieroeideticacy, casting it as a concept of central importance to the psychological experience of creating and appreciating music that posits itself within the esoteric. We will begin by 'reverse engineering' one of Versluis' historical case studies in order to isolate particular themes or 'building blocks' implicit in the concept. We will then explore the work of sound artist Kim Cascone through a hieroeidetic lens, with particular attention to his concepts of auditory 'grain' and 'subtle listening'. From here, we will take a reflexive turn, to explore how an initiation into Cascone's work has affected my own recent collaborative musical work. Finally, we will discuss the implications of musical hieroeideticacy, with particular regard to notions of authenticity, experience and the formulation of 'ritual drone'.

---

4   Ibid.

5   Versluis identifies three types of readers of esoteric works: closed readers, whose 'predetermined theses [...] disallow their imaginative entry'; sympathetic readers – who willingly 'enter into a work imaginatively'; initiated – 'who see the work as mirroring a process that they seek to undergo in themselves.' (Restoring Paradise, 14). Rather than use the term 'readers' or 'audience', I have followed Kim Cascone (interview, 2016) and used the more general term percipient to imply an audience of actively engaged (e.g. sympathetic or initiatory) listeners: those who can perceive – and participate in – the hieroeidetic field.

6   Restoring Paradise, 26.

7   Restoring Paradise, 4-5.

8   Katharine Norman, "Real-World Music as Composed Listening", Contemporary Music Review, vol 15, parts 1 (1996).

Rituals for Evoking Specialness: Outlining Hieroeidetic Creativity

Like Versluis' engaged readers, drone musicians and listeners are attracted to the music by its immersive, enveloping, cathartic qualities, which weaken subject-object boundaries. It may be argued that the same could broadly be said of many listening experiences, but—in addressing the fact that all literature is imaginative, but not all literature is hieroeidetic—Versluis suggests that what makes the hieroeidetic distinct is a question of intent on behalf of both the creator and percipients: the creator encodes their experiences in the art, and the percipient—by an active act of imaginative co-creation—may also connect with their own reflection of the artistic gnosis, from which further metaphysical insights may be developed.[9] Hieroeideticacy may be broadly defined, then, as an active relationship with an artwork within the imagination—an imagination that is felt to be set apart from commonplace 'fancy' in some way: it allows the percipients to experience what is perceived to be another reality.

One artist mentioned by Versluis who deserves particular attention in order to more clearly define the qualities of hieroeideticacy, is the English visionary painter Cecil Collins (1908-89).[10] Collins' work is inextricably bound up with the notion of hieroeidetic knowledge: he describes his creative process as being engaged with the 'theatre of the soul', which describes the interior, imaginative world in which he explores the 'ritual' play of the various archetypal figures involved in his paintings.[11] For Collins, these figures are not simply fictions or allegories, but the "actual emotions of the reality of existence, realised in concrete forms that can be experienced."[12] For Collins, artwork may arise from inner encounters with these images, or by projecting them onto chance patterns, as in his 'matrix' paintings. Either way, Collins perceives that the imaginative act involved in his work bridges the mundane and transcendent worlds, and opens the possibility for, both artist and percipient, of a 'sacramental' encounter with higher worlds.[13] It is the possibility of a rapport with 'higher worlds' through an active engagement with an artwork that is the essence of the hieroeidetic quality.

A closer study Collins' life and art may lead us to propose three areas that support the production of hieroeidetic art:

Complex Aesthetic Experience – Although the Collins' mind was often orientated toward interior and transcendent realities, many of his formative stemmed from epiphanies in the natural world.[14] For example, two of Collins' key symbols—the bird and the tree—developed form an epiphanic experience of a primal unity when he saw and heard a bird singing on a tree branch "and suddenly realised that the tree was the shape of the bird's song, they were one."[15] In this moment, the natural world was transfigured, and the bird and tree

---

9   Versluis, Restoring Paradise, 13.

10   Versluis, Restoring Paradise, 129-135.

11   Much of the material in this section is elaborated on in my paper "Singing Messengers: Re-considering the Role of 'Poetic Imagination' in the Creative Process" (presented at Creativity: A Multidimensional Approach, Leeds Beckett University, June 16, 2016), which is available on request.

12   Cecil Collins. The Vision of the Fool and Other Writings. (Ipswich: Golgonooza Press, 2002), 88.

13   Versluis, Restoring Paradise, 131-2.

14   The parallels with the Romantic encounter with nature (cf. Wordsworth and Coleridge) are obvious, and Collins identified his own work with a continuance of the Romantic tradition.

15   Collins, The Vision, 56.

become symbolic of an invisible, primal unity. For Collins, and for the sympathetic percipient, these symbols initiate us into a new apprehension of the world, opening up the possibility of a similar 'sacramental encounter.' Experiencing a natural scene is one form of what might be called a complex aesthetic experience, from which symbolic insight potentially arises. We might also suggest that an imaginative rapport with stochastic forms—such as the chance brushstrokes that Collins' used to construct his 'matrix' pictures, or Max Ernst's decalcomania—could also fall under this theme of 'potential insight provoked by complexity.' We could consider this to be the exoteric layer of our scheme: it encompasses audible, legible or visible phenomena that demands an artist or percipient engage with it and respond to it, but in doing so not to simply judge its superficial qualities, rather to incorporate the phenomena into an inner-sense response.

Inner-Sense Cultivation – Collins describes the symbols in his 'theatre of the soul' as unfolding "gradually or suddenly, from the unknown"[16] and often "in my imagination [thought] right out to the very smallest details".[17] This vivid engagement with mental imagery could be considered in the context of what Ann Taves and Egil Asprem have described as 'inner-sense cultivation.'[18] This term is a broadening of Richard Noll's concept of mental imagery cultivation, as observed in the anthropology of shamanism, which emphasises that mental imagery is a skill: the 'minds' eye' has a form of foveal vision, which strengthens

with practice.[19] The use of the term 'inner-sense' also avoids assumptions associated with the term 'imagination,' and emphasises the qualitative difference between inner-sense experience and imagination as 'day dream' or the entertainment of abstract propositions. It is evident from Collins' own writings that he was engaging with his 'inner senses' instinctively from a young age, and that his various epiphanies, intuitions and visions formed the hieroeidetic field in which he worked. The inner-senses are Versluis' mesoteric 'field of imagination', where interactions with the work are played out in the psyches of the percipients.

Sacramental Encounter, or Ascriptions of Specialness – Many artists develop work from their imagination, or from an experience of natural things. However, what defines the esoteric artist is that the goal of such creativity is not simply to document a scene, but to encounter, or re-encounter, a gnostic experience, or altered state of consciousness, often ascribed to a transcendent or transpersonal source (such as Collins' 'emotions of the reality of existence'). Such encounters are somehow set apart as 'special': they may be imaginative insights, vivid flows of imagery that seem to come from 'beyond' oneself, or less easily articulated life-affirming, re-vivifying experiences. These experiences may even seem more valuable to the artist than

16   Ibid. 149.

17   Ibid. 157.

18   Ann Taves & Egil Asprem, "Experience as Event: Event Cognition and the Study of (Religious) Experiences," currently in press, to be published in Religion, Brain, & Behavior (2015): 13.

19   Richard Noll. "Mental Imagery Cultivation as a Cultural Phenomenon: The Role of Visions in Shamanism", Current Anthropology, Vol. 26, No. 4 (1985): 446. For a more recent treatment of the development of the skill of inner sense cultivation, see Tanya Luhrmann & Rachael Morgain, "Prayer as Inner Sense Cultivation: an attentional learning theory of spiritual experience", ETHOS, Vol. 40, No. 4 (2012): 359-389. By suggesting the use of the term inner sense cultivation, as opposed to Noll's mental imagery cultivation, the attributes of hieroeidetic creativity and imagination suggested above are not so tightly bound to co-creation around mental imagery (the chief concern of Noll and Versluis), but may work with a broader range of phenomena including eidetic audition and other inner sense impressions.

the production of work itself.[20] However, without 'special' encounters of these types being ascribed to it, a work or creative process cannot be said to possess a quality of hieroeideticacy. This is the esoteric experience, in which inner-sense perceptions are 'set apart' as authentic gnostic experiences.[21]

In summarising these themes, it should be noted that I have incorporated some concepts derived from Ann Taves' theoretical framework for the study of religious experience. Drawn from a variety of anthropological, sociological and psychological approaches, Taves emphasises that religious experience is not sui generis—a unique phenomena to the difficult-to-define area of religion—but rather is a subset of a larger range of experiences that we set apart as in some way 'special', which may also include esoteric experience.[22] The process of 'setting things apart' by ascription is central to this: the focus being on why individuals set such experiences apart as special.[23] It is worth noting here that the attributes outlined above form what Taves has called a 'composite ascription' or 'path': a set of 'building-blocks' that connect to describe practices deemed efficacious toward a particular goal—a ritual

process with a start (complex aesthetic experience) and a goal (sacramental encounter).[24] We can see that for both artists, and percipient, an experience deemed 'special' is at the heart of what distinguishes the hieroeidetic from forms of creativity and reception which are not invested in the esoteric. For the purposes of this discussion, we will consider a work to be hieroeidetic if it facilitates an ascription of specialness through the engagement of inner-senses via a complex aesthetic experience.

Tuning in to Dark Stations: Hieroeideticacy in the work of Kim Cascone

Between 2007 and 2015, the American sound artist Kim Cascone (b. 1955) produced a series of essays and compositions that suggest strong connections to the form of hieroeidetic creativity outlined above.[25] Additionally, Cascone developed these ideas into a series of workshops entitled Subtle Listening: Ear Training for Artists, which he delivered at artistic and educational institutions across Europe. We will begin by surveying his work in terms of the above building-blocks of hieroeideticacy, followed by a reflection on my own experiences as a participant in his workshops, and subsequent 'initiated' response to his work.

---

20 Collins writes that some of his interior imagery is so rich that it need not even be painted (Collins, The Vision, 157).

21 It is unintentional, but perhaps significant, that the three attributes mentioned here can be seen as corresponding to the 'three worlds' of Renaissance esotericism: in the microcosm body, soul and mind; in the macrocosm elemental, celestial and intellectual worlds (Cornelius Agrippa, Three Books of Occult Philosophy (trans. J.F.), London: Gregory Moule 1651, I.i; I.lxi)

22 Ann Taves, Religious Experience Reconsidered: A Building-Block Approach to the Study of Religion and Other Special Things (Princeton: Princeton University Press, 2009), 26-45.

23 Taves describes special things as variously: anomalous experiences of agency; anomalous places, objects, experiences or events without agency; ideal things. Within these are things further set apart, or sacralised, such as spiritual beings/deities; qualities deemed mystical or spiritual; absolutes (Religious Experience, 45).

---

24 Religious Experience, 46-48.

25 These essays are: "The Grain of the Auditory Field", Junk Jet, No. 1 (2007); "Errormancy: Glitch as Divination", The End of Being (2012); "The Avant Garde as Aeromancy", The Idea of the Avant Garde (ed. Marc Legér), Manchester University Press (2014); "Subtle Listening: How Artists can Develop New Perceptual Circuits", Infinite Grain (2014); "Transcendigital Imagination: Developing Organs of Subtle Perception", Interference, Vol. 4 (2014). Reference will also be made to the musical composition Dark Stations (2013).

One feature of many of Cascone's essays is that they encompass exoteric and esoteric readings. The Grain of the Auditory Field (2007) is, on the surface, a critique of the state of digitally-mediated sonic arts, particularly those that involve the presentation of field recordings. Yet read more closely, the language indicates a variety of esoteric sympathies. The paper begins with a reflection on complex aesthetic experience: Cascone describes a flock of birds trapped in a shopping centre, which becomes a meditation on the commingling of natural and man-made sound and the nature of attention in listening.[26] Following this, he proposes an attitude critical of contemporary "commodity fetishism", which "blinds us to the 'grain' of the world around us."[27] This is a similar opinion of modern culture to that of the Traditionalist school, to which Collins and many other artists involved in esoteric creativity also adhere to varying degrees. Indeed, Cascone cites Ananda Coomaraswamy in this respect, whose work is often typified by emphasising the importance of myth, symbol and imagination over the trappings of modernity.[28] Cascone's central thesis is that by digitally recording sound, we somehow deprive it of its soul, or grain.[29] The artists' task is to allow the sound to "induce sympathetic vibrations […] when we allow this energy to flow through us we create meaning and are able to perceive the grain of the auditory field."[30] Considering the nature of Cascone's subsequent work, we may take this as an exhortation to develop a form of inner-sense cultivation: a reflexive, imaginative approach that enables the grain, or 'inner mystery', of the sound to unfold itself for artist and percipient.[31] The upshot may be a sense of special experience (- sacramental encounter -) informing the work: "If we are lucky, at some point the grain transports us via a cross of sensations that deepens us or adds to the quality of our lives. Eventually we want to share that transcendental feeling with others."[32]

In 2012's Errormancy: Glitch as Divination, the esoteric associations are more explicit. The theme here is that glitches, accidents, and the random-access of sound materials can be invoked as 'conjurers of symbols' that unveil 'subliminal content'.[33] In terms of hieroeidetic attributes, we are dealing with complex aesthetic experiences (the 'invocation' of glitches), and their imaginative reception. When Cascone also draws parallels with magical crystal-gazing and the tendency for visions seen in a 'shewstone' to shuffle "the psychic space of the observer, allowing the artists to establish a direct link with the supernal realm"[34], the connection with inner-sense cultivation and the possibility of special experience are also apparent: a process Cascone elsewhere refers to as 'artistic divination'.[35]

These ideas are most developed in two pieces published in 2014, Subtle Listening and Transcendigital Imagination. Both of these works can be read almost as manifestos of hieroeideticism in the field of sonic arts. Subtle Listening begins with a reflection on Cascone's first encounters with meditation in 1975, during

---

26 Grain, 1.

27 Grain, 2.

28 Grain, 4.

29 Grain, 3.

30 Grain, 2.

31 Ibid.

32 Ibid.

33 Errormancy, 2-3.

34 Errormancy, 2.

35 Aeromancy, 2. Aeromancy presents an allegory that can also be read through a lens of Traditionalism and its relation with notions of authenticity.

which he hears the sound of a flock of migrating birds flying back and forth. Taking his teacher's advice to "acknowledge the distractions, don't focus on them" he lets the sound of the birds take shape in his mind's eye as "an undulating, spiky, amoebic shape, travelling back and forth in arcs and loops."[36] He senses that he has "switched into an altered and slightly mystical reality."[37] The parallels with the proposed hieroeidetic building-blocks are apparent, and inform the inner-sense exercises that Cascone suggests elsewhere in Subtle Listening, and in his related workshops. For example, exercises like 'listening to voices in the sound of flowing water' use complex aesthetic experiences as a form of pareidolia, which yields further material to explore inwardly.[38] Inner-sense cultivation is further developed in exercises that ask participants to imagine the 'auditory field' of a painting, imagine the 'sound shapes' of words, and—in Cascone's workshops—to enter a loosely guided meditation and develop a soundscape from the sounds perceived therein.[39]

Transcendigital Imagination concludes the series of essays, returning to the theme of field recordings and the loss of 'soul' or 'grain' somewhere between capture and playback. It also possesses the same potential exoteric and esoteric readings as the Grain of the Auditory Field. This time, however, the connections to esotericism are more evident—the 'soul' (or 'grain') is asserted to be found in a heightened state of perceptual awareness, which Cascone describes as "the supersensible, mundus imaginalis, imaginal perception,

active imagination, subtle realm, participatory consciousness", and quotes F. David Peat to the effect that "once the barriers between inner and outer, inscape and landscape, are dissolved, and fixed responses give way to fluid and complex actions, then a new form of active perception can be practiced."[40] Peat's use of the term 'inscape' refers to an awareness of "the authentic voice, or inner-dwellingness of things and of our experience of them"[41]—perhaps akin to what Paracelsus called evestra: the qualities of things that can only be perceived through a mode of imaginative perception—the meeting on the mesoteric field of the hieroeidetic.[42]

During this period, Cascone was also performing his piece Dark Stations (2013), a 42-minute composition 'for meditating audience', diffused within a triangle of speakers encompassing listeners and a central subwoofer. Composed of inter-modulating electronic tones, the closest comparison would perhaps be Eliane Radigue's similarly meditative Adnos (1974). Compositionally, Dark Stations is deeply embedded in esoteric concepts, such as speculative music (for example, the presence of sun and moon frequencies, see fig.1), spiritual communication (the use of 'spiricom' frequencies), and invisible, atmospheric phenomena (the use of Schumann resonances). The musical content is itself 'subtle' and cannot be enjoyed in a passive way: rather, it demands alternate listening strategies, such as an adoption of a meditative, yet receptive state akin to the "altered and slightly mystical reality" that Cascone mentioned in his own experiences of sonic meditation.[43] The work is co-creative in the hieroeidetic sense: Cascone provides the environment and

---

36 Subtle Listening, 2. As an 'originary event', leading the experiencer on to more esoteric modes of thought, this has similarities with Cecil Collins' aforementioned experience of unity perceived between bird and tree.

37 Ibid.

38 Subtle Listening, 4.

39 Subtle Listening, 3-4.

40 Transcendental Imagination.

41 F. David Peat, Synchronicity: The Speculum of Inscape and Landscape (n.d.).

42 Restoring Paradise, 60.

43 Subtle Listening, 2.

sound, which we are urged to respond to on the imaginative field between ourselves and the work. Cascone says that own his experience of the work is one of re-centering, reflecting the form of special experience generally ascribed to meditative practices:

When I test a meditation piece that uses binaural beats I'd sometimes have CEV's (closed eye visuals) of intricate fractal-like mandala patterns […] When I'm in that space there is a nourishing effect, I also find it a good time to dump unneeded things into the abyss.[44]

The works surveyed here give us a sense of how Cascone's approach fits into the concerns of hieroeideticacy, particularly with regard to how the perception of sound, rather than visual or literary media, is used to stimulate the experience of the 'inner-sense'. The writings also often have an autobiographic introduction, which helps us identify the spiritual practices and forms of originary event that led to Cascone developing such a relationship between sound and imagination.[45] Such biographical details are also useful to situate his practices both socially and psychologically. This is particularly important with regard to Taves and Asprem's assertion that inner-sense cultivation is a skill: that certain practices enhance the intuition and the vivacity of imagery, and that the confidence to recognise and explore altered states of consciousness may also be considered skills in this context.[46] Furthermore, the use of complex aesthetic inputs (the natural soundscape, glitches, beating frequencies), their interpretation through the 'inner senses', and the ascription of insights yielded therefrom to unconscious or 'subtle realms' demonstrates a congruence with the type of complex ascription, or ritual path, that typifies the hieroeidetic approach.

The Imaginal Mirror: Subtle Listening and the Hieroeideticacy in Hawthonn

Having surveyed Cascone's work through the frame of hieroeideitcism, we will now take a reflexive turn in order to explore upon my own recent work, which has developed from—or was initiated by—encounters with Cascone's workshop and concert work.

In 2013, I invited Cascone to give a performance of his Dark Stations piece at Leeds Beckett University, and found it an unexpectedly uncanny and affecting experience. Seated in our 'black box' performance space, within the triangle of speakers, I gradually relaxed into the piece, as the frequencies generated interacted with the environment, and which also phased in accordance with the subtle movements of my own body. As the relaxed-yet-perceptive state unfolded, my focus was drawn toward the front-right of the auditory field, where a series of intermodulating waves seemed to have meshed into a semblance of speech: a strange, cracked voice, whispering "You sleep with you, you sleep with me." My wife, Layla, was pregnant at the time, and I found myself making a powerful association between this voice, and the voice of my then unborn son, who—being in utero—was, consequently, sharing the bed with us.

---

44   Cascone, Kim. Interviewed by Phil Legard, via email. 05/08/16 – 09/08/16.

45   On originary events, see Religious Experience, 156-60.

46   Ann Taves & Egil Asprem, "Event Cognition and the Study of (Religious) Experiences", Religion, Brain & Behaviour (Pre-publication postprint article), 2015.

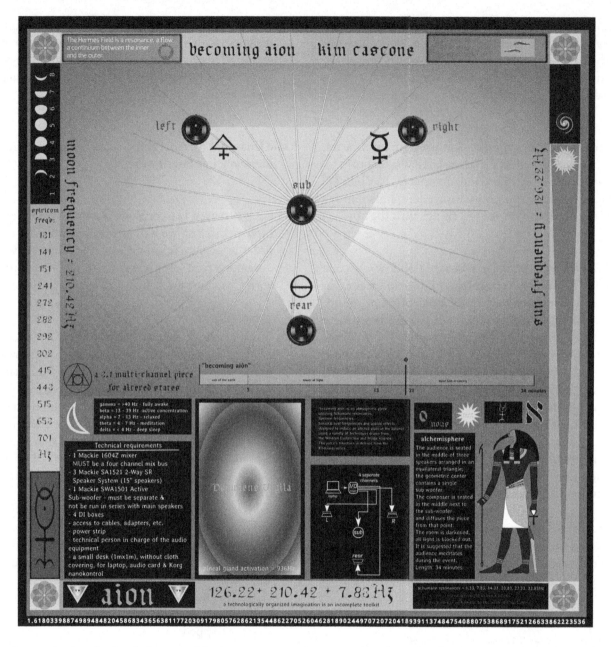

Fig. 1. Cascone's plan for *Dark Stations* (aka *Becoming Aion*), executed in the style of visionary artist Paul Laffoley. Used with permission of Kim Cascone.

I invited Cascone back to the university in April 2014, to lead a two-day Subtle Listening workshop participated in by final-year and post-graduate music students, and myself. This involved a variety of 'sound-shape' exercises, which can be seen as serving a particular purpose with regard to cultivating the experience and understanding of mental imagery within a group of varied skill, in order to prime them for the guided meditation that marked the culmination of the workshop.

Seated in a circle, Kim's meditative narrative evoked a cosmic terrain, which served as a point of ingress for our own imaginative encounter.[47] For myself, this encounter seemed to lead me through a series of mythic spaces: burial chambers, subterranean oceans, and caverns, all bathed in shimmering blue light.

Following this, my second experience of the Dark Stations composition was—perhaps as a consequence of having my sense for inner imagery 'primed' by the meditation earlier in the day—far more rich in imagery, as well as a particularly intense feeling of bodily awareness within the inner landscape. During the concert, I drifted through a variety of cathedral-like spaces, seemingly carved from a malleable, ivory-like material, patterned with fractal pits and strata. The vividness and peculiarity of the vision was striking, and—as with the pareidoliac voice in the prior session—developed an ascription of 'specialness': these were experiences that I would have deemed unlikely to have occurred without the music and the altered states of consciousness that the concert setting enabled. I am also moved to describe the events of the second workshop and concert as initiatory, in that contact with the teacher (or initiator) and working through the exercises in the workshop ultimately informed the modus operandi of the Hawthonn project, co-created with Layla Legard. The engagement with subtle listening took me from being a sympathetic percipient, to being a 'subtle composer'.

The name Hawthonn is a compound of the 'hawthorn', and 'Jhonn'—as in Jhonn Balance (born Geff Rushton, 1962-2004), the troubled visionary artist who comprised one half of the cult experimental group Coil. The Hawthonn project marked the tenth anniversary of Balance's death and the scattering of his ashes (along with the internment of a pair of blackbirds) around a hawthorn tree at Bassenthwaite, Cumbria, by his then-partner Ian Johnstone. The project set out to use the techniques of subtle listening as tools to develop a visionary engagement with emergent symbols and imagery, and ran from Summer Solstice 2014 to the 13th November of the same year—the date of Balance's death.

---

47   Such a meditation seeks to stimulate mental imagery and lead the percipient to a point where they can 'take over' and explore their own emergent images. There are a number of precedents in Western esoteric traditions, notably in the concept of 'pathworkings', or guided visualisations, which developed from Western esotericism in the early 20th century. Adam Maclean posits that the term pathworking has its genesis in the works of Dion Fortune and the Fraternity of the Inner Light ('Pathworking and Inner Journeys', The Hermetic Journal, vol. 22, 16-21). The Golden Dawn technique of tattvic skrying, for example, is an open-ended procedure, that begins with a number of visualisations, such as passing through the symbol as though it were a door, and making certain gestures 'astrally', ultimately taking the skryer into a symbolic landscape (see Israel Regardie, The Tree of Life (Minnesota: Llewllyn 2004, 197-200).

Emblems

1st - 10th April, 2014, Phil Legard

Fig. 2. Emblems (2014), graphic score developed from the author's experience of Kim Cascone's guided meditation.

Cascone has previously used the occult process of scrying (- gazing into a magical mirror of crystal -) as a metaphor for the visionary and creative processes involved in his work. For example, in Errormancy he writes:

The shiny surface of a jet shewstone, the dim flicker of lamp flame in a darkened room, the fogged interior of a crystal sphere—these devices acted like a receiver, carrying bits of wisdom from an a-temporal, non-spatial, non-manifest reality: the supernal realm or mundus imaginalis.

Dark Stations itself was explicitly described in programme material as "a scrying mirror into which the viewers' unconscious is projected then reflected back to them,"[48] and it was the potential of the 'surface' of a composition to become a tool for scrying that underpinned the work of Hawthonn. Being unable to visit the Bassenthwaite site itself during the given time-period, the work was conceived as a form of imaginative pilgrimage to the memory of Balance, enabled by scrying processes, and inspired in part by the work of Martin Locker, who has studied medieval traditions of 'internal pilgrimage'.[49]

Throughout the development of the project, a series of scrying compositions, which we termed holophones, were developed.[50] The first holophone, Alpha, was composed on June 21st, and listened to over a five-day period. It contained a series vocal extracts from an interview with Jhonn Balance conducted as part of the 1988 documentary The Sound of Progress. In this interview, a young Balance self-consciously discusses dreams, visions and 'neo-surrealism'. The vocal extracts (each less than half a second long) were split over stereo channels and crossfaded in to create a continuum of juxtaposed pairs. The intention here was to use Balance's own voice to evoke the phenomena of phantom words—a form of auditory pareidolia.[51] At

---

48   Kim Cascone, Dark Stations (promotional material), 2013.

49   Martin Locker, "Movement Through Stillness: Imagined Pilgrimage in Medieval Europe" (presented at the EMICS conference Stasis in the Medieval World, UCL Institute of Archaeology, April 13, 2013).

50   A nod to the visual hologram, the term holophone was intended to convey the sense of shifting images and viewpoints that the sounds were intended to facilitate.

51   This approach was inspired by Diana Deutsch's phantom word experiments (on Diana Deutsch, Phantom Words and Other Curiosities, 2013, La Jolla: Philomel Records), as well as Cascone's subtle listening exercises, such as hearing voices in a stream.

the end of the five-day listening period, the following list of phantom words had been compiled:

(It's) time, A guess, Amprodius, Burial, Chaos case, Cocidius, Copper moon, Curious, Daemon, Destroy stamen, Destroyer, Experience, Figures, Fingers, Going at you, Gotcha, Hideous, Hiss, Hornets, I'm staying, I'm studying, Integrate, Is is is is…, It's strange, Kala, Kia, Kiss, One-six-seven, Palace, Predator, President, Processor, Propagate, Proper moon, Provenant, Provident, Red alert, Resident, Resonant, Same room, Shadow, Shadowing, She knows, She'll go in, She's gone, Sitting room, Stamen, Stockading, Straining, Sugaring, Tame, Taming, Tangle, The chaos, The gardens, This is, This this this this…, Time, Time is tangled, Trapping 'em, Tremendous, Turning off, Upsetting them, Your guidance.

From this list, evocative words and phrases were selected as particular 'nodes' of interest for further exploration, these included: Burial, copper moon, palace, shadow, the gardens and time is tangled.

At this time, we also discovered a partially-decayed fox in our garden, and bleached its skull and vertebrae. This struck us as a 'meaningful coincidence', given that Balance's partner, Ian Johnstone, adopted a vulpine stage persona named Mr. Todd. The creation of a rattle from fox skull and vertebrae evoked associations with shamanic journeys, and informed the composition of the second holophone, Beta, in which repetitive, phasing rhythms were used to create an evolving series of patterns, accompanied by image-to-sound transformations from photographs of hawthorn foliage, and field-recordings of the sea and blackbirds. Whereas Alpha had behaved as pareidoliac evocation, the intention of Beta was to use it as a tool for imaginative journeys. In this instance, listening sessions were initiated with a form of semi-structured meditation, or pathworking, in which:

I imagine myself to be climbing to an upper room in a grand Victorian mansion, which overlooks the sea. I can hear distant waves and, unexpectedly, the call of a blackbird.[52]

To look out of the window is a surprise. I see not the distant sea and the town rolling off toward it, but instead look upon the self-illumed landscape. It is a window to another place, previously only glimpsed in an obsessional dream.

Here comes the psychopomp—a decaying fox of immense size, all matted dark brown fur and exposed bones. Despite its eyeless sockets, it knows the way.[53]

The intention was to visualise riding the fox into another realm, and to use this as a stepping stone to explore emergent imagery, akin to the guided meditation that Cascone had led. From the sessions with holophones Alpha and Beta, the first composition developed for the album, which added vocal passages to the music of the Beta. The lyrics were informed by the imagery of Alpha and subsequent symbols drawn from the 'self-illumed landscape', of Bassenthwaite's 'imaginal mirror':

---

52   This is a reference to the house Jhonn Balance shared with partner Peter 'Sleazy' Christopherson, at Weston-Super-Mare.

53   Phil & Layla Legard, Hawthonn Journal. (Leeds: Larkfall, 2015), 7-8.

Follow the fox
Follow the fox
Through tangled time,
Through the clouds of ash
And the copper moon,
To the palace of birds.
To a shadow garden
Where the hawthorn grow.[54]

---

54   Hawthonn Journal, 8.

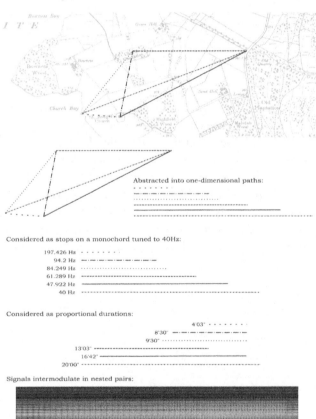

As time passed, the exploration of 'imaginal Bassenthwaite' became more central to the project. A third holophone, Gamma, was composed specifically as a drone that would be in some way symbolic of the locale, and which could become the focus for deeper explorations of the landscape. A series of 'significant' locations were plotted on a map of Bassenthwaite and connected together (see figure 3). It was then supposed that the longest of these distances represented a monochord tuned to 40Hz. The other distances could then be interpreted as 'stops' on the monochord, yielding frequencies above the fundamental. Using a Max/MSP patch, the resulting frequencies were then arranged and intermodulated to yield complex timbres and rhythms.

While Alpha was constructed to induce auditory pareidolia—a form of acoustic séance—Beta and Gamma came to constitute a pair of tracks to be employed in imaginatively journeying to and exploring internal landscapes. This form of imaginative pathworking, along with the intense, obsessional nature of the project also provoked dreams, reflecting the same interior landscapes, for example the dream of the 22nd of September:

Somehow Layla and I have found ourselves moving to the countryside, to a small, low house, built of sturdy stones and annexed to the side of a church.[55]

Fig. 3. A plan for the Gamma holophone, showing the mapping of geographical loci to frequencies.

---

55   The church of St. Bega, Bassenthwaite.

Of course, there is a secret passage: it leads into what, upon reflection, must have been a cistern or drain of some sort. A ledge leads along the side of the chamber, beneath which a shallow, muddy rivulet trickles. We have to stoop and edge along, holding on to the cracks between the brickwork to avoid falling. At the end of the ledge, there is a door.

This door leads into a very dark chamber. There is a four-poster bed to the right, a window ahead, and a mirror next to the window. There is a high-backed chair in front of the mirror. I sit down in the chair. I decide not to look in the mirror, but instead out of the window. The sky is a deep, dark blue. A forest is silhouetted against it. Above the trees are two bright stars—intuitively I feel they are part of the constellation of Aries. The stars become the eyes of a face, looking at me from the sky. The black and blue face of a youth.[56]

The face in the sky became a recurrent symbol toward the end of the project, as in the lyrics to the final track, Thanatopsis: "Think of a star / think of a star daemon."

Unlike Cascone's Dark Stations, the holophones were not intended for public performance: their purpose was to inform the development of an album that would both possess an imaginative potency, and be accessible to a wider audience. The holophones were a creative tool, providing us with an acoustically conjured hieroeidetic field in which to develop relationships with emergent images and symbols, which ultimately included: hawthorn, church, fox, star daemon, madman, white horse and night-mare.

The holophones did enjoy a limited release with the first 72 copies of the album, and material from them was incorporated into parts of the resulting album. The music of the album still broadly centres on the drone idiom, and as such provoked its own responses from reviewers: they generally avoided mystical superlatives in favour of expressing high degrees of imagistic content, which perhaps demonstrate the persistence of the hieroeidetic field in the finished work, for example:

[The opening track is] "[a] half-dream, half-distant field recording of a pre-Christian ritual in some Stonehenge-like clearing on a hillside […] Layla acts as a kind of benevolent Siren, guiding me through a fog of buzzing drones."[57]

"Deep bass drones are like the muddy soil beneath our boots, hiding magickal manuscripts and the corpses of the restless forgotten dead. A fox skull calls the faithful to prayer, as ritualistic shakers frame Layla's incantations like an ivy trellis."[58]

[The final track is] "a full circle from rural and earthborn to something lunar and cosmic and then back again."[59]

The most interesting response in this regard came from the author David Metcalfe, whose review-essay bound his experience of the album to a series of synchronicities, and assertions that come across as intuitively

---

56 Hawthonn Journal, 16-17.

57 Anthony D'Amico, review of Hawthonn. Brainwashed, 24 January 2016, http://www.brainwashed.com/index.php?option=com_content&view=article&id=10744:hawthonn&catid=13:albums-and-singles&Itemid=133.

58 Jason Simpson, review of Hawthonn. Forestpunk, 30 August 2015, https://forestpunk.wordpress.com/2015/08/30/hawthonn-hawthonn/.

59 Grey Malkin, review of Hawthonn. Active Listener, 2 June 2015, http://active-listener.blogspot.co.uk/2015/06/hawthonn-hawthonn.html.

aligned with the hieroeidetic field with which this chapter has been concerned:

… it is a testament to the power of such methodologies that immediately upon engagement with Hawthonn, the imaginal landscape evoked in the recordings became so immanent and accessible.

Within an imaginal landscape the geography is mapped through associative meaning rather than physical landmarks. While those around me continue to exist in their own perceived web of meaning, by allowing myself the freedom of associative thinking I can actively realign my own representational references and enter into a meaningful conversation with the symbols that encircle the album and its creation. We see through a glass darkly, and techniques such as those employed in the conception of this album provide a lens to adjust our vision.[60]

Conclusion: Ritual Drone and Hieroeidetic Fieldwork

This chapter has explored the concept of hieroeideticacy in a number of areas. In the theoretical writings of Kim Cascone, it manifests as the use of 'imaginative perception' to interpret the acoustic environment, or as an artistic methodology to explore other 'complex' phenomena, such as glitches. In his music, however, the intention is to conjure a hieroeidetic field in which the audience can use their own inner-senses: for Cas-

cone this is a centering, nourishing experience which may be accompanied by the perception of sound-shapes; in my own listening the acoustic space opened up the opportunity to explore a flow of imaginative imagery.[61] This fed into my own notion of the regular, 'ritualised' use of such acoustic spaces to engage in a sustained imaginative process that would be fundamental to the unfolding of a creative project.

All of these approaches are focused on the experiential value of the act of imaginatively-engaged listening as an esoteric practice, although for Cascone and myself these acts are also embedded within the creative process. The listening engagement with the holophones has been referred to as ritualised with serious intention, rather than simply an attempt to 'occlude' the creative process. To revisit Taves' building-block paradigm, we can discern that there are a number of ascriptive processes involved in this type of engagement with sound and creativity. One ascription is to the value of the process: that these works conjure an imaginative field in which a source of inspiration—whether unconscious, imaginal, or supernal—may be encountered. A consideration of the efficacy of this process forms a composite ascription, or a series of related blocks that are constituted to have an effect—a ritual process, which fuses the presumed power of sound, the act of meditative listening, and the awareness of 'inner-sense' perceptions, with the sense that these insights are qualitatively different from common imaginings and daydreams. These ascriptions of revelatory efficacy frame a particular way of responding to the world and art. Versluis' formulation of hieroeideticacy also fits Taves' ascriptive approach well, since it

---

60 David Metcalfe, "Blackbirds and Fox Bones – Notes from an Imaginal Pilgrimage". Modern Mythology, 31 May 2015, now archived at: http://joinmycult.blogspot.co.uk/2015/05/blackbirds-and-fox-bones-notes-from.html.

61 The two approaches could perhaps be called apophatic and kataphatic: Cascone's being focused on the production of a spiritually affective space, my own on the production of imagery ascribed to something beyond my own mundane consciousness.

may also be interpreted as the sacralising, or setting apart (hieros), of the imagination (eidolon).

These qualities, for which an active, committed engagement with the music is a necessity, could be formulated as defining a form of ritual or initiatic drone music. Kennet Granholm has already suggested 'ritual black metal' as a sub-genre within black metal, primarily made by active occultists who use their practices as a signal of artistic authenticity.[62] While the artists involved in Granholm's work discuss the experience of performance in terms of a "communion between us and the forces unto which we direct our praise",[63] the creative processes behind the music are not explored, since Granholm's methodology focuses chiefly on the 'performance' of esotericism. Additionally, the requirements of the musical genre of black metal perhaps preclude the type of meditative, reflective listening that the sympathetic or initated percipient requires in order to engage with the hieroeidetic field. However, the relationship between esoteric practices, musical materials, the hieroeidetic field they conjure, and how artists feel this is manifests in their creative work, could also be applied to the study of the ritual black metal genre from an emic perspective, in complement to the etic assessment of performative authenticity.

Versluis' concept of hieroeideticacy is a 'perfect fit' for visually-orientated media, such as painting and literature, which generally depend on a relaxed and reflective environment, and an insular—or hermetic—sensibility. It may be suggested that areas such as drone and acousmatic music, in which the emphasis is on individual listening, rather than the anarchic communitas of many rock concert experiences, provide a similarly enveloping hieroeidetic field. Hopefully the suggestion in this chapter that Versluis' concept of hieroeideticacy can support an ascriptive approach to esoteric creativity and reception will suggest further methods by which we may explore the experiential nature of contemporary musical esotericism.

---

62   Kennet Granholm, "Ritual Black Metal: Popular Music as Occult Mediation and Practice," Correspondences, Vol. 1. (2013), 5-33.

63   Granholm, Ritual Black Metal, 23-26. Statements such as these also border on what Owen Coggins has identified as an 'implicit mysticism' and has studied in drone metal – a metal sub-genre with arguably a stronger 'hieroeidetic field' ("The Invocation at Tilburg: Mysticism, Implicit Religion and Gravetemple's Drone Metal", Implicit Religion, Vol. 18, No. 2 (2015)). A consideration of the hieroeidetic field in such situations may also provide insight into esoteric relationships between creators, audiences and music.

References

Agrippa, Cornelius. Three Books of Occult Philosophy (trans. J.F.), London: Gregory Moule, 1651.

Cascone, Kim. "The Grain of the Auditory Field," Junk Jet, No. 1 (2007). http://junkjet.net/readjj/read_kimcascone.html

Cascone, Kim. "Errormancy: Glitch as Divination," The End of Being (2011). http://theendofbeing.com/2012/04/19/errormancy-glitch-as-divination-a-new-essay-by-kim-cascone/

Cascone, Kim. Dark Stations (promotional material). 2013.

Cascone, Kim. "The Avant Garde as Aeromancy." In The Idea of the Avant Garde (ed. Marc Legér). Manchester: Manchester University Press, 2014.

Cascone, Kim. "Subtle Listening: How Artists can Develop New Perceptual Circuits", Infinite Grain (2014). http://sonicfield.org/2014/03/subtle-listening-how-artists-can-develop-new-perceptual-circuits/

Cascone, Kim. "Transcendigital Imagination: Developing Organs of Subtle Perception", Interference, Vol. 4 (2014). http://www.interferencejournal.com/articles/sound-methods/transcendigital-imagination-developing-organs-of-subtle-perception

Cascone, Kim. Interview with author via email, 05/08/16 – 09/08/16.

Coggins, Owen. "The Invocation at Tilburg: Mysticism, Implicit Religion and Gravetemple's Drone Metal", Implicit Religion, Vol. 18, No. 2 (2015).

Collins, Cecil. The Vision of the Fool and Other Writings. Ipswich: Golgonooza Press, 2002.

D'Amico, Anthony. Review of Hawthonn. Brainwashed, 24 January 2016. http://www.brainwashed.com/index.php?option=com_content&view=article&id=10744:hawthonn&catid=13:albums-and-singles&Itemid=133.

"Grey Malkin". Review of Hawthonn. Active Listener, 2 June 2015. http://active-listener.blogspot.co.uk/2015/06/hawthonn-hawthonn.html

Granholm, Kennet. "Ritual Black Metal: Popular Music as Occult Mediation and Practice," Correspondences, Vol. 1. (2013). http://correspondencesjournal.com/issue-1-1/

Hanegraaf, Wouter J. "Textbooks and Introductions to Western Esotericism", Religion, 43:2, 178-200

Legard, Phil and Legard, Layla. Hawthonn Journal. Leeds: Larkfall, 2015.

Legard, Phil. "Singing Messengers: Re-considering the Role of 'Poetic Imagination' in the Creative Process." Paper presented at Creativity: A Multidimensional Approach, Centre For Applied Social Research (CeASR), Leeds Beckett University, June 16, 2016.

Locker, Martin. "Movement Through Stillness: Imagined Pilgrimage in Medieval Europe." Paper presented at the EMICS conference Stasis in the Medieval World, UCL Institute of Archaeology, April 13, 2013.

Luhrmann, Tanya and Morgain, Rachael. "Prayer as Inner Sense Cultivation: an attentional learning theory of spiritual experience," ETHOS, Vol. 40, No. 4 (2012).

Maclean, Adam. "Pathworking and Inner Journeys", The Hermetic Journal, vol. 22 (1983): 16-21.

Metcalfe, David. "Blackbirds and Fox Bones – Notes from an Imaginal Pilgrimage". Modern Mythology, 31 May 2015. http://joinmycult.blogspot.co.uk/2015/05/blackbirds-and-fox-bones-notes-from.html

Noll, Richard. "Mental Imagery Cultivation as a Cultural Phenomenon: The Role of Visions in Shamanism", Current Anthropology, Vol. 26, No. 4 (1985).

Norman, Katharine. "Real-World Music as Composed Listening," Contemporary Music Review, vol 15 (1996), part 1.

Peat, F. David. Synchronicity: The Speculum of Inscape and Landscape (n.d.). http://www.fdavidpeat.com/bibliography/essays/synch.htm

Regardie, Israel. The Tree of Life. Minnesota: Llewllyn, 2004.

Riley, Danny, "Northern Noise: Looking for the Perfect Drone with Northern England's DIY Transcendentalists," Bandcamp Daily, 14 July 2016. https://daily.bandcamp.com/2016/07/14/drone-music-in-northern-england/

Simpson, Jason. Review of Hawthonn. Forestpunk, 30 August 2015. https://forestpunk.wordpress.com/2015/08/30/hawthonn-hawthonn/

Taves, Ann. Religious Experience Reconsidered: A Building-Block Approach to the Study of Religion and Other Special Things. Princeton: Princeton University Press, 2009.

Ann Taves & Egil Asprem, "Event Cognition and the Study of (Religious) Experiences", Religion, Brain & Behaviour (Pre-publication postprint article), 2015.

Taves, Ann and Asprem, Egil. "Experience as Event: Event Cognition and the Study of (Religious) Experiences," currently in press, accepted for publication in Religion, Brain, & Behaviour (2016).

Versluis, Arthur. Restoring Paradise: Western Esotericism, Literature, Art, and Consciousness. New York: SUNY Press, 2004.

Violacea, Xylocopa, conversation with author, August 25, 2016.

Discography

Cascone, Kim. Dark Stations. Unspace Records, 2016 (2013), Digital (stereo reduction of 2013 3.1 audio piece). https://itunes.apple.com/us/album/dark-stations/id1118247812

Deutsch, Diana. Phantom Words and Other Curiosities. Philomel Records, 2013, CD.

Hawthonn. Hawthonn. Larkfall, 2014. Digital. https://xetb.bandcamp.com/album/hawthonn

Radigue, Eliane. Adnos I-III. Table of the Elements, 2002. CD.

SUSTAIN//DECAY

ᛉ ∴ Ø ∴

61

63

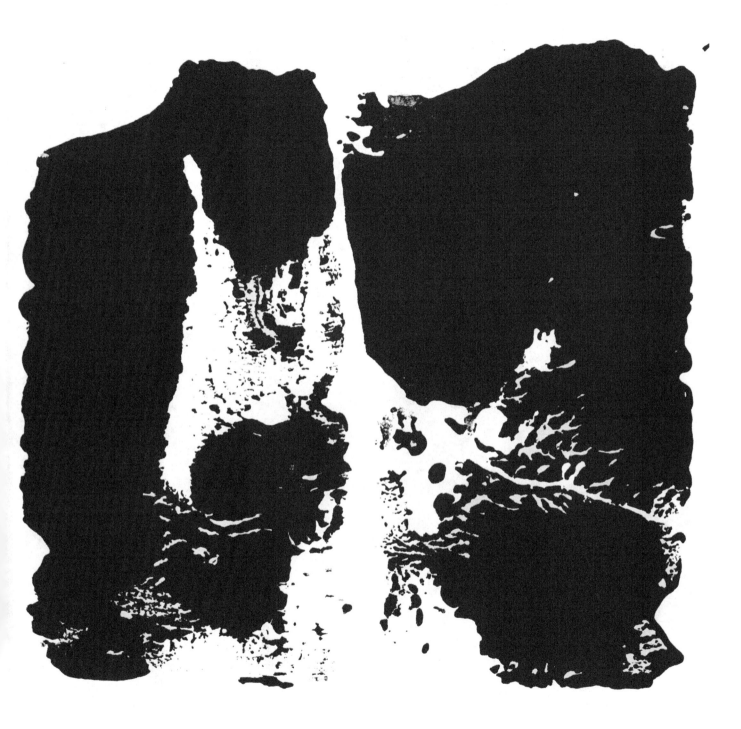

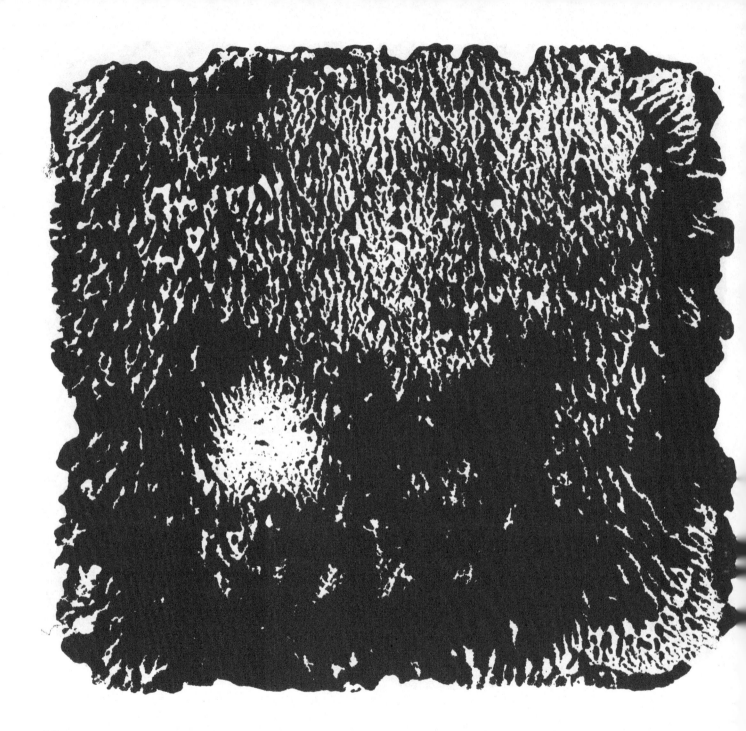

69

ISOLUMINANCE

Kristine Wolfe

Sounds of 'Mysterious Provenance'[1]

That sense of unreality was all the more wonderful because the next day I heard sounds as unaccountable as were those lights, and without any emotion of unreality, and I remember them with perfect distinctness and confidence (Yeats, 2004, p. 139).

In the visual realm, objects that shimmer and glow have always captured the imagination. They are common in many religious art traditions, where the divine body is depicted as glowing or shimmering. Shimmering is understood in certain religious traditions as the "light of nature" and the energetic representation of the genus loci or "spirit of place" (Morphy, 2013, p. 2). In the Yolngu art of Australia, it is called the bir'yun, and reveals where the barrier between reality and the supernatural is weakest. Howard Morphy describes the bir'yun as "the flash of light, the sensation of light one gets and carries away in one's mind's eye, from a glance at likanpuy miny'tj" (the Ancestral beings). From a physical perspective it is the "sensation of light ... They see in it a likeness to the wangarr (Ancestral past) ... the shimmering effect ... which project[s] a brightness that is seen as emanating from the wangarr (Ancestral) beings ... this brightness is one of the things that endows the painting with Ancestral power" (Morphy, 1989, p. 28). Christian mystics such as Saint Hippolytus have also seriously considered the transmutative properties of mystical shimmer:

Wherefore it is constrained, by all its reflection and understanding, to collect into itself the lustre and scintillation of light with the fragrance of the spirit. And it is possible to behold an image of the nature of these in

---

1   This paper is a version of a chapter I wrote on isoluminance in my dissertation titled Sonic Mysticism and Composition, 2016

the human countenance; for instance, the pupil of the eye, dark from the subjacent humours, (but) illuminated with spirit. As, then, the darkness seeks after the splendour, that it may keep in bondage the spark, and may have perceptive power, so the light and spirit seek after the power that belongs to themselves, and strive to uprear, and towards each other to carry up their intermingled powers into the dark and formidable water lying underneath. (Hippolytus, 1868, p. 172)

Examples of this can be seen in medieval paintings of holy people in Hindu and Buddhist art, as well as in the Yolngu art practice. The divine is represented by light with a shimmer or a glow to represent the spirit.

In Zen Buddhism, the concept of luminescent darkness or serene reflection—one's Buddha nature—is commonly described as having the same qualities as the moon's shimmering reflection in water. The moon is not tangible in its reflection, but the reflection expresses the presence of the moon. This reflection, like the Dharma "is unbounded, like empty space. It reveals Its form by conforming to an object, Like water reflecting the moon" (Dogen, 2007 p.571).

In sound this phenomena has been largely overlooked for many reasons. One of the primary reasons being that similar phenomena are not viewed as such because of the very real fact that the visual and audible are different senses. Phenomenologically, it is difficult to train the visually-focused mind to notice subtle changes in an ephemeral soundscape. To make matters more complicated, listeners are accustomed to accepting whatever sound emanates from recordings. All of these issues (and more) set the stage for a listening attention that is not likely to notice when an otherworldly sound flutters past the ear in the soundscape.[2] The purpose of this article is to shed light on the subject of sounds heard as light and to inspire the listening attention to notice and reflect on these sounds.

Light frees wisdom from the darkness of ignorance. Torches illuminate surfaces that were hidden from view by reflecting their light off them. Sound, like light, reveals space and information through the medium of reflection.

---

2   Listeners are left with the memory of the event which, while magic in itself, is the subject of another article

Shimmering and glowing in medieval, Buddhist, and Yolngu art		
Anunciation by Simone Martini and Lippo Memmi	Dambulla rock temple caves Sri Lanka	Djambawa Marawili Garrangali 2010 etching and screenprint

When the sound wave from a hand clap is reflected from that distant wall, we hear the reflection as a discernible echo. The distance to the wall determines the delay for the arrival of the echo, the area of the wall determines the intensity, and the material of the wall's surface determines the frequency content... The echo is the aural means by which we become aware of the wall and its properties... The wall becomes audible, or rather, the wall has an audible manifestation even though it is not itself the original source of sound energy. (Blesser, 2009, p.2)

In Errormancy: Glitch as Divination, Kim Cascone suggests that the supernatural may be attempting to communicate through small flickering glitches in digital error such as an unsteady screen. The "cluster of glitches" forms "an outline," defines an "area," and traces "a route through uncharted space." This space is virtual, invisible, an "n-dimensional 'potential space,'" and this error can be used to "navigate this space," with the intent of seeking "unexpected patterns, chance juxtapositions," and "subliminal content" (Cascone, 2011). With isoluminant sound, sounds that resonate in peculiar ways can be understood, much like the glitches and flicker, to be the echoes bouncing off an invisible space and listeners can use these sounds like sonar to "become aware" of all dimensions of the world.

Isoluminance

Colorimetric research suggests that the eye determines the shape and location of an object (what it is and where it is) using chromaticity (color-matching) and luminance (brightness) of an object. In basic terms, chromaticity is the specific color (hue and saturation) of an object. Luminance is "a statistic designed to ex-press the fact that lights of equal power but different wavelengths do not all appear equally bright" (Arend, 2015). Information regarding visual objects in space is thought to be processed using a combination of these two "streams" of information—the ventral stream and the dorsal stream. The ventral stream "plays a critical role in the identification and recognition of objects" while the dorsal stream "mediates the localization of those same objects" (Wilson & Keil, 2001, p. 873) and (Mishkin & Ungerleider, 1982).[3] In a basic sense, the dorsal stream is considered the "where" pathway, deals with "location and movement for action," and is largely unconscious (Van de Gaer, 2015). The ventral stream is the "what" pathway, focuses on object recognition and form analysis, and is considered a conscious process. According to Margaret Livingstone in Vision and Art - The Biology of Seeing, luminance is associated with the dorsal stream and is thought to aid in the determination of motion and the location of an object while the ventral stream focuses on form (Livingstone, 2002, p. 194). Brightness corresponds with location and color with form. An example of this is shown below in Victor Vaserly's 1970 Gestalt 4. Darker shaded squares are perceived to be 'behind' lighter squares despite all of the squares being the same size and all of them located on the same physical plane.

---

3   Reality is more complex. For more information, see: http://ai.ato.ms/MITECS/Entry/goodale

This cognitive habit of associating luminance with distance can be short-circuited and is the underlying principle behind camouflage and most two-dimensional visual art that uses color to give the impression of space. This effect is called isoluminance and is defined as a phenomenon when a perceived object "is made up only of variations in chromaticity, without accompanying variations in luminance" (Lindsey & Teller, 1990, p. 1751). Isoluminance can cause a disruption or even a "loss of motion perception in color vision" (http://dx.doi.org/10.1016/S0042-6989(03)00115-9). Some scholars, such as Conway and Livingstone, argue that this perceptual incongruity is due to "perspective and reflections chang[ing] second to second as we move our eyes across a scene... there would have been little biological benefit to incorporate the rules for... illumination into our visual computations" (Conway & Livingstone, 2007, p. 479). Studies in vision and neuroaesthetics such as Turano and Pentle's On the mechanism that encodes the movement of contrast variations: velocity discrimination and Teller and Lindsey's Motion at isoluminance: discrimination/detection ratios for moving isoluminant gratings have shown that when objects are processed using only one "stream," a "wide variety of visual functions are compromised" (Lindsey & Teller, 1990, p. 1751).

This ambiguity of location has great creative potential, evidenced by its common use in most visual arts. While giving the impression of dimension, these kinds of effects can also give objects a shimmering appearance. Anjan Chatterjee, a scholar in neuroaesthetics, more explicitly discusses the perceptual and creative experience of shimmer:

...the shimmering quality of water or the sun's glow on the horizon seen in some impressionist paintings ... is produced by isoluminant objects distinguishable only by color. This strategy plays on the distinction between the dorsal (where) and ventral (what) processing distinction ... The dorsal stream is sensitive to

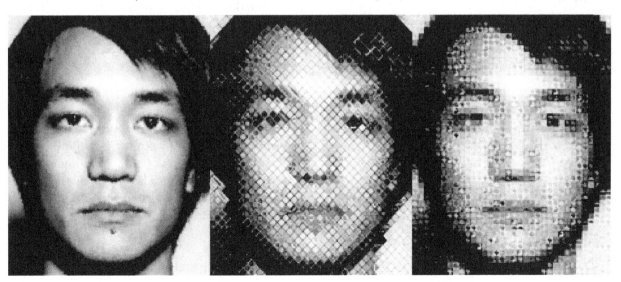

73

differences in luminance, motion, and spatial location, whereas the ventral stream is sensitive to simple form and color. Isoluminant forms are processed by the ventral stream but are not fixed with respect to motion or spatial location, as the dorsal stream does not process this information. Thus, isoluminant forms are experienced as unstable or shimmering. (Chatterjee, 2011, p. 53)

The conflation of location and identification can lead to interesting and somewhat supernatural impressions of objects in space, because the eye can easily identify the presence of an object but cannot determine where the object is as easily as it normally can. Sometimes the object is interpreted to be from another, possibly spiritual, realm.

Shining Sounds

Isoluminance, glow, and shimmer are terms used specifically to refer to light, but there are analogous experiences when processing certain sounds. In contemporary spectral and post-spectral composition, for example, composers conjure non-localizable tones, harmonic sound, and ringing spectra. When doing this, they:

> *creatively personify these sounds as phantoms*
>
> *describe them using visual language, and*
>
> *refer to the sounds as though they were made of light.*

Tristan Murail, for example, "compares the effect of [his] overtone chord with the condition that occurs when the sun is at its zenith: it casts no shadows" (Haas,

2007, p. 3). Jonathan Harvey describes sound presence as halos in his Passion and Resurrection: "I supplied all the characters with a spectrum that moved above their lines in parallel, composed of from one to twelve partials according to the dullness or brilliance of the halo I imagined them to have" (J. Harvey, 1999, p. 53). Heinz Holliger describes his Siebengesang as "shimmering torrents, full of purple stars" (Griffiths, 2011, pp. 214-215), and Hans Zender describes the effect of just-untuned third as "luminous": "for many music lovers it is a revelation to discover that intervals like the just major third … have a luminosity, which compared to the color of a tempered interval is like a radiant red compared to a muddy red-brown" (Hasegawa, 2011, p. 2). The work of Kaija Saariaho is heavily influenced by her experiences of the arctic sky and mysticism. Her works such as Mirage, Light and Matter, Changing Light, and Notes on Light are all brilliant examples of this.

Composer Liza Lim explores the relationship of sound and light in depth in her shimmer pieces. According to Lim, shimmer is also "akin to the structure of natural forces like weather … A surface is not a static plane but part of a shifting system that registers ripple effects, shimmering, and turbulence patterns from the movement of forces below" (Lim, 2009b, p. 3). Just as a glowing object emits a steady light without a discernible origin (and thus alludes to unseen forces at work), a shimmering or glowing sound is created by or gives the impression of an underlying force or combination of forces. Sounds created by the careful manipulation of bowing and string vibration can be thought of as shimmering.

Striated, shimmer effects are created in the interaction between the competing planes of tension held in the retuned strings as they are affected by fingers and the varied playing surfaces of the two bows traveling at changing speeds, pressure and position. (Lim, 2009a, p. 2)

In this context, the surface of the supernatural realm is represented by the fundamental tone produced by the bows and the physical plane of the string. Vibrating strings shimmer, and the manipulation of the periodic "surface" of the bowed tone and string conjures new, ringing tones.

This is only a subset of the vast numbers of composers and sound artists where light and sound play an important role. This collection, while not exhaustive, was presented to give several concrete literary examples of the strong synesthetic and quasi-mystical link between light, flicker, glowing, pitch, space, and timbre in the creative sonic imagination.

Isoluminant Sound

There are differences between an "object" in vision and an "object" in sound, as well as differences in how location information is processed by the two faculties. I argue that:

The ephemeral location and identification issues that hallmark the experience of isoluminant phenomena are similar to both sound and the mystical-ephemeral

There is evidence that composers perceive sounds of comparable qualities in a similar way.

Furthermore, as a creative trope, isoluminance works well within the context of sound and fills the imagination with dreams of sounds that have as Harvey said, "mysterious provenance."

Just as there are two "information streams" that help the viewer identify objects visually, there is evidence that there are somewhat-equivalent "streams" that aid the listener in the identification of sounds. Jennifer Bizley and Yale Cohen have discussed this at length in their article, The what, where, and how of auditory-object perception. They assert, "substantive auditory-object processing has been identified in the dorsal pathway, and substantial information about auditory space has been found in the ventral pathway" (Bizley & Cohen, 2013, p. 4). Esoteric visual art represents the mystical (that which exists in an incorporeal, paradoxical, and invisible realm just outside the fabric of reality) using isoluminance and replicating the ephemeral experience of shimmer in the work. If there is a similar phenomenon in sound, there should exist at least some evidence that listeners interpret the experience of disembodied or otherwise locationally obtuse sound objects mystically. Furthermore, there should be a means to replicate the source of the experience. Fortunately, there is evidence of both due to recording.

In these next few sections, I will talk about the mysticism of the disembodied sound, the many senses and uses of presence in sound, and, finally, the quasi-mystical interpretations of the sound object and the meaning of blurring the sound object in a way that conveys space.

Incorporeal Sound

The disembodied sound was interpreted as mystical in the early days of electronic and recorded sound before it became common to hear a voice without the source. Robin Maconie describes these traits in the context of early perceptions of the gramophone:

...the gramophone was a medium in the mystical as well as actual sense of storing and retrieving at will voices from the dead. To hear a voice speaking from a disc was construed in the terms of a séance or rite of communion with the eternal, since the sound of a person's voice was understood to be a mirror of the soul. (Maconie, 2012, p. 12)

Barry Blesser argues that because of the assumed objective credibility of technology and the notion of scientific and technological progress, the "mystical experience of sound without a visible source reappeared" (Blesser & Salter, 2009, p. 121), and its reappearance marked a turning point in the human experience. Recording devices capture sounds from both natural and supernatural sources, just as monochords conjured and replayed the audible perfection of the divine plan. The recording device, like a photograph, is imagined as something that "mechanically repeats what could be repeated existentially ... the event is never transcended for the sake of something else ... it is the absolute Particular, the sovereign Contingency ... the This ...the Occasion, the Encounter, the Real, in its indefatigable expression" (Barthes, 1981, p. 4). This aura of credibility of the recording within the impermeable past gives the viewer/listener a near-mystical impression of raising the dead and conjuring a past, which, as with music, "was an event that was perceived in a particular situation, and that disappeared when it was finished ... The effect of recording is that it takes music out of the time dimension and puts it in the space dimension" (Eno, 1983, p. 1).

For a brief period, the visitation from an incorporeal sound was interpreted as the strange and profound experience it was. Unfortunately, for the modern ear it is very difficult to appreciate or notice a phantom sound because the ear and mind are quite used to sounds masquerading as both space and image in recording. As Stockhausen clearly pointed out: "most listeners... say, well, the walls have not moved, so it is an illusion.. the fact that you say the walls have not moved is an illusion, because you have clearly heard that the sounds went away... and that is the truth"(Stockhausen, 1972, pp. 107-108).

Presence

Phenomenologies of presence, mutuality, and recognition are complex philosophical subjects and will not be discussed in detail. Instead, I am going to focus on the various forms of presence and explain how visual impressions of presence exist in the experience of sound. The reason that I am discussing sound presence in relationship to isoluminance is to show that sounds are perceived as quasi-mystical objects that can be obfuscated and rendered ghostly. Rather than existing only as ghostly sounds, these ghostly objects must be re-framed in one's attention as single sound objects/presences/beings that are echoing off an invisible realm. This transformation can happen in timbre, through attention, or some combination of both.

… we are able, depending on context and motivation, to attend to particular sounds and establish an auditory aura: a penetrating, invading presence that is more than the sounds, more than the space and more than the sounding thing(s) within it. By physically penetrating the body and the spaces it occupies, sounds can command and encourage us to obey. We can become dramatically engaged in listening, participating with our whole bodies. (Mills, 2014, p. 43)

Presence, in sound, is a noun, an adjective, or a verb, and thusly takes on different connotations depending on the context. In many ways, all uses of the term combine in sound. In sound art, presence and its variety of possible meanings is used creatively and somewhat interchangeably to create networks of meaning and possibility in a work. I will focus on four primary uses of the term in music and investigate how they function in the context of shimmering, revealing, and attention.

Presence, as a technical term, is a setting on an amplifier. It is also a term used to describe an audio process that "boosts the upper mid-range frequencies to make the sounds of voices and instruments with similar tonal ranges seem more 'present'" (Jackson, 2008, p. 75). In film and television, it is used to describe the characteristic sound of silence in a particular room. Philosophical concerns of realness in media aside, recorded sound is being altered to make a sound seem more lively. Along with indicating the existence of something, presence also carries social, religious, paranormal, and mystical connotations. Presence, in a Buddhist tradition, is a state of attention.

The division of processes… is simply to make it easier to bring our awareness into the passing moments, to give us something to look toward, to train us to use inevitable experiences as a support for the practice of pure presence. (Rinpoche & Dahlby, 2004, p. 181)

A presence can also refer to any unknown that has been noticed and has the potential for communication. This is an important definition for this discussion because it primes the attention to interpret a sound object as something that has agency and intention. Presence is an admission of inherent human sociability and attention to others: "the presence of an Other comparable to us, to whom we are subjected, enjoined to pay a kind of exclusive attention" (Connor, 2012, p. 1). The term is often used to refer to ghosts or the somewhat perplexing feeling of "not being alone" while alone. Walt Whitman uses presence to refer to the spirit of nature: "How it is I know not, but I often realise a presence—in clear moods I am certain of it, and neither chemistry nor reasoning, nor aesthetics will give the least explanation" (Whitman, 1891, p. 105).

In its verb form, presence appears almost exclusively in mysticism and divination. To "presence" something or bring something "into presence" is to conjure or summon something using a ritual or spell. This definition is also important to this discussion because it enforces the double-coded creative and communicative meaning of the word in the perception of an isoluminant sound object. J. L. Nancy describes painting as if he were conjuring ghosts:

Painting presents presence and always, saying nothing, says: here is this thing, and here is its presence, and here is presence, absolute, never general, always singular. Presence which comes, the coming into presence, the coming-and-going, ceaselessly coming and going from its own discreteness to the discreteness of every time that is "proper" to it. (Nancy, 1993, p. 348)

Liza Lim uses the verb in her essay, Staging the Aesthetics of Presence, regarding the Aboriginal practice of Dreamtime: "'[Dreamtime] is an originary force of creation that underlies all things and can be presenced in all times, mythical, historical, and contemporary" (Lim, 2009b, p. 2).

Presence, when used to refer or think about sound, can take on all of these connotations because hearing can be an indicator of physical and metaphysical presence.

Sound is a present absence; silence is an absent present. Or perhaps the reverse is better: sound is an absent presence; silence is a present absence? In this sense, sound is a sinister resonance—an association with irrationality and inexplicability, that which we both desire and dread. Listening, then, is a specimen of mediumship, a question of discerning and engaging with what lies beyond the world of forms. (Toop, 2010, p. vii)

This can be a disturbance in an environment of sound, a presence within or indicated by the existence of sound within the environment, or it can be the individual characteristics of the sound environment that are unique to that environment—like a genus loci or spirit of place. This is a personal and imaginative understanding of the world, where the listener "'lends an ear' to resonate with, and become[s] immersed in, the mobile, vibrating, modulating, sonorous presence that results in the setting in motion of place" (Scarre et al., 2006, p. 42).

In Phenomenology of Spirit, Hegel argues that individuals become conscious of themselves only through noticing other perceived autonomous beings. Shimmering and glowing, in both sound and light, are fundamental to the experience of consciousness because of the way they appear to reveal information about the shape, motion, and environment of a presence.

The aura of stillness common to drones exists for most small whole number ratios. Jonathan Harvey considered equal divisions of the octave as meditations on a specific point of stasis and says the unison "becomes a musical expression of suspension in space … it is itself a form of prayer, a means for experiencing unity. It is not a code for pointing to something" (J. Harvey, 1999, p. 71). Morton Feldman uses a similar set of descriptions when defining his work based on the aesthetics and philosophy of the "Single Sound." In his view, single sounds take on characteristics reminiscent of glowing. Recall his earlier statement that a single sound is "frozen, at the same time it's vibrating" (Feldman, 2000, p. 84). In sound, unisons, like pure tones, are "frozen" and are meditative because they exude pure time. As "sound beings," they have an indisputable impression of spirit, as Musicologist Daniel Thompson quotes Harvey (quoting Takemitsu): "the single sound is complete enough to stand alone—if we are prepared to listen in the manner most appropriate to apprehend its 'spiritual' qualities" (Harvey, 1999, p. 78) and (Thompson, 1999, p. 494). This is similar to the Buddhist conception of the singular pure mind reflected in meditation:

…there is no "thing" that can be grasped as the source of the light nor a "thing" that reflects the shining. Neither is the darkness or silence a "thing" that can be grasped. This is because in the face-to-face encounter with the Eternal of meditation there is no separate self, just the serene, profound, illuminating light. (Master, 2016, 15)

Isoluminant Unisons

Sonorities such as the blurred unison (single sounds that are perceived to be obfuscated) have inspired many composers to work with phantoms, alternate visions of reality, and shadow instruments. Individual sounds are seen as a presence, an object (or a religious icon), and ritual. While individual sounds are a presence in themselves, the modulation or blurring of them reveals their spirit, intentionality, and echoes, which bounce off the walls of other worlds. A useful metaphor for this modulation of dimension in the 'single sound' is the binaural or stereographic image.

Each frame is comprised of two dimensions, but when presented together the third dimension is revealed. In much the same way, glowing or shimmering sounds hint at three-dimensional spaces that do not exist in the everyday experience of the listener. This extra dimension is a source of presence; it can fuel a sense that there is an otherworldly vitality to a sound.

Defining Isoluminant Sound

Isoluminance is relatively clear-cut in the visual domain, but it exists as more of a spectrum of potential qualities in the audible realm. In this article, I define

Image: Eugene LaRue, Sentinel Rock, Glen Canyon, Utah

"audio-luminance" as the spatial and locational information gathered from a sound and "audio-chromaticity" as the perception of "thingness" (i.e. violin-ness). An isoluminant sound would be easily identifiable as a sound object but impossible to locate in space ("Where is that sound coming from?"), or a sound that seems to have spatial qualities separate from the known listening space ("Why is there reverb in my anechoic chamber?"). Within this context, isoluminant objects exist almost outside of the realm of space, time, and form. This conflation of the where within the space of what can conjure new objects identified as beings communicating from another realm. This is similar to the poetics of the shimmering sunset:

In their illumination and their obscurity, the transparent colors are without limits, just as fire and water can be regarded as their zenith and nadir ... The relation of light to transparent color is, when you come to look into it deeply, infinitely fascinating, and when the colors flare up, merge into one another, arise anew, and vanish, it is like taking breath in great pauses from one eternity to the next ... It is these, however, that are able ... to produce such pleasing variations and such natural effects that ... ultimately the transparent colors end up as no more than spirits playing above them and serve only to enhance them. (Goethe, 1926) quoted in (Benjamin, Jennings, et al, 2008, p. 234)

In hearing, space and location (especially at liminal points in perception) are more vague than in the visual. Sounds can also be heard to be emanating from many more places than can be seen. In the next section, I will discuss a few basic cases of sounds that can be altered to sound like they are resonating in unusual ways and/or are hard to locate.

Basic How-To-Conjure

Through introductory listening and experimentation, I found that I could create prototypes of isoluminant sounds using sine tones. While somewhat static and unsatisfying, these sounds are easily replicated and fairly uncomplicated to produce and can lead to more creative individual listening techniques and strategies. It is almost impossible to present an ideal case at this time because:

from the perspective of the listener, there may be no difference between a disembodied sound and a mystical sound in a recording,

individual listening strategies may not be adequately developed to hear the sounds in the mystical frame, and

in many cases, individual differences in hearing will effect what sounds can be heard

This is not a judgement on listeners or listening skills. The purpose of this article and the introductory presentation of these techniques is to inspire the reader go out and explore his or her individual listening practice as it relates to one's individual experience of sound In the mystical, this would be similar to cultivating the inner sense, learning to recognize when something speaks, and hearing what is spoken. It is more important to seek out the sounds that the individual reader hears as having presence, dimension, intentionality, shimmer and glow than it is to learn to hear preconceived sounds as such.

Isoluminant effects (where-ness mingled with whatness) can be created through changes in instrumental timbre, pitch, or gesture. Common methods such as "ring tone" modulations, difference tones, sampling rate resultant tones, shepherd tones, and timbre-specific harmonic effects produce hidden sounds that can be combined with these tones to reflect on invisible spaces and beings. In general, glowing and shimmer tones are specific pitch groups similar to "chorusing tones" (Leedy, 1991, p. 204). Glowing pitches, which Carlos calls chorusing tones, are "[o]scillations of about 0-6 Hz" and oscillations "around 6-16" are categorized as "roughness" (Carlos, 1987, p. 33). Shimmering tones begin to arise out of timbres that Carlos calls "roughness," but in my experience, this quality is extremely timbre dependent. These tones can arise from temperaments like meantone, with their "noticeable but not unpleasant beats" (Leedy, 1991, p. 204). In the pitch domain, I have found that glowing tones begin to be produced when perfect intervals are altered between the range of a schisma (+/-1.954 cents or 32805/32768) in simple waveforms to slightly less than a quarter tone (around +/-35 cents or slightly less than a 49/48 ratio) against an unaltered complex tone. Adding additional altered overtone pitches (doubled in respective unevenness) will amplify the effect and produce a more resonant result. Like reverberation, the conception of space surrounding the overtone sonority is altered by de-tuning the pitch of the sonority. In this link there is an example of an overtone chord where an impression of a resonant space is made apparent through slight alterations in pitch around this limit of a schisma. I have included an example here:

https://www.youtube.com/watch?v=ZRARCvF1Dq8

Overtone chords built using specific intervals conjure spatial effects using difference tones. When combined with other forms of aliasing from sampling rates and speaker bodies, these effects produce sounds that have an air of space to them that is not reducible to the parts alone. These voices create imaginary space.

https://www.youtube.com/watch?v=DIviriIm-kUM&list=PLmHRIo_H-52_6jDcSAC7BlK-sN-miK00f-&index=1

In the video, the change in pitch mimics a change in space that the ear has learned to hear through experience of listening to spaces. As Stockhausen said, "the wall has moved" and the room has changed shape because one has heard the change in shape. In listening practice, the next question might be: "To where? What is the wall made of? What is the shape of this space?"

Image: Phillip K Smith III: Lucid Stead

Conclusion

In this article, I have focused on two main types of isoluminant sounds: 1) sounds that are difficult to localize and 2) sounds that present impossible spaces. There are more types of isoluminant-type sounds to be explored and future practice-based research will involve delving deeper into the qualities and experiences of isoluminant sounds. I will also research the writings and work of sound artists and composers outside of contemporary academic music. I will also study the effects of infrasound and stochastic resonance in the perception of mystical sounds, and investigate the characteristics of specific sites where these types of sounds have been heard.

With practice and attention, isoluminant sounds are not difficult to find and it is possible to train the ear to recognize when sounds come from strange or unusual places. Sound objects can be altered in sound or in mind to exist in a liminal space where the recognition of the object itself becomes difficult; further, the listening attention can be primed to hear subtle details and construct an image of the sound object and space around this new attention. These kinds of effects can be created using many sound techniques and not necessarily through any particular manipulation of cognitive processes.

That being said, the ubiquity of light and shimmer metaphors that I have already uncovered in sound art underscores the importance of learning to understand the underlying visual, perceptual and experiential specifics of isoluminance. In my view, this feeling of a spirit that can be perceived yet remain out of reach gives new meaning to David Toop's account of a sound that "came from nowhere, belonged nowhere, so had no place in the world except through my description" (Toop, 2010, p. vii).

Bibliography

Arend, L. (2015). Luminance And Chromaticity. from http://colorusage.arc.nasa.gov/lum_and_chrom.php

Banks, J. (2012). Rorschach Audio: Art & Illusion for Sound: Strange Attractor Press.

Benjamin, W., Jennings, M. W., Doherty, B., Levin, T. Y., & Jephcott, E. F. N. (2008). Kunstwerk im Zeitalter seiner technischen Reproduzierbarkeit: Belknap Press of Harvard University Press.

Bizley, J. K., & Cohen, Y. E. (2013). The what, where and how of auditory-object perception. Nature Reviews Neuroscience, 14(10), 693-707.

Blesser, B., & Salter, L.-R. (2009). Spaces speak, are you listening?: experiencing aural architecture: MIT press.

Boethius. (1100). De Musica.

Bolin, L. (2011). Plasticizer. Beijing.

Burkert, W. (1972). Lore and Science in Ancient Pythagoreanism: Harvard University Press.

Burtner, M. (2005). Ecoacoustic and shamanic technologies for multimedia composition and performance. Organised Sound, 10(01), 3-19.

Carlos, W. (1987). Tuning: At the crossroads. Computer Music Journal, 29-43.

Cascone, K. (2011). Errormancy. Glitch as divination. The End Of Being. from http://theendofbeing.com/2012/04/19/errormancy-glitch-as-divination-a-new-essay-by-kim-cascone

Chatterjee, A. (2011). Neuroaesthetics: a coming of age story. Journal of Cognitive Neuroscience, 23(1), 53-62.

Connor, S. (1999). The Impossibility of the Present: or, from the Contemporary to the Contemporal. Literature and the Contemporary: Fictions and Theories of the Present, 15-35.

Conway, B. R., & Livingstone, M. S. (2007). Perspectives on science and art. Current opinion in neurobiology, 17(4), 476-482.

Curran, J., & Liebes, T. (2002). Media, Ritual and Identity: Taylor & Francis.

Dawes, G. W. (2013). The rationality of renaissance magic. Parergon, 30(2), 33-58.

Deutsch, D. (2003). Phantom words and other curiosities: Philomel Records.

Dogen, Eihei. "Shobogenzo." Trans. H. Nearman. Mount Shasta, CA: Shasta Abbey Press. http://www. urbandharma. org/pdf/Shobogenzo. pdf (2007).

Emmerson, S. (2007). Living Electronic Music: Ashgate.

Erickson, R. (1975). Sound structure in music: Univ of California Press.

Feldman, M. (2000). Give my regards to Eighth Street: collected writings of Morton Feldman: Exact Change.

Fineberg, J. (2000a). Guide to the basic concepts and techniques of spectral music. Contemporary music review, 19(2), 81-113.

Fineberg, J. (2000b). Spectral music: aesthetics and music: Overseas Publishers Association, published by license under the Harwood Academic Publishers imprint.

Gann, K. (1996). The Outer Edge of Consonance: Snapshots from the Evolution of La Monte Young's Tuning Installations. The Bucknell Review, 40(1), 152.

Gann, K. (1997). Just Intonation Explained. Retrieved 1/17, 2016, from http://www.kylegann.com/tuning.html

Gaver, W. W. (1993). How do we hear in the world? Explorations in ecological acoustics. Ecological psychology, 5(4), 285-313.

Gellman, J. (2001). Mystical experience of God: A philosophical inquiry: Ashgate.

Gilmore, B. (2003). "Wild Ocean": an interview with Horatiu Radulescu. Contemporary music review, 22(1-2), 105-122.

Gilmore, B. (2007). ON CLAUDE VIVIER'S 'LONELY CHILD'. Tempo, 61(239), 2-17.

Goethe. (1926). Gesammelte Shriften, IV: Die Literarische Welt.

Grey, J. M., & Gordon, J. W. (1978). Perceptual effects of spectral modifications on musical timbres. The Journal of the Acoustical Society of America, 63(5), 1493-1500.

Haas, G. F. (2007). Mikrotonalität und spektrale Musik seit 1980 (R. Hasegawa, Trans.). Mainz: Schott.

Harrison, M. (2007). Music In Pure Intonation. Retrieved 1/17, 2017, from http://www.michaelharrison.com/Pure_intonation.aspx

Harvey, J. (1999). In quest of spirit: thoughts on music (Vol. 11): Univ of California Press.

Harvey, J. (1999). In Quest of Spirit: Thoughts on Music: University of California Press.

Harvey, J. (2000). Spectralism. Contemporary music review, 19(3), 11-14.

Hasegawa, R. (2008). Introduction:'Sound for the Sake of Perceptual Insight'. Contemporary music review, 27(1), 1-5.

Hasegawa, R. (2011). Gegenstrebige Harmonik in the Music of Hans Zender. Perspectives of new music, 49(1), 207-234.

Hasegawa, R. (2012). "Le vertige de la durée pure": Time and Harmony in Gérard Grisey's Vortex Temporum. In E. S. o. Music (Ed.).

Hasegawa, R. (2015). Clashing Harmonic Systems in Haas's Blumenstück and in vain. Music Theory Spectrum, mtv014.

Heather, P. (1954). Divination. Folklore, 65(1), 10-29.

Hippolytus. (1868). The Refutation of All Heresies. University of Lausanne: T. & T. Clark.

Jankelevich, V., & Abbate, C. (2003). Music and the Ineffable: Princeton University Press.

Katz, S. T. (1992). Mysticism and Language: Oxford University Press.

Katz, S. T. (2013). Comparative Mysticism: An Anthology of Original Sources: OUP USA.

Keating, T. (2002). Open Mind, Open Heart: The Contemplative Dimension of the Gospel: Continuum Pub.

Kozel, S. (1994). SPACEMAKING: EXPERIENCES OF A VIRTUAL BODY. from http://www.art.net/~dtz/kozel.html

Kramer, G., Walker, B., Bonebright, T., Cook, P., Flowers, J. H., Miner, N., & Neuhoff, J. (2010). Sonification report: Status of the field and research agenda.

Krohs, U., & Kroes, P. (2009). Functions in Biological and Artificial Worlds: Comparative Philosophical Perspectives: MIT Press.

Lachenmann, H. (1980). The 'Beautiful' in Music Today. Tempo (New Series), 3(135), 20-24.

Leedy, D. (1991). A Venerable Temperament Rediscovered. Perspectives of new music, 202-211.

Lim, L. (2009a). Invisibility.

Lim, L. (2009b). Staging an Aesthetics of Presence. Search: Journal for new music and culture, 6.

Lindsey, D. T., & Teller, D. Y. (1990). Motion at isoluminance: discrimination/detection ratios for moving isoluminant gratings. Vision Research, 30(11), 1751-1761.

Livingstone, M. (2002). Vision and art: the biology of seeing: Harry N. Abrams.

Luhrmann, T. M. (1991). Persuasions of the Witch's Craft: Ritual Magic in Contemporary England: Harvard University Press.

Maconie, R. (2012). Saving Faith: Stockhausen and Spirituality. Retrieved from www.jimstonebraker.com/Saving%20Faith.pdf

Martel, J. F. (2015). Reclaiming Art in the Age of Artifice: A Treatise, Critique, and Call to Action: North Atlantic Books.

Martin, F. (2006). Sacred Scripture: The Disclosure of the Word: Sapientia Press of Ave Maria University.

Master, R., and P. T. N. H. Jiyu-Kennett. "Serene Reflection Meditation." (2016).

Mercer, J. E. (1913). Nature mysticism: George Allen Limited.

Mills, S. (2014). Auditory Archaeology: Understanding Sound and Hearing in the Past: Left Coast Press.

Mishkin, M., & Ungerleider, L. G. (1982). Contribution of striate inputs to the visuospatial functions of parieto-preoccipital cortex in monkeys. Behavioural brain research, 6(1), 57-77. doi: http://dx.doi.org/10.1016/0166-4328(82)90081-X

Morphy, H. (1989). From dull to brilliant: the aesthetics of spiritual power among the Yolngu. Man, 21-40.

Morphy, H. (2013). Shimmering Light Jörg Schmeisser Bilder Der Reise – a man who likes to draw: Macmillan Art Publishing.

Morton, T. (2007). Ecology without nature: Rethinking environmental aesthetics: Harvard University Press.

Nancy, J. L. (1993). The Birth to Presence: Stanford University Press.

Norman, K. (2005). Poetry of Reality: Taylor & Francis.

Norman, S. J., Ryan J. (2013). Touchstone. STEIM Writings. from http://steim.org/steim/texts.php?id=2.>.

Oliveros, P. (2005). Deep listening: a composer's sound practice: IUniverse.

Parry, R. (2014). Episteme and Techne. In E. N. Zalta (Ed.), The Stanford Encyclopedia of Philosophy (Fall 2014 ed.).

Partch, H. (1949). Genesis of a Music; with a Foreword by Otto Luening: University of Wisconsin Press.

Partch, H., & McGeary, T. (2000). Bitter music: collected

journals, essays, introductions, and librettos: University of Illinois Press.

Radulescu, H. (2003). Brain and Sound Resonance. Annals of the New York Academy of Sciences, 999(1), 322-363.

Rinpoche, T. W. (1998). The Tibetan Yogas of Dream and Sleep: Snow Lion Publications.

Russell, B. (2013). Mysticism and logic: Courier Corporation.

Rutherford-Johnson, T. (2011). PATTERNS OF SHIMMER: LIZA LIM'S COMPOSITIONAL ETHNOGRAPHY. Tempo, 65(258), 2-9.

Scarre, C., Lawson, G., & Research, M. I. f. A. (2006). Archaeoacoustics: McDonald Institute for Archaeological Research.

Schafer, R. M. (1993). The Soundscape: Our Sonic Environment and the Tuning of the World: Inner Traditions/Bear.

Simmel, G. (1950). The stranger. The Sociology of Georg Simmel, 402-408.

Smalley, D. (1996). The listening imagination: listening in the electroacoustic era. Contemporary music review, 13(2), 77-107.

Sontag, S. (1969). The aesthetics of silence. Styles of radical will, 3, 34.

Steiner, G. (2013). Real Presences: Open Road Media.

Steiner, R. (2007). Knowledge of the Higher Worlds and Its Attainment: Filiquarian Publishing, LLC.

Sterne, J. (2003). The Audible Past: Cultural Origins of Sound Reproduction: Duke University Press.

Stockhausen, K. (1972). Four criteria of electronic music: Allied Artists.

Stockhausen, K., & Maconie, R. (1989). Stockhausen on Music Lectures and Interviews.

Sussman, H. (2007). Idylls of the Wanderer: Outside in Literature and Theory: Fordham Univ Press.

Tarasti, E. (1994). Music Models Through Ages: A Semiotic Interpretation. International Review of the Aesthetics and Sociology of Music, 25(1/2), 295-320. doi: 10.2307/836948

Thompson, D. N. (1999). Beyond Duality: Stasis, Silence, and Vertical Listening. Current Musicology, 67, 487-517.

Toop, D. (2010). Sinister resonance: The mediumship of the listener: A&C Black.

Truax, B. (2012). Sound, listening and place: The aesthetic dilemma. Organised Sound, 17(03), 193-201.

Van de Gaer, M. (2015). Dorsal - Ventral Stream. Facial Masking, Alignment & Dyslexia. from http://www.sharp-sighted.org/index.php?option=com_content&task=view&id=70&Itemid=133

Vernallis, C., Herzog, A., & Richardson, J. (2013). The Oxford Handbook of Sound and Image in Digital Media: Oxford University Press.

Virilio, P., Violeau, J. L., & Moshenberg, D. (2012). Lost Dimension: MIT University Press Group Limited.

Voegelin, S. E. (2006). Sonic memory material as. Organised Sound, 11(01), 13-18. doi: doi:10.1017/S1355771806000033

Wessel, D. L. (1979). Timbre space as a musical control structure. Computer Music Journal, 45-52.

Whitman, W. (1891). Complete Prose Works: D. McKay.

Wilson, R. A., & Keil, F. C. (2001). The MIT Encyclopedia of the Cognitive Sciences: MIT Press.

Winkelman, M. (2015). Shamanism as a biogenetic structural paradigm for humans' evolved social psychology. Psychology of Religion and Spirituality, 7(4), 267-277. doi: 10.1037/rel0000034

Winkelman, M., & Baker, J. R. (2015). Supernatural as Natural: A Biocultural Approach to Religion: Taylor & Francis.

Wolin, R. (1994). Walter Benjamin, an aesthetic of redemption (Vol. 7): Univ of California Press.

Yeats, W. B. (2004). The Celtic Twilight: Cosimo, Inc.

HISSEN

SCORE FOR A SPATIAL COMPOSITION

machine scream
turn to stop and release
extend voice no teeth or lip obstructions
                                                            clog
call to beyond the walls

fill white
overlay

wipe a frictionless plane circular until dry and keep wiping
                                                            spasm
accelerate rotations

                                    push as slow as possible to an end without hesitations

shake a glass or metal container
sweep the same place until too tired
break frequency
in and out
white then pink then brown for a while or waves

                go up slow and down fast and then up fast and down slow

                        pay attention to one and then two and then none or all

                                                            stare
                                                            lose energy and keep going
                                                            again and again

fire a toy gun or pretend to to break a duration

                                                become impeded
                                let out   with intermittent breaks until none
        put lips in the way
                a low or a high or both

                                        call with a sort of anguish no one will respond
                                        sweep the same arc until too tired

        600 to 400 to 600 to 400 for a while

        sort of respond to a call

                        higher and higher and quieter and quieter

                                twirl

90

rub rubber on rubber
rotate vertical on horizontal
play a baby mobile or a fairground quietly
let a melody come home

beat something once
metal on metal of the same kind
irregular continuous frictions
repeat a little sore

go back as far as can
increase time intervals

come to top
menace with air maybe a word
together and regular

break at the wrong time
break at the right time

watery creaks
drop in a steel container   do not swallow for some time with a microphone
bend

talk without words

let some saliva out
air through a mouth or instrument   stroke a rod along ridges
10000 to 14000 and hold
warn with a long horn
move closer to someone
push
fill a container maybe a mouth
send a signal and let it die
shake
increase animates with the same little buzz
turn on the tv in the other room
harder walls
no walls for a while
a low voice from not here
break it and then lose it
cough a few times same durations
a church call

a body part on a surface on and off
creak a door a wire or a leg let it go somewhere and break
get in the way of a propellor
hold it sort of

respond to that voice in a while

pluck

send air through a small opening
take some space and add more

something through another thing
open and hold

turn up
yank something rubbery

small metallic objects in a glass container
backward and forward and

12000 to 13000 to another you cannot hear
strike
a sweet melody to remember and expect
a voice with inhuman urgency

sing or play a keyboard or glockenspiel or something similar
exhale through a recognisable wind instrument or two thumbs
block
layer a crying machine
400 to 300 to 400 to 300 to 400 and so on
fail
a sphere down a slope or against a corner or toward the sky
squeak and repeat

a train or something coming
stop listening
listen to all at once if possible
join

sing along in head

approach

eat wet

a little shaky
conjure a sort of melancholy

let out some flies

close mouth more
drop

sirens

meet an expectation

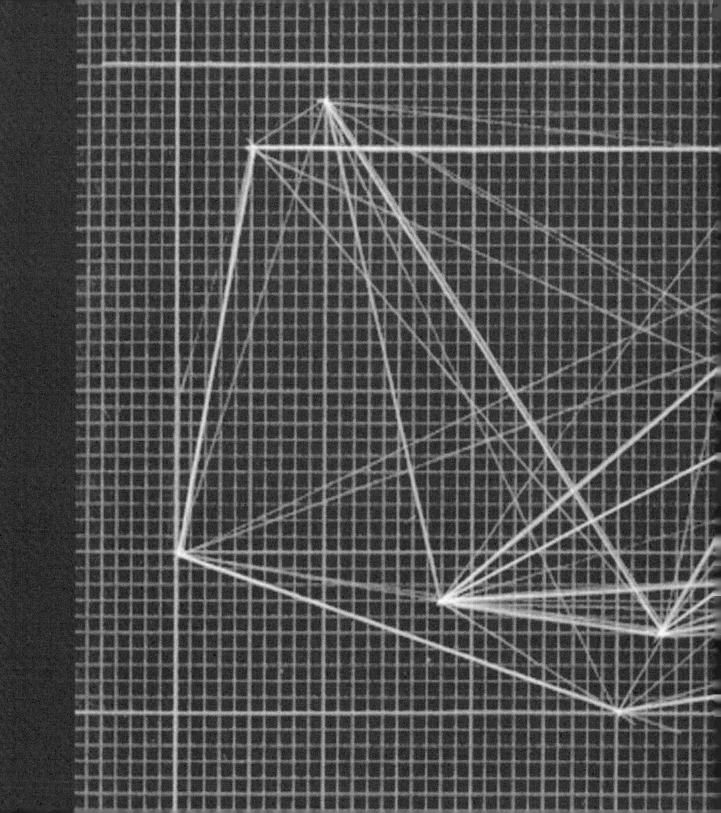

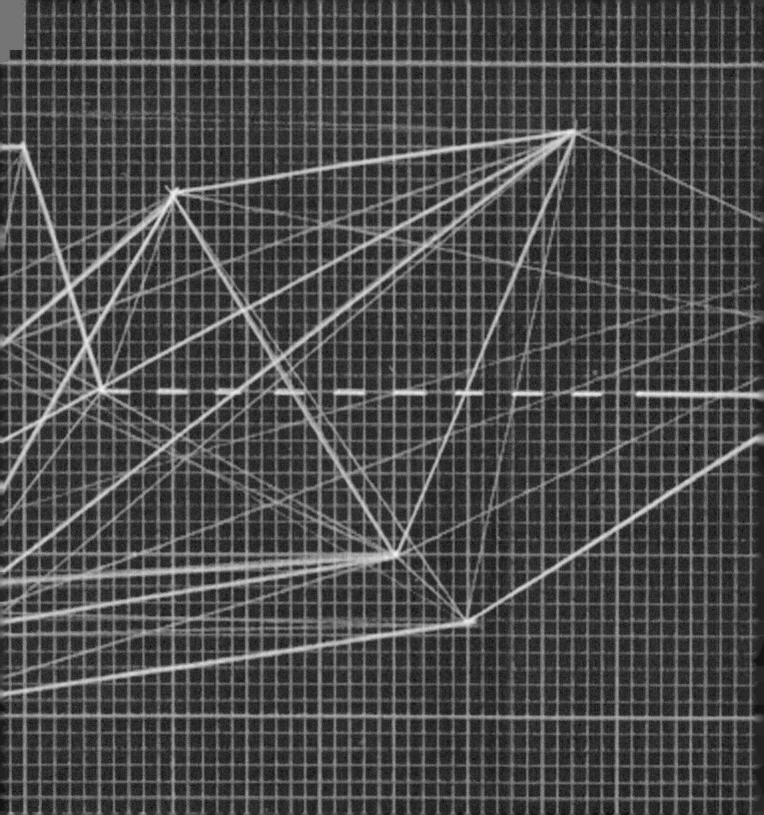

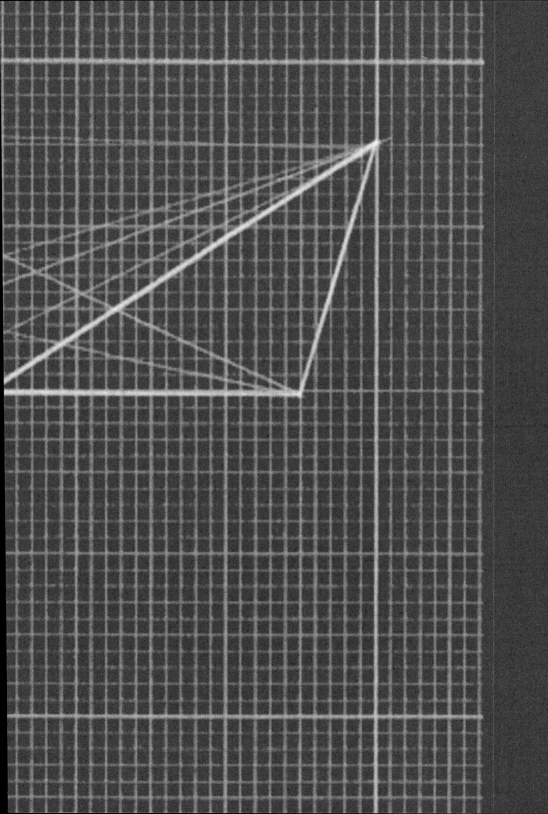

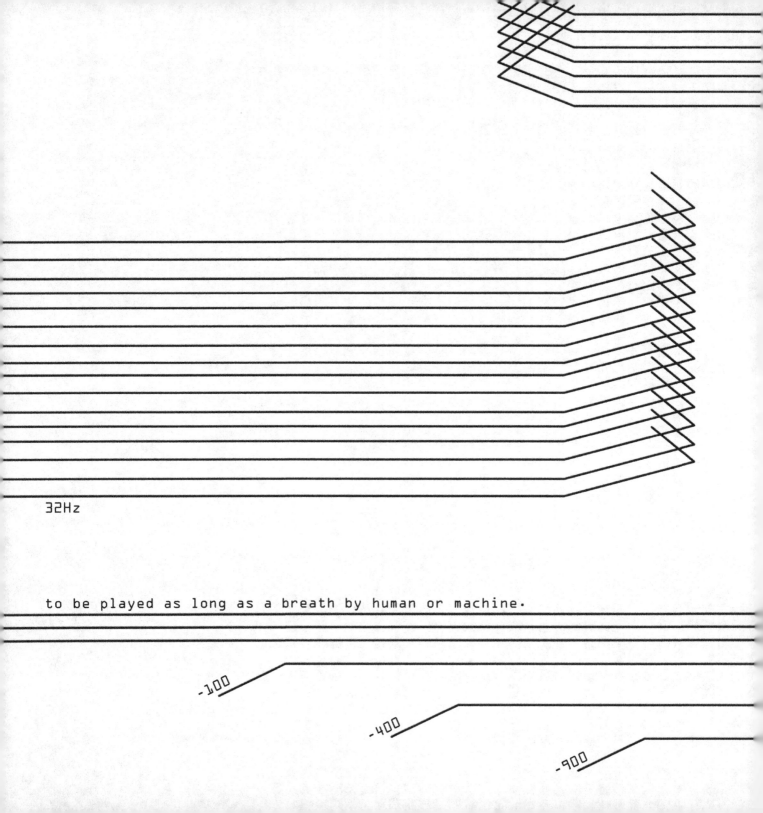

32Hz

to be played as long as a breath by human or machine.

-100

-400

-900

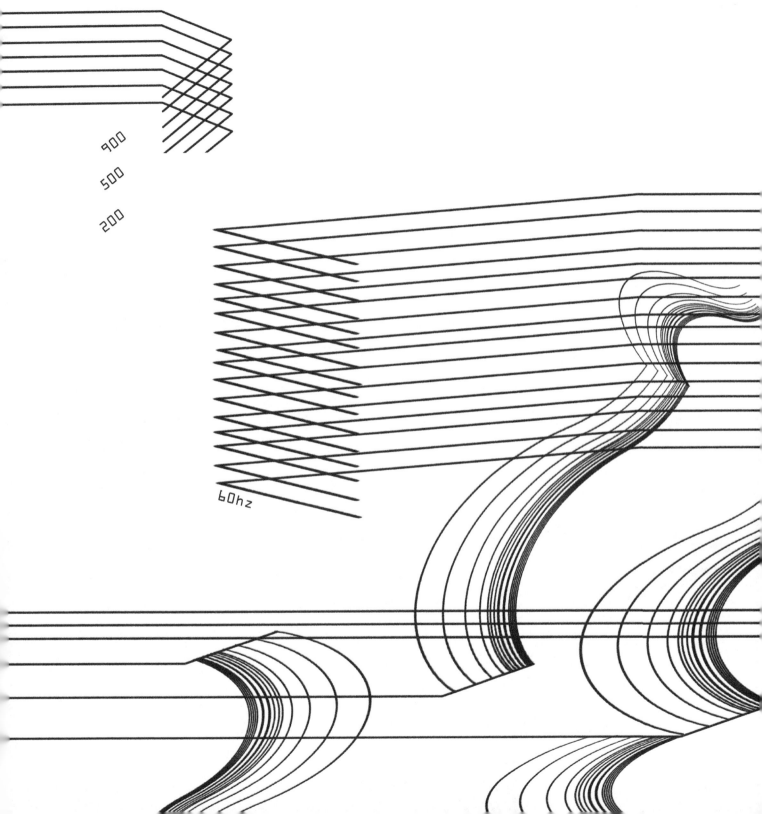

900

500

200

60hz

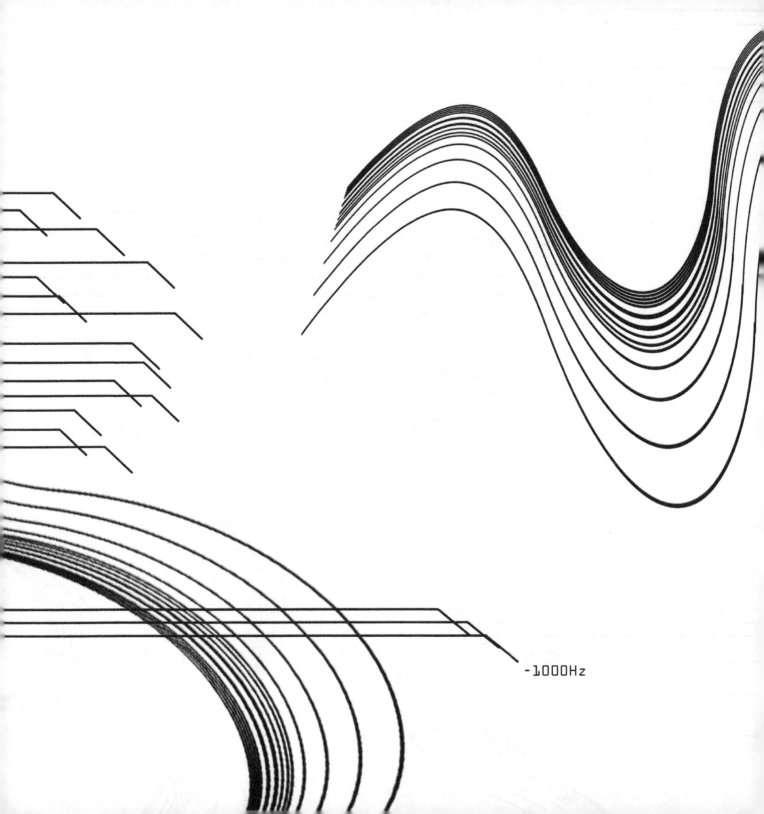

-1000Hz

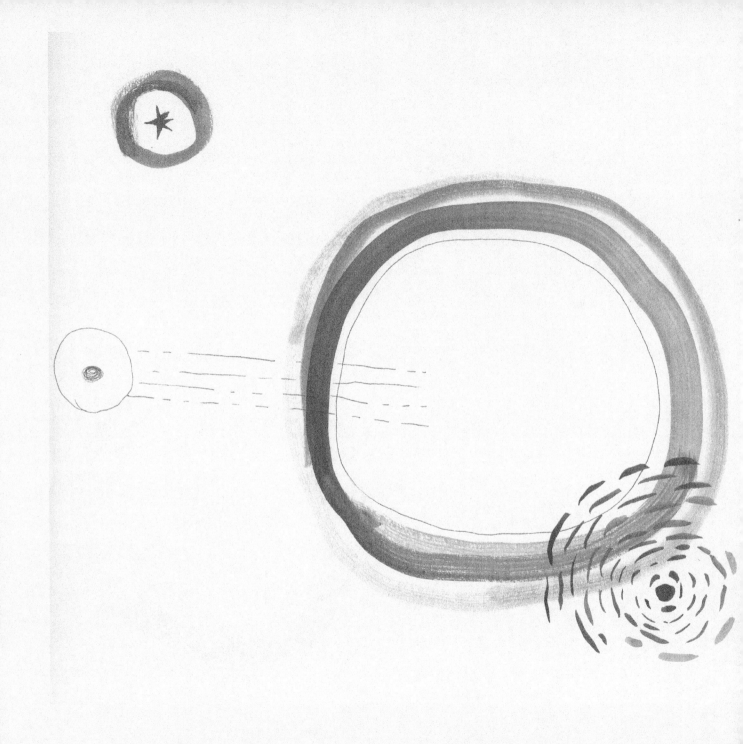

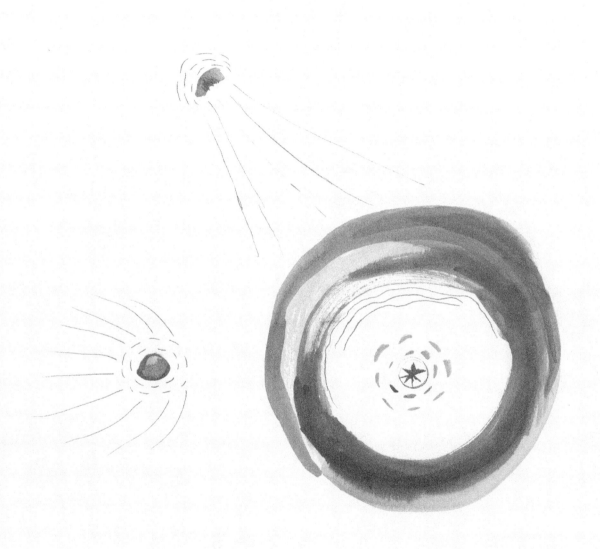

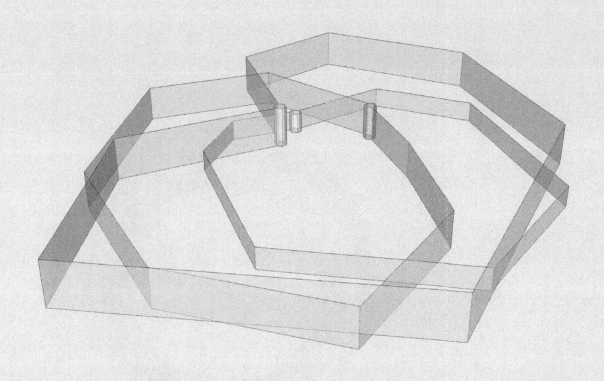

Score for a spatial composition
for three performers in an undefined space

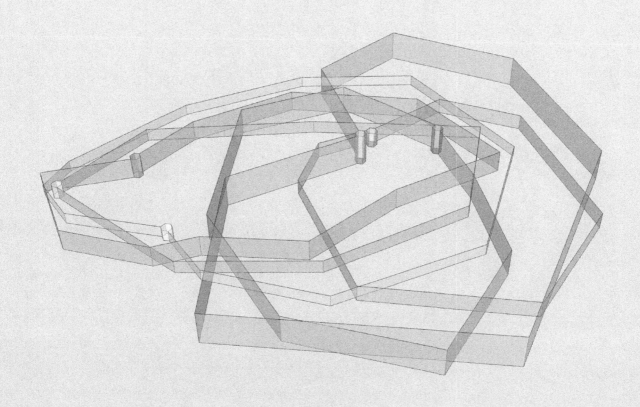

Three more performers join intersecting and
morphing the quality of sound produced

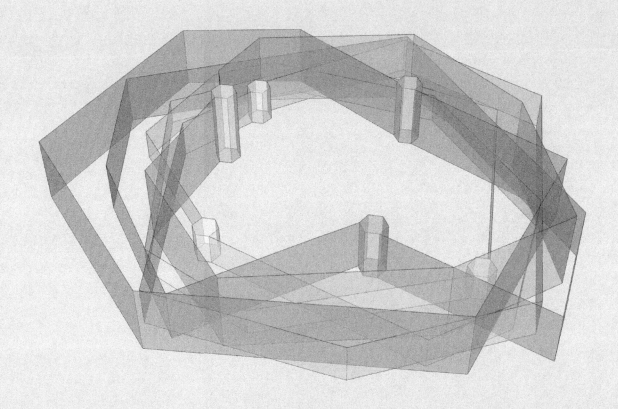

All six performers tune to each other
and the resonant frequency of the space

SONIC GNOSTIC: A PUN IN 2 PARTS

Eyvind Kang

the Gnostic, the difference of Appearance and Reality widens into the difference of a Bad God and a Good God
the Sonic, the difference between sound and hearing re-inscribes itself in the gap between mind and brain.

2 is further bifurcated:

2a) Sound in the Air//Sound in the Ear
2b) Sound in the Brain//Sound in the Mind

the secondary Bifurcations are mirrored by Mediations at every level:
the Mediation in 2a consists of air Pressure (Acoustic)
the Mediation between 2a and 2b is the Cochlear Fluid (Acoustic Electric)
the Mediation in 2b is the Neuroplastic Reservoir (Electric)

At each stage, a further Bifurcation between Good God and Bad God, (or between Angel and Demon) occurs.

the Acoustic as sound pressure waves in a medium
the Acoustic as sound pressure waves in the cochlea
the Electric as neural transductions in the cochlea
the Electric as sound in the mind, or thought waves

Synaurality, which in one of its proper modes plays on the proportionality of Acoustic to Electric sounds by combining them in relation to the dynamic combinations of Mediations 2a and 2b.

thus the pairs:
Bad//Good
Good//Bad
Bad//Bad
Good//Good

Good God	Bad God
Truth	Seeming

Brain	Mind
Sound	Hearing

1.1 Bad and Good Gods (in Zoroastrian vocabulary *Ahriman* and *Ahura Mazda*) correspond to Appearance (Seeming) and Reality (Truth).

2.1 The Appearance of Sound can be described in the form of 4 tetrads, or squares of opposition:

Truth	Seeming
Brain	Mind

Sound	Hearing
Good God	Bad God

105

PLEROMATICATALYST
RITUAL INTOXICATION TOWARD THE UNIVERSAL FIELD

James Harris

//Sunn O)))—*It Took the Night to Believe*//		Interweaving
vibrate		Interwoven
believe		Interweaving
	To understand me, you must close your ears to what I am saying.	
vibrate	//F. Zalamea—*Wittgenstein Sheaves*//	Interwoven
defile		Interweaving
vibrate		Interwoven
believe	The confession of the being not to come into being continues to sound within myself	Interweaving
vibrate	//Keiji Haino—*Pathetique IV*//	Interwoven
defile		Beginning and end
		Beginning and end
	The Eleusinian initiates were not going to learn anything, but they were to suffer …	Interweaving
	//Aristotle via Mylonas//	Interwoven
		Beginning and end
	//Keiji Haino—*Beginning and end, interwoven*//	

106

Ocean of graves, ebb and flow.
//Conan—Dying Giant//

Deep in layers unwarm drifting
Lower in depths still descending
On wide billows slowly floating
In colder streams smoothly drifting
Beauty unleashed
Light wind flowing
Heard Silence
A dance to abyss would soon follow
Once another would soon swallow
Darkness as the light most silent
Silence as the darkest of voices
From Silence and anything
To Silence and nothing
Is the path of final solitude
//Skepticism—Aether//

"Did I not tell you that you would not have patience with me?"
//Al-Khdir to Moses, Quran—18th sura, ayat 60-82//

The Greeks ended a nine-day fast with the drinking of the kykeon, a psychedelic brew containing ergine, at the height of the Eleusinian Demeter-cult's annual inner rite. Coupling the pinnacle of the Greeks' most solemn religious ritual with a difficult-to-synthesize drug that amplifies visualisation at the expense of linguistic faculties not only elegantly explains how the secret of the chemical makeup of the potion was maintained for thousands of years, but also why Homer might say that //deep awe of the gods checks the voice.//[A1] To experience a lavish month-long participatory ritual recreation of the loss of paradisiacal conditions that made way for the samsaric cycle of seasons, wordlessly, under the influence of a starvation-amplified hallucinogen surely would have failed only rarely to incite perceived divine contact: levelling boundaries between initiates, between god and mortal, between inner and outer. Mylanos suggests that no surviving representation could have been accurate, referencing both the people's pervasive fear of divine retribution and the self-occulting nature of the chemical silence of those //awful mysteries which no one may

1: suturing

in any way transgress or pry into or utter//[A2] as if echoing the I Ching's statement that the Tao that can be spoken is not the Tao. The unexplainable has always driven religious law-making, and even making art representing the secrets of the Greater Mysteries was a heresy punished by death. This makes details exceedingly scarce, however music was said to //take on the mystical colouring//[A3] of rituals in which it is performed due to the //chameleon-like//[A4] attributes of the Muses and //the power (of music) to influence and shape its environment.//[A5] Through the Muses' "presence" in this cultic environment the μουσική would take on aspects of the rite, and from this one might extrapolate certain rhythmic, cyclic, solemn, silent, and organic elements that may have been present in Eleusinian music that easily draw a speculative comparison to drone.

In the essay Pleromatica, Gabriel Catren's "phenoumenodelic scene" in which we are to conceive existence is the product of a series of un-groundings, from the Copernican suspension of Earth's solar primacy to the //*relativistic crisis of the spatiotemporal background.*//^△^ While these un-groundings individually subvert previously supposed //*fixed god-given structure[s]*//^△^ and //*aprioristic motionless Ur-frames*//^△^, Catren sketches a chaining of these gestures that progressively undermine the paradigm of differentiating between inner and outer in a *speculative absolutism.*

This chain of underminings is the maximally general subset of neuronihilism, an arsenal of cognitive subversions, subtractions, and negations that may be applied to thought in order to shear away misconceptions regarding the experiential field of an endophysical observer. Here we further intensify the un-grounding and remove the ultimate Ur-referinertial-frame: the sociocultural image of closed-individuality and object-dualism that occults and obscures intuitive awareness of a universal and impersonal field of experience:

2. *cutting*

{brahman
{atman
{the tao
{the Gnostics' pleroma
{the Platonic ideal form-world/animus mundi
{the Sufi "Black Mind" of Allah
{the Aztec teotl
{the mystics' "union with God"

... among others, are *theophysical metaphors* for a *non-oriented, non-performable, yet permissible* state of (un)be(com)ing we call the *pleromatica*, borrowing another term from Catren, despite how many names it already goes by. In the pleromatica the concept of an "Ur-frame", which may also in many respects be equated to the "self", is sublimated into an un-framing process: //*the transmutation of the immobile Ur-frame into an ark continuously going under—the coming of the one and only number that cannot be any other.*//^△^

On the other end of the known world, India was already dozens of centuries deep into the open celebration of Shiva as the "Lord of Bhang." The public consumption of the cannabis-infused drink known as bhang in reverence to Shiva was and still is ubiquitous during certain festivals and stands as an exuberant counterpoint to the Eleusinian secrecy, however they share a solemnity. Maha Shivaratri, or the "Great Night of Shiva", is an annual festival in which the devotees remain awake all night chanting prayers, fasting, doing Yoga, and meditating in remembrance of Shiva. Devotional songs known as bhajans (a word that can mean both divide and attach) are performed, and mantras are repeated ceaselessly through the night as //we meditate on the Three-eyed reality which permeates and nourishes all.//[B1] A god known for radical inclusivity, this manifests itself in two particular aspects sutured into a single

form. First: a Death-God aspect, as Shiva was accepting of everything that is rejected, rotting things such as corpses, alcohol and even marijuana as something rejected by mankind. As the Atharvaveda declares, everything that is rotting creates an intoxication—the state of mind that occurs when one orients oneself toward death—and this aspect leads all kinds of creatures to worship him. Ghosts, ghouls, goblins, devils, demons, the poorest, the outlaws, the oppressed—all those beings rejected by everyone find communal space in Shiva's continuous meditations on the world. This is conjoined with the dancing Natesha or Nataraja form, the dance of creation which spontaneously self-creates from eternal stillness, coupling motion with stasis and guiding the destruction of destruction by creative imagination. The overlaid images of permanent trance and permanent dance accessible to any entity willing to strive alongside the "destroyer of ignorance and illusion."

We label this state *non-performable* because acts of differentiation cause decoherence of this "substrate," this pleromatica that is *constantly, spontaneously, attempting differentiation*. This provides a glimpse into understanding why it has proven so resistant to instrumental measurement as the choice of observational frame of reference *is itself* a differentiation. One may not "perform" actions leading to this state, but may only experience it passively after performing modulations on the surface-self that allow the Outside to "leak in." We label it *non-oriented* because it does not inertially or conceptually index any frames of reference, rather being achieved by iterated negations and categorical integrations on almost any axis. In other words, this state is achieved by collapsing or decomposing inertial, cognitive, sensory, linguistic frames of reference, or the protogeometric compression and integration of disparate signals into more general or universal categorical schemes. Co-opting and mirroring a note from Nick Sousanis, we refer to such anti-gestures as *flattenings* of the experiential field. In the brain, the thalamus performs a colossal number of iterations per second of an operation akin (or possibly identical) to what is known to mathematicians and physicists as a "Heisenberg cut" on the undifferentiated flow of incoming signal that seem to be almost entirely arbitrary determinations of differentiation between observer and observed, between figure and ground, between object and signifier. One of drone music's defining features is its ability to flatten in the audio-space of the experiential field: decelerating the cutting and temporally extending the frame of reference. This can become so extreme as to, in J-P Caron's words elsewhere in this volume, *//exceed both the superior and inferior temporal limits that a (human) subject is capable of indexing//*[1], overwhelming the frame, overfilling it to bursting.

This correlates well with how the outer layer of the thalamus, the *thalamic reticular nuclei (TRN)*, is a group of neurons responsible for aligning several multimodal topographical mappings from corticothalamic feedback, ascertaining a coarse unity, a "fuzzily logical" overlapping of maps (maps of present, past, anticipated future cuts) from across every functional network that has a thalamic projection. The local binding problem is solved within the TRN and its own feedback loop of neuronal projection linking the "*supervisory attentional system*" to this function. This suggests that freedom from this individualized and idiosyncratic matrix of correlation is challenging because the human-type "matrix" of cut-nexuses exhibits a strong gravitation toward a singular identity, disregarding substantial elements of the foundational signal that do not correspond to the singular as superfluous to immediate experience, cutting them out in a bandwidth-saving gesture. The local binding problem as usually stated, in this view is contextually incomplete as everything begins "bound" in a unitary signal and we *negentropically* cut into this eternal flow toward *unihilification* in order to abstract arbitrary objects and differentiated signals. Every isomorphic cut reifies the seeming persistence of an object, and the closed-individual experience of "everyday human consciousness" is nothing more than the temporal persistence of the intersection of all these cuts constantly being made in the pleromatica. What masquerades as the binding problem is what may be thought of as harmonic overtones of a Bayesian basin of attraction generated from carving out so many of these cuts in identical shapes over time. The human-type entity *katabasically* sinks toward the most extreme and reified cuts and must conceptually climb untold numbers of unholy mountains to see the surface again.

As the Taṣawwuf or Sufi sect of Islam spread into the east, its wandering monks began to intersect with cannabis-loving India. Contact between wandering Sufi and the Hindu sadhus led to the infusion of hashish into Persia, and Shaykh Haydar tells his followers //Almighty God has bestowed upon you a special favor the virtues of this plant, which will dissipate the shadows that cloud your souls.//[C1] Devotional life for the Sufi consists of musical sessions of synchronized, frenetic dancing or spinning where the dancers become oblivious to all but the spiritual state, rhythmic repetition of the dhikr (mantras formed from the names of God or its attributes), and deep communal and solitary meditation, all frequently supplemented by hashish. Qawalli music is the repetition of Qual, or "utterances of the prophet", and as the Sufi believe their saints are free of space and time certain forms of qawalli are considered "announcements" of the arrival of the faithful, who are never dead, just gone into some other state from

where they visit whenever they are mentioned. In these trance-formations, the Sufi //is to collect all of his bodily senses in concentration, and to cut himself off from all preoccupation and notions that inflict themselves upon the heart.//[C2] Similar to the counterculture movement of the 1960's, the rejection of hashish by the mainstream of Islamic thought was as much attributed to its association with the impoverished and outcast as its alleged ill effects and both Sufism and hashish became intertwined with the spiritual, political, and symbolic struggles of the lower, poorer, social classes. //According to Karamustafa, they regarded the drug as "a means to find respite from the unreal phenomena of time and space and to attain the hidden treasure of reality."//[C3]

Drone liquifies the mountain and inverts the difficulty of the climb. We may imagine an Ovidian Sisyphus so mesmerized by the sound of Orphic dronesong that he dismisses dreams of happiness and simply refuses to roll the stone, committing himself to eternal mantric zazen atop a perpetually sinking spherolith.

Following Catren further, he claims that //the transcendental a priori structures of human experience are a posteriori products of the immanental natural dynamics of the impersonal field//[Δ], that the //human transcendental type, far from being characterized by some sort of pre-phenoumenal necessity, results from a contingent local subjectivization of the experiential field itself.//[Δ] These local subjectivizations are "excitations" of the field, excitations whose structure defines particular frames of subjectivity. According to this line of reasoning, the human mode is just one of any number of potential subjective modes //according to which the field of impersonal experience locally […] frames its narcissistic self-experience.//[Δ] A phenoumenodelic experience—any experience that //involves a shift of the very transcendental structure that renders a transcendent experience possible//[Δ] —is an unfurling of the pleromatica out of the hyper-enfolded stratifications of a typical human-type structure's knotwork of frame-cuts: an experience in which one perceives reality from the perspective of Nature as if one is Nature, rather than merely a component of it. We speculate that as this cutting is decelerated the world-model becomes progressively synchronized with the executive functions, resulting in either seeing executive function in any or every mental object including the entire world-model, to the oppositionally extreme state of perceiving zero possibility of agency, and even both simultaneously.

Panpsychism and anatta synoptically align to form the droneswarm hyperobject: concurrently connective and fragmentary in a multiperspectival multidentity mutating flexibly between the One, the Many, and the Zero like a murmuration of starlings.

Within the phenoumenodelic experience we are exposed to the complex noumenal threading through every phenomenon and find a symmetry between inner and outer: imaginative world-building takes on robust sensory characteristics and may be perceived as "real", while outer experience is shown to be generated in a highly similar "imaginative" gesture as more and more mediation qua reference-frames is stripped away. At the deepest extreme of these experiences, we "transcend transcendence" onto the void-plane, the //positive death at zero-intensity//[2], a brain state of maximal network connectivity between world- and self-models. This is attained by flattening the divide between the two, engaging in a persistent cognitive suturing of the two models into a single continuous field by operations that realize the aforementioned deceleration of the TRN and the thalamus. This reduces and eventually eliminates the differentiation of incoming signal by functionally eliminating the node at which the "Heisenberg cut" is performed. This apparently causes every functional network to receive a copy of the whole signal rather than only receiving the slices of the signal it would normally process, flooding the cortex with feedback and reducing available bandwidth for the construction of a self-model in direct correlation with the reduction in mediative frames. We may from here, assert the witnessing of the simulated or real annihilation of any number or type of "virtual selves" or components thereof, "deaths" of various aspects and elements of the self-model (breaking of frames) up to and including the entirety of the

//To become warriors, the cohiuanos must abandon all and go alone to the jungle, guided only by their dreams. In this journey, he has to find out, in solitude and silence, who he really is. He must become a wanderer dream. Many are lost, and some never return. But those who return they are ready to face what is to come.//[d1] *Referring to those that seek ayahuasca as* //pilgrims to an apocalypse//∞, *Richard Doyle called the infamous jungle potion* //perhaps the most difficult experience of my life that didn't involve somebody (else) dying.//∞ *He goes on to say* //I had palpably and unmistakably died—the accounts of ego death were not at all greatly exaggerated.//∞ *Known as the "vine of the dead", ayahuasca is hardly a recreational drink—its ability to* //erode the distinction between the living and the dead//∞ *generating frightening and terrible visions of underworld and innerspace distinctly overlaid, interpolated, seamlessly blended with transcendent numinous imagery of jungle holism,* //converging rainbows of twisting triple helical anaconda assemblies//∞, *shamanic*

space-travel, and an operatic continuum of animal-alien-insect song wherein all sounds are perceived to be in a kind of perpetual "conversation" with each other. The whistled and sung icaros of the ayahuasquero mimic the sound of the forest, guiding and shaping the experience in a technics of avianimal insectoid melodrone. Among the visual tropes found repeated in ayahuasca-fuelled art are beings of all varieties gathered together in //a common and thoroughly violet projectile vomit.//∞ *Doyle reminds us that the word dose has its roots in "dosis" which means "a giving", and that this purge has not only become an integral part of the modern folklore, but has been definitively implicated in the mechanism of ayahuasca's efficacy as the active chemicals are heavily amplified on an empty stomach. To be dosed with ayahuasca is to let go of an interior and in doing so form a commons with the group, to give one a* //capacity to open.//∞

possibility for existence itself that correspondingly drags our linguistically-mediated "meatspace" with it into the Void.

These "deaths" progressively dismantle the unitary observer, removing boundaries, barriers, limits, and other self-identifying traces from the field of awareness, uncovering more and more of the raw signal-field out of which a "reality" is carved. These experiences provide a strong argument in favor of the DeWitt-Graham-Wheeler version of Hugh Everett's Many-Worlds Interpretation of quantum mechanics by showing in an intuitive fashion that classical reality is entirely perspectival (in a geometric or topological sense) and results from ignoring information about the exact state of the environment. Aldous Huxley's "reducing valve" model of consciousness was an idealization of this, while Catren's work lists several methods of //*varying, deforming, or perturbing*//[Δ] our human-type transcendental structure in order to achieve a //*partial trans-(in the sense of transversal)-umweltization of experience*//[Δ], which then allows for the reformulation of our cutting to move across perspectives: transecting, transcending, transforming perspective rather than merely re-cutting the same perspective ad infinitum.

Catren's list of phenoumenodelic technics covers everything from biotechnical expansion of sensory apparatus to meditation and fasting, but this inquiry deals with a particularly direct route toward the pleromatica. We consider the cross-cultural human propensity to ritualize forms of intoxication as a distinctly democratic

transmodern approach, following Zalamea, to understanding //*knowledge as transformation*//[3], and to experiencing a phenoumenodelic non-orientation that privileges flux, motion, process, symmetry and its breaking —a pendular motion between the differential and integral and their possible alignments— over any individual static frame of reference. We view neurochemical (re)mediation and sonic deceleration as isomorphic operations of ritual intoxication that exponentially amplify when combined.

These ritualizations combine deep expressions and reifications of traditional and/or cultural identification with the //*postmodern dissonances*//[4] of breaks, contradiction, ambiguity, locality—diagramming the amplitwist contamination of an expanding scope of cognition over time and generating a large-scale flattening of the dualistic separation between supposedly metaphysical "quantum" unity and the classical world of objects and abstraction. This annihilat[ing/ed] unity of identity carves out space for reformulating what is meant by self while simultaneously re-minding, re-cognizing a self's historical context, turning cultural and temporal trajectory, the self itself, and all its ramifications and coalescence into entia rationis— generating a dynamic map of the connectome and routing it through the audiovisual cortices. It is within these maps we can explicitly track a "coincidence of oneself" (cf. Deleuze/Guattari) in the perichoresis of a tripartite meta-physics of metamathematical metaphilosophy that succeeds in "getting behind, or above" (cf. Husserl) the ordinary modes of thinking to the structure of mentation itself.

Bill Burroughs and Brion Gysin turned their apartment on Rue Git le Coeur into the inner space of their imagination. Boxes of notes. Pages, photocopies, photos, littered the place. Permutations of linguistic patterns organized and reorganized and cut up photocopied copies of copies in every stage of vivisection and reconstruction littered every surface. Never-to-be-completed works stacked atop and amidst future masterpieces buried and forgotten. Windowless, cannabis and tobacco smoke filled, either one of them potentially gazing steadily into a mirror or into the smoke or at the ceiling for hours on end, sometimes acting out sequences of writings, bits of dialogue. Scissors and hypodermics flashing. Chemical neuro-missionaries bringing the good news of permanent timewar and post-linguistics to "wise up the marks" lost to the linear Control system of the Word-Virus. They tuned their outer environment to match

their inner, performing a symmetry between a linguistic framework and imagery; re-cognizing the word, the symbol, as operative visual art, coding, encoding, recoding, and decoding. They scryed smoke and mirrors in a churning language-threshing black box of hyperperspective, a tentacular multidentity sigilizing an inside-out third-minding of the gaps between their brains. //I'm all these characters, I'm an octopus!//[E1] *exclaims Burroughs in a fit of depersonalization, while Gysin "Let the Mice In" to gnaw solid holes in ephemeral self. Claiming that the future leaks in through every cut, the "Self-Portrait Jumper" and El Hombre Invisible undertake magically- and chemically-charged metamorphoses in the "Grey Room" to cut down past thought, the brain, and blood and bone to render themselves simultaneously immortal and unseeable. The sucking emptiness of a needle a black counterpoint to entheogenesis, the* //droning black hole of molecular mysticism's abortive escape//[E2] *provides the zen-like detachment from the self—while paradoxically generating the most severe of attachments.*

Examples of the flattening operation of which we speak can be as banal and everyday as a pile of disparate objects that are all an identical color, the moiré that emerges when two geometric patterns align in interesting ways, and tessellations of entire fields; or as singular and unique as extended time in a sensory-deprivation isolation tank or the creation of a mandala in which all worlds or all Buddhas are symbolically aligned in a cyclic, generative, and unicursal artistic organon that epitomizes transience. Drone music, particularly forms such as drone metal and other heavily amplified varieties, either drowns out or mimics ambient environmental sounds, flattening aural differentiation and rendering the audio field a single contiguous object of thought rather than a collection of objects.

It is in this sense that our flattening can be thought of as a form of compression, as ways to reduce cognitive expenditure in order to both make more bandwidth available for use and also reduce the effort required to *cognize cognition*. Compression of all signal to one source is shown in these extreme experiences to be a step shy of cognition of the full field, narrowly missing awareness of the possibility of the removal of the individualised signal. This loss is an integral component of the process and it is through ritual subsumption of the individual into the larger categorical structure of tribe/void/god/etc. that we complete this black circuit of non-negative negation, the negation of negation, and bring into focus the equality of being and non-being.

//That wonderful operation of hypostatic abstraction by which we seem to create entia rationis that are, nevertheless, sometimes real, furnishes us the means of turning predicates from being signs that we think or think through, into being subjects thought of. We thus think of the thought-sign itself, making it the object of another thought-sign.

Thereupon, we can repeat the operation of hypostatic abstraction, and from these second intentions derive third intentions. Does this series proceed endlessly?—CS Peirce, letter, 1906//

//There was neither non-existence nor existence then; there was neither the realm of space nor the sky which is beyond. What stirred? Where? In whose protection? Was there water, bottomlessly deep? There was neither death nor immortality then. There was no distinguishing sign of night nor of day. That one breathed, windless, by its own impulse. Other than that there was nothing beyond. —Mandala 10, hymn 129, verses 1-2, as translated by Wendy Doniger O'Flaherty, in The Rig Veda : An Anthology (1981).//

//Every sentence I utter must be understood not as an affirmation, but as a question. —Niels Bohr, A Dictionary of Scientific Quotations (1991) by Alan L. Mackay, p. 35//

//How wonderful that we have met with a paradox. Now we have some hope of making progress. —Niels Bohr, The Man, His Science, & the World They Changed (1966) by Ruth Moore, p. 196//

2.5 grams psilocybin mushrooms // Sunn O))) Ready Room, St. Louis 2016: The density of the fog was nothing compared to the density of the sound. Oceanic waveform oscillating to waveformless depth, wavelength simultaneously infinite and infinitesimal. Visceral body-crash amplitude: in the fog awareness of audience is eroded; inside the wavefront the body is gnawed away until the only perception is wave and wonder. Fog and sheer volume collude to concentrate attention on the megalith semicircle of speaker cabinets and amplifiers. Cloaked form covered in mirror shards attenuates the gaze further: Attila presiding over this //spinning thunderous vortex//[F1], this //great viscous cloud smothering hope//[F2], this ritual depersonalization, with seismophonic inc(h)antation. Planar LED beams and lasers attached to Attila's fingers cut strange mutating topological patterns in the haze. Chant-wave intersects, resonates, cancels, interpenetrates and interlocks with bass-waves; a physical rendering of sound in which one perceives absence as intensely as presence— //a perfect silhouette dilates full.//[F3]

The aether, so many times disproven as to be comical, turns out not to be measurable "out there" because it is "in here." It is not in physics, but within the ceaselessly howling oscillatory dynamics of neuroscience's (un)ground that we may be able to understand this illusory field upon which our representational "simulation" is projected, and only through flattening—by quite literally levelling—the entire simulation may we come to know the mechanism of this simulation. Flattening the simulation destroys the "world", crushes the transient individualized "ego", and permits the full flowering of intuition and identity. Perhaps quantum theory's observer problem disappears with the individualized observer?

//In the Great Death heaven and earth become anew. —Nishitani Keiji, Religion and Nothingness//

In conclusion, it is a pervasive thesis among spiritual thought, that to *even perceive* certain truths one must undergo certain transformations—that even empirical data may be corrupted by perspective that persists in the myth of separation and refuses to acknowledge that any observer is both container and contained, that every observer is embedded in a field of illusion that can be brought to standard awareness and manipulated, and even overcome, but only at the expense of so many typically Western forms of observation and communication. To ritualize intoxication stacks both transformative experience toward holism and a neurochemical shift away from object-dualism into a complex symmetry between the real and the ideal. On this pleromatic hyperplane, the gravity of temporal and sensorial binding-into-one is banished, destabilizing the ability to perceive oneself as a single Cartesian human individual moving inside an environment and restructuring identity toward a flexible multidentity in which an entity may experience smooth or abrupt, volitional or involuntary transfigurations between perceiving itself as one, as none, as a swarm, as but a single component of a superorganism, as the controller of a superorganism, or as indistinguishable from the environment as well as several points in between and

even foldings of this continuum such that multiple configurations may seem to overlap or intersect. These phenoumenodelic experiences aggressively demonstrate a vast spectrum of nonhuman identity, ranging from non-existence, to non-differentiation, to the unitary, to multiple enclosed identities, to being one among many identical identities inside a larger body, to an infinite enclosure wherein the self is identified with the entirety of existence. Drone music and ritual can provide pilot waves for guiding these transformations as the balancing act of drone's mutations and torsions align with the flexion of identity, while the cyclic and sacrificial spectacle of ritual generates a somatic, tangible convergence of inner and outer experience. The mind in tracking representations of these metamorphoses forces an added layer of environment/entity neurosymmetry, allowing for expanded cognition of the experiential field itself, an alignment of the lenses of imagination and sensory input in what may be considered a "spiritual de[a/p]th perception" or the Sellarsian "synoptic" alignment granting one *//not the inside knowledge of an elite but [...] a universal openness to movement, difference, sensation.—Sadie Plant, Writing on Drugs//*

REFERENCES

Δ: Gabriel Catren, *Pleromatica: Elsinore's Drunkenness* https://www.scribd.com/document/294147204/Pleromatica-or-Elsinores-Drunkenness-Gabriel-Catren

1: J.-P. Caron, *On the Transcendental Significance of Time-Stretching* https://voidfrontpress.org/portfolio/the-abstracts/

2: Nick Land, *Thirst for Annihilation: George Bataille and Virulent Nihilism* (London: Routledge, 1992), 81

3: Fernando Zalamea, *Peirce and Latin American "razonabilidad": forerunners of Transmodernity* http://lnx.journalofpragmatism.eu/wp-content/uploads/2009/11/09-zalamea.pdf

4: *ibid.*

A1: "Homeric Hymn," *from* G. E. Mylonas, *Eleusis and the Eleusinian Mysteries* (Princeton: Princeton University Press 2015).

A2: http://www.maps.org/images/pdf/books/eleusis.pdf

A3: P. Murray/P. Wilson, eds: *Music and the Muses, the Culture of Mousike in the Classical Athenian City* (Oxford: Oxford University Press, 2004), 33-34.

A4: *ibid.*

A5: *ibid.*

B1: http://www.swamij.com/mahamrityunjaya.htm

C1: Michael Muhammad Knight, *Tripping with Allah* (Berkeley: Soft Skull Press 2013), 47.

C2: Muhammad Emin Er (Author), Joseph Walsh (Translator), *Laws of the Heart, An Introduction to the Spiritual Path in Islam* (Shifa Publishing, 2008), 77.

C3: *Tripping with Allah*, 47.

D1: *Embrace of the Serpent* (Buffalo Films, 2015)

∞: Richard Doyle, *Hyperbolic: Divining Ayahuasca* http://aaaaarg.fail/upload/richard-doyle-hyperbolic-divining-ayahuasca-1.pdf

E1: William S. Burroughs and Brion Gysin, *Third Mind* (New York: Grove Press, 1982), 50.

E2: Joshua J Benjamin, *The Devil in My Veins*, forthcoming, voidfrontpress 2017.

F1: Sunn O))) "Aghartha" *Monoliths & Dimensions* (Southern Lord, 2009).

F2: Sunn O))) "Bàthory Erzsébet" *Black One* (Southern Lord, 2005).

F3: Sunn O))) "It Took The Night To Believe" *Black One* (Southern Lord, 2005).

Swans
THE GREAT ANNIHILATOR
Invisible Records 1995

Coil
MUSICK TO PLAY IN THE DARK VOL. 1
Chalice Records 1999

Anoxia Cerebri
ACCESS TO TOOLS
CDC Records 1987

Vatican Shadows
DEATH IS UNITY WITH GOD
Hospital Productions 2014

Sunn O)))
MONOLITHS & DIMENSIONS
Southern Lord 2009

Veš, Slikar, Svoj Dolg II
MUSIC FOR THE SPECTATOR
FV Založba 1989

MFH
MASKS
YHR Tapes 1980

Velimir Khlebnikov
THE RADIO OF THE FUTURE
http://imaginaryinstruments.org/the-radio-of-the-future/
https://www.youtube.com/watch?v=dj9AUrwq_OM

Raksha Mancham
CHÖS KHOR
Musica Maxima Magnetica 1993

AudiØVOID

The Message
https://the-message.bandcamp.com/

Rainforest Spiritual Enslavement
FOLKLORE VENOM
Hospital Productions 2013

Rainforest Spiritual Enslavement
GREEN GRAVES
Hospital Productions 2016

Sunn O)))
KANNON
Southern Lord 2015

Vishudha Kali
PSENODAKH
Fight Muzik 2003

Aural Holograms
VOLUME 1
Aural Hypnox 2007

Black Mountain Transmitter
BLACK GOAT OF THE WOODS
Aurora Borealis 2009

Die Sonne Satan
FAC TOTUM
Slaughter Productions 1993

Fister
VIOLENCE
Gogmagogical 2013

Drone Box

In 1234 Pope Gregory IX outlawed the tritone in church music. It was a restless interval, known as Diabolus in Musica and was cautiously avoided in the theory of the "old authorities". It was but one facet of the phantasmagoric dimension of nature which belongs to no regime. But it played an essential role in the formation of the Roman Catholic Church; a defile of the structure and purpose of ecclesiastical architecture, and programmatically varied structures of the western tradition. Pythagorean and Egyptian beliefs register in the Biblical story of the Garden of Eden as the spiraling Fibonacci growth of the Serpent and the circular pentagram and golden-ratio core of the Apple. Nature was understood as the foremost agent of evil in the world and our inmost chamber.

As with any discourse, one must understand the purpose of the material and the authority's target audience. In the Middle Ages, the Roman Catholic Church was the most powerful social force and was very successful in establishing and promulgating a franchise whereby the ecclesiastics could reach God through the brand of the Church. It was through this marketing and distribution network that the Church was able to socially engineer vast populations. The study of self and nature was the greatest sin. What does it mean to hide something from oneself or to deceive oneself in terms of ecclesiastic partitions and barriers? This is a difficulty faced by all theories that begin with man or a part of man alienated from his relation with nature. We all know that we can be ourselves only in and through the natural world. There is a sense in which nature will die with us although it will go on without us. The Roman Catholic Church, too, died with nature and was survived by it.

Tritone omission was the first principle—the foil, if you will—behind the dominion of the Church. The role the tritone played in unifying the canon of Roman Catholic music was similar to the role tragedy played in unifying Athenian culture, which says nothing about any possible connection between artistic achievement and the archetypical institution of Catholicism. The tritone was the model for all canon law and became the legislative model used to prosecute paganism in general. It was the ethical justification behind the Church's mission to eradicate free harmony in music. Catholic discourse constitutes a modality of fractio-harmoniphobic language: the tritone became subject to the signifying economy in which canon law constituted a closed resonance chamber of the Church. But this pagan resonant interval was considered sacred by the architects of the Church, and to preserve their dark secrets they encoded cymatic[1] symbols into the architecture of the Church. The Fibonacci ratio 13:8 or 1.625 is embedded into the architecture of Churches, the Rosslyn Chapel being but one example. This is the first non-resonant Fibonacci ratio. This begins the convergence of the subsequent Fibonacci ratios which lead to the golden ratio (~1.61803) found in the pentagram and "golden triangle."

The Church was well aware that the tritone could reveal the symmetry in music harmony and open the door to the "carnal knowledge" of harmonics in the body and elsewhere in nature, and this is why its cymatic architecture was designed to buffer the defile of the tritone. There can be no fractional, or unstable, resonance at

or near the infinite frequency proportion of the golden ratio. After the ratio of 13:8 the ratios of adjacent numbers in the Fibonacci series converge into the infinite golden ratio and damping increases, gradually canceling all fractional standing waves and leaving only whole number harmonics.

The tritone can be thought of as Foucault's grin which hangs about without the cat. It is a quality without an abiding substance, a free-floating attribute that suggests the possibility of radical communion without the substantializing and hierarchizing grammar of cymatic space. The Church's architecture is nothing but a regulatory fiction, a chamber which amplifies the Angel's symbolic resonance while minimizing Pantheistic drone with anti-harmonic damping effects. The immanent rebellion of the fractional standing waves of Pantheistic drone is static, as in the Athenian political concept of stasis (στάσις); that is, rebellion or civil war. Although this form of drone implies restlessness, it remains static and stops the endless signifying economy of the Church. It represents a suspension of God and angelic resonance. It is hiatus in the normality of the functioning Church. The radical externality of the tritone becomes the rat's nest in the church walls. It is in the last instance heresy.

The tritone is problematic within the resonance chamber of the Church because it is a standing wave which occupies space but cannot be counted as a whole number. It is a fractional number of dimensions in an optimally directional space and its drone varies continually in every direction without tangent. The orthogonal walls of the church seek to count and limit, to order the natural into coherent bodies. This creates a galvanizing tension, a principle of work antithetical to the "inertia or non-work" of Pantheistic drone. The

---

1   Cymatics, from Greek: κῦμα, meaning "wave", is a subset of modal vibrational phenomena. The term was coined by Hans Jenny (1904-1972). In 1967 Jenny published two volumes entitled Kymatic, in which, repeating Ernst Chladni's experiments, he claimed the existence of a subtle power based on the normal, symmetrical images made by sound waves.

fractional standing waves of the Diabolus in Musica perforate the Church into a Sierpensky's sponge. On pure sudden days like innocence we behold the saints and their priorities keypunched in the air.

Halfway between man and God, the Diabolus in Musica has absolute torsion: it is both the possibility of stasis and the sprawling occupation of its power. Not merely a refraction of nature, it designates the peril beyond Catholicism that might prevent in a definitive manner the denouement of Truth, an ominous hiatus threatening the inmost sanctum of man. The blinding light of the Church obscures the shadow of the Diabolus in Musica to obfuscate its brooding power; until the existence of Truth in nature has been secured, the tritone haunts the whole of canon law. How could the Roman Catholic Church reduce the tritone to a mere foil? For the medieval church, it was the element in which nature was born to its own truth, the realm where Catholicism would have to assert its absolute sovereignty. But what taxonomic principle could possibly order a flood? The church supports an overwhelming and ultimately meaningless historicism.

The Roman Catholic Church and its opposite, the Diabolus in Musica, are powers which erupt from nature itself, without human mediation. The architects of the church were puppets on string, animated entirely by nature's drives. Nature has little regard for the individual, even seeking to annihilate and release him through the mystical oneness of fractional harmony. In relation to these unmediated natural drives in nature every discourse is an imitation; either a Catholic zealot's or a Pagan architect's—or both at once. Alone and alienated from the chorus, oneness with the inmost chamber reveals a symbolic fractionated wave. The orthogonal surface of the Church stands in

opposition to the stasis of Pantheistic drone, which is channeled by the chorus towards its appropriate addressee.

What is at stake here is an unfathomable silence. The cymatic symbols hidden by the architects of the church form a sort of unconscious; like hieroglyphics on the walls of the church they patiently wait to be deciphered. An unfathomable silence, rendered by the cymatics of the resonance chambers of the church, acts as an insurmountable obstacle to the Pantheistic drone and its meaning. The architects are precarious figures at the borders of silence mandated by the Roman Catholic Church.

Separated by the thin surface of pantomime, the resonance chambers themselves are little more than slight deviations from the sacred architecture of the ancients But in this pantomime, where the truth of nature is only maintained within an unfathomable silence, the church is met with the ironic perversion of its own truth, at the moment when it passes from the sin of interiority to the form of social condition. Pantheistic drone then takes on the form of an evil unconscious— no longer one which exiles man from divine truth, but one which brings mystification and clarity simultaneously, that disenchants the truth about the self that the church has entrusted to angelic resonance; an evil unconscious which operates by dissolving back to the world the cymatic structure of the Truth.

The possibility of the tritone is no longer lodged in perception, but in expression, and the irony is to see the dull mass at the mercy of the immediate and the sensible, alienated in the mediation that it is. The cymatic structure of the church drafts maps of the sensible, trajectories between the angelic chorus and the silenced tritone, relationships between modes of speech, modes of silence, and modes of social participation. It defines variations of perceptions and abilities of the mass.

The fractional standing waves of the tritone thus muzzled, the church takes hold of the docile social body. The silence of the tritone widens the gap between man and his inmost chamber, it opens up space for wild gapings, trajectories, and ways in which the mass recognize their image in the resonance of the church. The church reconfigures the functionality of sound. It sets up a silent dialogue between Pantheistic drone and whole number harmony. That dialogue itself comes undone, and the silence is absolute. There is no longer communion with the dark secrets of nature, there is only an absence, for it is the lacunary of canon law, and therefore not music at all; its only trace, in the evil unconscious finally silenced, is sin. And it is only from this quality that a dialogue is possible, after sin had been classified and dealt with.

The absence of the tritone, as a fundamental structure of nature, has as its correlative the act of admitting sin. If there is to be any exchange in the eroding monologue, is it any wonder that the formulations can only be a reference to sin? In this unfathomable silence, sin had taken over the very source of Pantheistic drone. It is only legible in the part of itself that is heard. The rest is reduced to silence. The tritone no longer exists except as that which is silenced in the inner sanctum of the church. The social body that is formed in the church does not encourage reciprocation. It is simply that of a deaf ear, gaping, censoring, roving pitilessly close the better to hear its own voice, while remaining sufficiently distant to avoid any contamination. The

science of nature, as it was to develop in the church, was only ever of the order of isolation and classification. It was never destined to be a reciprocal interaction.

The remotest semblance of dialogue took the form of the excision of the phenomenon of angelic resonance, so essential to the Roman Catholic Church, substituting its silent magic with the powers of divine truth. Or perhaps it would be more accurate to say that the church doubled the absolute silence of the tritone with the indefinite monologue of its resonance; the structure of a canon without response.

Silence, or the reification of the tritone, was key to the dominion of Catholicism. The inmost chamber of being is silenced, translated into whole number harmonies that resonate angelically in the chamber of the church. The voice of the pagan, the dark, fractionated, dissonance is curbed. There are examples of this throughout the cannon of the church. For instance, the martyr Saint Eustace who, according to the golden legend from the forest, saw transfigured in the antlers of a stag the crucifix. He was so overcome with awe that he converted immediately. The antlers of that mythic beast, the gnarly formations crowning the skull of the pagan saint of the woods, symbolized nothing; they were the erratic background noise, the morbific secret of a world that challenged the orthogony of Catholicism. The stags living in the branches Yggrdasil came down to earth to proselytize.

Following his vision Saint Eustace baptized his family, but over the course of his life his faith was challenged. The gnawing calamity of the world consumed his wealth, his household, and ultimately his family; yet, like Job, he remained devout. Saint Eustace's devotion progressed to such a degree that he even challenged the ethical justification behind the Church's mission to eradicate paganism. His decision to refuse pagan sacrifice proved fatal. Saint Eustace bowed only before the stag. It was the dark secret of the world that first penetrated his inmost chamber, but his faith could only be reified as devotion to the church in canon law. It was the stasis of the antlers, the cymatic structure of Pantheistic drone that awed Eustace. This is the irony behind the church's roasting him to death inside the hollow bull.

The hollow bull is one of the oldest, perhaps the first, musical instruments of the church. It is a simple concept, following a certain medieval fascination of rendering inanimate objects animate. The hollow bull was animated by the screams of heretics. Like the minotaur it was a symbol of labyrinths, power, and sacrifice. It was a torture device that doubled as a rudimentary instrument. Legend has it the first heretic[2]

was executed by order of the Catholic Church inside the hollow bull. It was the true Diabolus in Musica.

On the back of the hollow, brazen bull was a hinge trap door that opened onto a chamber inside. Once the pagan heretic was locked within the belly of the beast, a flame was lit beneath, and the victim was cooked alive. Inside the dark space claustrophobia, panic, acute stress, and tachycardia would build up into crescendos of panic and pain until the heretic eventually passed out from dehydration trauma and roasted. The extreme heat cooked him from the inside out.

Inside the head of the hollow bull was a labyrinthine system of brass tubing that converted the high frequency screams of the heretic into the low frequency bellows of an infuriated bull. The exact configuration of the device is unknown, but historical writing describes the eerie transformation of the heretic's screams. The screams could not be heard through the dense metal, but once the fire superheated the air inside, the heretic would struggle to reach a mouthpiece at one end of the tubing built into the bull's head, siphoning air from outside and exhaling while screaming.

The hollow bull was a microcosm of the church itself. It opened a lacunary reserve[3], which designated and demonstrated this hollow where heresy and silence implied each other, one being the foundation of the other, and animated nothing other than their cymatic relationship. It was a non-musical instrument because it was a torture device (an instrument which only

---

2   The builder of the hollow bull was the first victim: 'This Phalaris burned to death Perilaus, the well-known Attic worker in bronze, in the brazen bull. Perilaus had fashioned in bronze the contrivance of the bull, making small sounding pipes in the nostrils and fitting a door for an opening in the bull's side and this bull he brings as a present to Phalaris. And Phalaris welcomes the man with presents and gives orders that the contrivance be dedicated to the gods. Then that worker in bronze opens the side, the evil device of treachery, and says with inhuman savagery, "If you ever wish to punish some man, Phalaris, shut him up within the bull and lay a fire beneath it; by his groanings the bull will be thought to bellow and his cries of pain will give you pleasure as they come through the pipes in the nostrils." When Phalaris learned of this scheme, he was filled with loathing of the man and says, "Come then, Perilaus, do you be the first to illustrate this; imitate those who will play the pipes and make clear to me the working of your device." And as soon as Perilaus had crept in, to give an example, so he thought, of the sound of the pipes, Phalaris closes up the bull and heaps fire under it. But in order that the man's death might not pollute the work of bronze, he took him out, when half-dead, and hurled him

---

down the cliffs.' Diodorus of Sicily, World History, 9.19.1

3   The sickness and the cure are rendered inseparable. The only way to "play" this musical instrument is to step inside.

existed in the act of torture, an act which said nothing but resonated canon law)—i.e. an articulation of the heresy which, strictly speaking, said nothing. A fold of the heresy which was an absence of the heretic.

This medieval torture device became an instrument of canon law and social denunciation. The intention was to erect one form of cymatic speech as universal, which was to be imposed from within on other forms of heresy that were alien to it, and which contained the alienation that would inevitably traumatize would-be heretics. In the first place, it was to act as an awakening and a reminder, a traumatic spectacle that invoked a forgotten nature; in the second, it was to act as social upheaval, to dislodge individuals from their paganism. The goal was simple: a diabolic instrument for the purposes of moral purification. The labyrinthine tubes inside the bull's head operated a moral synthesis, assuring an ethical continuity between the dark secrets of the inmost chamber and the Truth, but enacting a form of social denunciation all the while that guaranteed Catholic morality a *de facto* universality, enabling it to impose canon law over all forms of heresy.

In its marvelous economy, the task of the hollow bull is doubly effective: it produces angelic resonance and destroys heresy, a task necessary to canon law born out of the death of heretics whose disappearance was desirable. The diabolical, restless tritone of men passed into the docility of the brazen bull. The irregularities of their senseless screams were buffeted and polished as smooth as bronze. Canon law here reached a paroxysm of perfection: the heretic was cooked alive, but each step taken towards his silence was useful to the church from which they were banished.

Just as the Church strictly forbade tritonic standing waves, relegating the Pantheistic knowledge of resonance to the secret knowledge of the Underworld, the hollow bull silenced heresy. In the very act of outlawing heresy both the Church and its microcosm indelibly bore features of what they negated; both adhered to the rigors of a geometry that was architectural and moral. Every partition of space in the Church and every meticulous inch of the tubing inside the bull's head took on the symbolic value of an earthbound hell.

ON THE TRANSCENDENTAL AESTHETICS OF TIME-STRETCHING

J.-P. Caron

I.

In the Tarkovsky film Stalker two men, a writer and a scientist, enter what is called in the film the Zone, which is a geographic stretch wherein the topology is always changing. That means that the region you are once in will not be the same once you come back to it, so as to need special guidance from those that are called the Stalkers. Their function is to bring you to a place inside it in which one can fulfil whatever desire one has, but only if one has the ability to formulate it in words.

What strikes one philosophically minded viewer of the film is the metaphor in play which can be thought of against Kant's 1786 text What does it mean to orient oneself in thinking?

However exalted the application of our concepts, and however far up from sensibility we may abstract them, still they will always be appended to image representations, whose 'proper function' is to make these concepts, which are not otherwise derived from experience, serviceable for experiential use. For how would we procure sense and significance for our concepts if we did not underpin them with some intuition (which ultimately must always be an example from some possible experience)? If from this concrete act of the understanding we leave out the association of the image—in the first place an accidental perception through the senses—then what is left over is the pure concept of understanding, whose range is now enlarged and contains a rule for thinking in general.[1]

So, in this Kantian account, concepts are in some sense to be used experientially—in some sense to be empirically filled as images that can furnish points of reference in thinking. The stability of such points of reference is, thus, required for them to be used in thinking. The world of the Stalker presents a contrast-

---

1   I. Kant, "What does it mean to orient oneself in thinking" In: Religion and Rational Theology. (translation by A. Wood and G. Giovanni) Cambridge University Press.

ing image in which there's no topological stability in which to locate oneself, thus presenting something of a non-conceptualizable region for thought, and yet, that demands the expression of desire, not just desire itself. The expression of one's own desire then demands one's own conceptual self-navigation through the non-conceptualizable Zone.

The aim of the present paper is to engage in the problems posed to sensibility and reason pertaining to the temporal points of reference while listening to drone music, particularly by investigating the modifications and mechanisms that are exposed in the procedure of extreme time stretching. The idea suggested itself to me through an interview that was published, between Lee Gamble and philosopher Robin Mackay wherein there was mentioned a supposed "transcendental significance of time-stretching."

We'd do conferences, and instead of reading an academic paper, we'd read out these blunted, cut-up texts over some dark drum and bass mix. We'd talk about cyberpunk fiction, sci-fi movies and the early days of the Internet; all of that was precisely what we called "abstract culture." I had a whole philosophical deduction about the transcendental significance of time-stretching![2]

Shortly after I'd read it, I emailed Mackay with questions about what was meant by it, to which he answered that he hadn't thought about it for a while, and it needed to be worked through again. I started immediately to think about this problem, having been involved for a couple of years in composing what I called my "time-stretch pieces." I have no intention to excavate what would be meant by Mackay himself, rather freely thinking about the problem myself and offering my personal results.

What calls one's attention in the expression is the word transcendental. It seems to refer to a procedure that would somehow reveal something to be a conditioning element of experience itself. The second important word is time-stretching, which is an assortment of digital audio processing procedures that enables the temporal extension of a determined soundclip without modifying its pitch. Time-stretching is a digital audio procedure that is dependent on the conversion of sounding signals into samples—ultimately into discrete elements over which are applied determinate operations. The whole phrase attributes a transcendental significance to time-stretching. One would be inclined to think that such transcendental significance should be deduced from the empirical transformation undergone by the objects to which such procedure is applied. That is, something essential about our a priori access to reality should be illustrated by the procedure.

II.

The most accurate and flexible electronic musical instrument ever designed is the digital computer. Just like the organ, invented centuries earlier, the power of the computer derives from its ability to emulate, or, in scientific terms, model, phenomena. Computer models take the form of symbolic codes. So, it does not matter if the phenomena being modelled exist out of the circuit of the machine or if they are pure fantasy. This makes the computer a perfect testing ground for

2   http://www.electronicbeats.net/lee-gamble-gets-deep-with-philosopher-robin-mackay/, visited in February 24, 2017.

the representation of musical structures on multiple time scales.[3]

The paragraph touches on several assumptions of what will come next. First, the possibility of transformation that comes with the use of computers, which is dependent on the use of symbolic codes—binary sequences of numbers representing objects. Second, the disjunction of digital modelling of pre-existing models in reality. And third, and consequently, the possibility of exploring unprecedented time scales by manipulating digital audio.

The present work deals with a specific procedure applicable to digital audio, time-stretch, and its philosophical consequences for the representation of time in music and music in works. For those who do not know what it's all about, just a visit to YouTube to find dozens of videos of famous songs 'stretched' with freeware time-stretching programs such as paulstretch (Paul's extreme time-stretch). [4]

Prior to the advent of digital audio, temporal extension procedures as applied to sound were only possible with simultaneous pitch transposition. For instance, in order to extend a certain recorded sound to twice its duration, one had to reproduce the sound to be stretched with half the speed—obtaining a sound with twice the duration, but also one octave lower. This is easily understood by understanding that there is an interplay between the frequency of a sound,

what we hear as "pitch", and time. A sound an octave on the piano above another sound is simply a sound with twice the frequency, that is, a periodic sound whose cycle repeats twice as much per unit of time as another. The additive spatial concept of "interval" is a projection of the temporal logarithmic concept of frequency difference (The "space" of frequencies is organized logarithmically, that is, from one frequency one can obtain any other not by adding intervals, as in a piano, but by multiplying frequencies.)[5]

In the context of digital audio, there is a symbolic representation of sound, ultimately, strings of numbers. In a less fundamental level, the sound is mapped into samples or windows. Which means that in digital audio, the sound we hear as a continuous signal, is chopped into a sequence of discrete elements. This enables a number of different interventions.

The first step of analysis is windowing, or segmenting a continuous sound into discrete particles. (...) By concentrating on one grain or window of sound at a time, the analysis can focus on local or short-time spectra. Like the frames of a motion picture, a series of windowed analyses yields a portrait of the spectrum evolution over time.[6]

The digital time-stretching procedure consists of a procedure of assembly and interpolation. The assembly consists, roughly, in the multiplication of samples that would represent a certain sound, maintaining the proportionality between its constituent moments. This procedure is a tributary of a representation of

3   C. Roads Microsound. The MIT Press, Cambridge, 2004.

4   Paul's extreme time-stretch is freely available here: http://hypermammut. sourceforge.net/paulstretch/

5   Cf. Harry Partch- Genesis of a music. Da Capo Press, 1979

6   C. Roads, op. Cit. p. 239

sound as a particle—the so-called granular synthesis. By dividing continuous sound into thousands of small corpuscles it is possible to perform sound syntheses by combining these corpuscles. Another method makes use of Fourier Transforms, which are formulas that allow one to decompose a complex signal into a multitude of simple signals. Thus, an extremely complicated waveform can be decomposed into a multitude of sinusoidal (simultaneous) forms theoretically. Through the transforms it is possible to locate peaks, elements of high amplitude and with greater importance in a certain sound recreating trajectories between them in a different temporal scale. Unlike the simple mechanical process of stacking more windows side by side, this spectral modelling process recreates a routing ("interpolates") between original points of sound retained as relevant to its identity, modulating the trajectory length according to the requested extension. The idea is to reconstruct the illusion of continuity between the different windows to produce the impression of one sound and not of a multiplicity. The analogy with cinema is adequate in that it works by a similar process: the display of a certain number of frames per second goes beyond the perceptual ability to isolate the frames, creating apparent continuity.

III.

It's perhaps interesting that I've begun a paper about time-stretching with the metaphor of the space of Tarkovsky's Zone. It's mostly because space furnishes the basic metaphor for localization, which is confirmed by its role in Kantian Transcendental Aesthetics as that a priori form that pertains to the external world and the external relations that is characteristic of physical objects. While time is necessary for both our interior world (inner thoughts or episodes) and the external,

the burden of establishing the difference between ourselves and that which is not ourselves lies in some form of spatial intuition.

That much Peter Strawson understood, and in his chapter "Sounds" from his book Individuals proceeds to investigate the possibility of a non-solipsistic consciousness in a no-space world.[7] That is, the possibility of differentiation of one's thought episodes and mind-independent entities in a world without space. The paradigm of a no-space world offered by Strawson is a purely auditory world. Obviously one should abstain all the elements that pertains to (empirical) space from such an auditory world in order for the thought experiment to function. So, more than a purely auditory world, it is a world where our intuitions of spatial localization are completely suspended. Strawson's idea being that maybe he can come up with an analogue of space that would do the job.

The job is, then, to be able to recreate, as a sign of mind-independent reality, the idea of numerical identity in such a world. That is, the idea not just of categorical identity between two similar sounds, but the possibility to differentiate particular sounds and, moreover, to re-identify particulars that have been absent from contact with the consciousness that is plunged in this no-space world. Strawson takes to be fundamental to objectivity-as-such the possibility of continuing existence-while-absent from perceptual contact.

---

7   Peter Strawson, Individuals. An essay in descriptive metaphysics. Routledge, 1991 (1959). For a more detailed analysis of the intrinsic sound space offered by Strawson, see my own "Into the full: Strawson, Wyschnegradsky and acoustic space in noise musics" In Goddard et al (org.) Resonances: Noise and contemporary music. Bloomsbury, 2013.

The fiction that he creates is the idea of a Master Sound. A Master Sound is something each consciousness has (much like space is something that is provided by the subject by Kantian Transcendental Aesthetics) that is perpetually modulating, increasing and decreasing gradually in pitch. The master sound works much like a radio dial—a metaphor for successive positions—as in when one browses through the frequencies finding radio programs and reidentifying them after returning to the same position in the dial. When the Master Sound attains a determined "pitch", a determined sound—different from the master sound itself—appears to our subject. Then it vanishes as the master sound moves on, reappearing when it returns to that same pitch. The idea being that one has to have independent criteria for constructing coordinates in whatever world one happens to exist. The master sound is supposed to offer such criteria, a criteria for successive "positions" in which one is supposed to re-encounter, and re-identify other sounds (the entities that populate this no-space world).

Gareth Evans, in his critique of Strawson[8], is not convinced by this account of objectivity. He believes one has to have a theory of physical objectualities in order to have objectivity. This theory includes a rough version of the doctrine of primary and secondary qualities. For Evans, Strawson's fiction does not prove that reidentification is necessary for objectivity, as one could simply substitute continuity for reidentification. In which case there's not a sufficiently robust concept of space in Strawson's world, and the reidentification it proposes is not one between objectualities, but a continuity between processes. And secondly, this

reidentification of processes in time after absentia cannot account for the differentiation between two simultaneous processes in different places.

What's important is to retrieve from Strawson's fiction the idea of an auditory world that is fraught with indexicals. That is, where it is possible to know one's way around in time the same way one knows one's way around in space.

IV.

Classical music (Bach, Mozart, Beethoven, etc.) allocates reference events at regular intervals (cadences, repetition) to periodically guide the listener within the form. Some popular music takes this to the extreme, reminding listeners repeatedly in a shorter interval of time. [9]

Roads refers here to an important element in the construction of musical time. In addition to the periodic articulation of minimal units—rhythmically articulated notes—the repetition of elements— melodies, cadences, themes at strategic points of the form articulates for the listener relations between parts, which in turn are intermediary level entities between the total form of the work, and its minimal units. This means that a musical composition is to some extent a particular topology which produces a certain image of time for us. Time is here constituted by the relation between events and perception. It does not refer to something that flows independently of the subject, external to the syntheses operated by consciousness, but places itself entirely within the latter, as a presupposed medium for its operations. The articulation of musical

8   G. Evans "Les choses sans l'esprit. Un commentaire du chapitre deux des Individus de Strawson" In. D. Perrin et L. Soutif (org. and translation) Cahiers de philosophie du langage, vol 7 "Wittgenstein em confrontation" Paris, L'Harmattan, 2011.

9   C. Roads, op. Cit.

elements presupposes time as succession while at the same time acting on it by synthesizing a specific image of it.

An interesting duplicity insinuates itself here: while succession is time's invariable form, different qualities of time are conjured by the listening experience. Interestingly, musicologist Jonathan Kramer proposes a whole typology of time for musical composition, which deals with contradictions between levels of temporal consciousness. [10]

The categories proposed by Kramer are resultant on the interplay of two different forces: linearity and non-linearity. They should be differentiated from continuity and discontinuity. Linearity is every form of development that is implicated in succession, such as the harmonic "resolutions" of tonal form. Non-linearity is not discontinuity, which is a rupture on continuity, such that one can have linear elements that are not contiguous to one another, but is anything that is outside the succession, organizing discourse without being implicated in time. For instance, the instrumentation of a musical piece. He then proposes four species of time operant in XXth century music: Linear time; Multiply directed Time; Moment Time and Vertical Time. Those can be organized in a diagram like the one below[11].

LINEARITY

LINEAR TIME	*MULTIPLY DIRECTED TIME*
CONTINUITY	**DISCONTINUITY**
VERTICAL TIME	*MOMENT TIME*

NON-LINEARITY

Which means, pure linear time results from linearity and continuity—linear forces express themselves contiguously; multiply directed time results from the interruption of continuity by discontinuous elements, each one with its own linear implications, which are resolved in different points of the form; vertical time is continuous without strong linear implications—the continuous present of Drone—and moment time is a succession of discontinuous "moments" with no linear implications between them—like Stockhausen's momentform, or grindcore's fast succession of moments with no linear implication .

A work in this context behaves as a coordination center for the operations of sensibility. It presupposes time as a condition for its constitution, but it acts upon our perception in order to guide us or, on the contrary, to make us lose ourselves by instituting or erasing flags or indexicals, which are moments in the form that provide criteria for the individuation of the form. The work thus presupposes a totality. It presents itself as an individualized and, to some extent, repeatable ex-

---

10   J. Kramer. The time of music. New meanings, new temporalities, new listening strategies. Schirmer Books, 1988

11   This graph was used for the first time in J.-P. Caron. Aspectos de tempo e espaço musicais em Giacinto Scelsi e La Monte Young. Masters in music, Universidade Federal do Estado do Rio de Janeiro, 2007.

perience, which would make it liable to be reified as an object. With the object it has in common its bounded nature. It begins and ends, after following a certain path which presupposes in the one who listens the ability to follow it with one's mind. From its totalization as limited experience it is deduced the correlation that is proper to the work, between an event, and that being that perceives it. Insofar as it presupposes in the subject the same processes it offers itself, the work is a correlational entity—it emerges within a normatively articulated social-perceptual practice.

In the twentieth century we can see attempts to break with the correlation pointed out, particularly in the work of John Cage, who intended to break the intentional chain of composer to the finished work, by the same token opening it to chance, and finally breaking the presupposition of syntheses to be performed by the listener. The listener is invited to adapt to a content that was not prepared for him. But it is quite clear that the operation proposed by Cage is placed within a practice of composition and listening of works, being a deviation that presupposes it as a norm. The very self-placing of the act within a concert raises the pretense of correlation again, only to offer a content that is not itself thought out as a result of a synthetic activity to be shared by composer and listener.[12]

My bet is that the time-stretch procedure can (and I emphasize here that it can, because it is a potential that is to be radicalized or not) function in a similar way. To seize the correlational work-constituting subjectivity of the listener, while offering him something that is

not presupposing the subjective synthetic activity so much, offering instead a product of a completely different synthesis: that of a kind of temporality that is the result of operations that are both short of and beyond the temporal level synthesised by the (human) subject.

V.

From 2007 onward I designed a series of time-stretch pieces. At the time it was harder to get good results and softwares like Paulstretch were not available, so I used a Csound patch that was provided to me by composer Rodolfo Caesar, with whom I had had electronic music lessons before. I modified the numerical values of the patch as well as other small modifications so that I would get the effects I wanted.

At that time it was a set of pieces that were to be time-stretched from another piece of mine, called 8' for Giacinto Scelsi. This piece was an investigation of what I perceived as the constants of a certain sound grammar proper of the Italian composer Giacinto Scelsi. This composer worked with prolonged concentration on sustained sounds, but in a way that, when observed with more care, were in fact tiny continuous trajectories that swept the frequency space between the points of stability of his sonorous discourse. A difficulty of stabilization is proposed to the ear that rounds this instability to its nearest stable points/pitches. This opened cognition to a space that was at the same time narrow and infinite. Unlike the space we find between the notes of the piano, which are discrete, i.e. there are gaps between the notes, entities perceived musically as different, in Scelsi there was a dwelling between the notes, but not in the form of a narrower grid (as

---

12   This reflection on Cage is pursued further in my doctoral dissertation L'indé-termination à l'oeuvre: John Cage et l'identité de l'oeuvre musicale. PhD dissertation. Philosophy. University of Paris 8, 2015.

we can find, for example, in a quarter-tone space), but rather as a perpetual slip between close frequencies, a slip that blocks the proper comprehension of its constituent moments. This for me constituted a very specific sound topology, in which there was the predominance of the continuum to the detriment of the discrete, of continuity to the detriment of contrast. And this would also have consequences for the perception of the time of the music. The less frequent occurrence of contrasts, abrupt changes that work in traditional listening as flags and indexicals, that is, as markers of time-points that allow the constitution of musical narrative form, would plunge us into a form of temporal stasis, although inhabited by the sonic dynamism already commented.

The score of 8′ for Giacinto Scelsi offered graphic lines that would mark continuous frequential trajectories to be performed by the instruments in narrow spaces. There were a number of factors left to the interpreters' choice, in such a way that a large number of phenomenally diverse pieces were to be generated from the same source chart. This same productive relationship between the graph and its sound realization, I wanted to have also between each recording and its temporal expansion. With each new 8′ performance, I was able to produce a different time-stretched version from its recording, varying both the recorded source and the factor of multiplication of the stretched piece. The series is defined by the procedure, but does not propose a unified experience. Different versions of both 8^2 (8′ multiplied by 8) and 8^3 (8′ multiplied by 8^2— circa 8 hours long) were produced, without a single one of them being counted as being the piece.[13]

What was desired by this process was to test the specific topology of Scelsi's music by stretching it temporally and seeing if this would entail a modification of the species of time (cf. Kramer supra) that are presented by this music. This much was achieved. The propounded image of an extended present that is typical of all droning music could be indeterminately stretched. Its topology was weak enough to subsist to this modification without entailing a temporal transformation it its species of time. But in the process another dimension of time made itself present. Not the intensive qualities of time but the extensive time of time intervals, and measuring, as the successive versions asymptotically approximated points of rupture of the synthesizing activity of one listening subject. By the factor of 4 the series would achieve multi daily duration, growing exponentially with each installment. By the factor of 5 we get almost 27 days of a single running musical form.

This extensive time, measured in time-units, irreducible to a specific quality of time as in the Kramer diagram, is what opens up musical form to an alien intelligence— one that is capable not only of synthesizing a certain time species from the perceptual input, as in drone music in general, but one that is capable of following the narrative form through its indexicals in the same way as one (a 'human' subject) follows Beethoven's 9th.[14] This means that, on the side of the subject there must still be the possibility of structural

---

13   Two of those can be heard online. 8^2 is featured in the album ST, released by Sinewave records, and can be downloaded in the link http://sinewave.com.br/2014/05/j-p-caron-st-2014/ And a much more radical, 8^3 version, produced from the same source as the previous version can be listened to in the link

https://jpcaron.bandcamp.com/releases

14   Ironically there is a 24 hours time-stretch of Beethoven's 9th, which illustrates perfectly the argument advanced here. 9 Beet Stretch can be listened to as a continuous stream here: http://www.xn--lyf-yla.com/. The continuous streaming form that was chosen is problematic, though, for the recognition of form, leading the listening act back to a form of ambient rather than structural listening, which is recognizant upon human limitations and the conversion of (extreme) extension into intensive time.

rather than ambient listening— the exigency of which opens the gate to the recognition of form by an apparatus capable of reconstructing form in such proportions; while on the side of the "work", there must not be mereological identity from part-to-whole. That is, the form must be articulated by differences among its constitutive parts and between these and the totality. One single sound stretched to a million years doesn't count— as each constitutive moment rehearses the work as a whole (what I am calling mereological identity from part-to-whole). [15]

Three ruptures comes about from this way of proceeding in relation to the model of the work as limited experience:

1. *Rupture of the temporal limits of the object.*

The series of works called 8' does not propose an upper bound for the duration of a specific version. This can last for days, or even centuries. Although the resulting object has definite edges, they far exceed the individual's ability to perceive them and must be inferred or presupposed by the listener. The process goes beyond the experience one can have of it.

2. *Rupture of the singularity of the object.*

More than one 8^2 can exist, as well as more than one 8^3 and so on. The names no longer refer to limited temporal experiences reified in single pieces, but to the procedures that produced them. Thus, a number of objects fall on the same concept, dissolving the one to one relationship of name and work. The name designates something that may appear in various forms, non-reducible to each other except for the knowledge of the procedure that engendered them.

3. *Rupture of the aesthetic appearance of digital music.*

The constructed character of temporality is assumed. Time is presupposed as a form of succession, but temporality is assumed to be artificial. The procedure makes use of digital audio, in which most of the music listened nowadays is currently consumed. On the one hand, while the .mp3 format strives to conceal its own artificiality, while optimizing storage information space, the extreme time-stretch procedure clearly displays the operation, and although it does not make it audible in itself, it displays a perceptual result that presupposes digital audio manipulation.

This means that time-stretching exists through the recognition of the constructed character of digital sound in order to activate—ideally beyond the human capacity of perception of that structure which is maintained (stretched)—a contrived traversing of the discontinuous representation of sound. This exemplifies human incapacities in at least two ways: a) by the sometimes extreme extension of the duration the identity of the original structure is lost on the listener because it exceeds her available identifying memory and b) by the micro-assemblage of digital samples it creates the impression of continuity by exceeding human limits of micro-temporal discrimination.[16]

---

15 Several other experiences with extreme duratons can be mentioned, but most of them balances towards ambient listening. Bull of Heaven's pieces come to mind http://www.bullofheaven.com/, as much as Jem Finer´s a thousand years long Longplayer http://longplayer.org/. The problem with such pieces is, again, an absorption of their narrativity into an atemporal concept. The use of recursive algorithmic procedures enables either the anticipation by the intellect of what it is to come, either the simple absorption of listening into the hearing of "ambiances".

---

16 While the vector of time amplification is illustrated by the extreme time-stretching procedures, the vector of time compression is illustrated by the many who are working on granular synthesis and the cognitive overload that are characteristic of some electroacoustic and noise musics.

Of course, this is not exclusive to time-stretching, as audio manipulation is ubiquitous in electronic music in general. But the way time-stretching achieves its result is particularly engaging when it comes to temporality—the tethering to a kind of imperceptible field of the construction of a hyper-process that is supra-perceptible, in the sense of being perceptible as the process it is only to a higher transcendental apparatus or an intelligence inhabiting another level of temporal processing.[17]

VI.

It is tempting to recuperate the extraction of time performed by extreme time-stretching from the subject via the mobilization of Kant's mathematical sublime. The idea is seductive in that the resulting piece seems a quite literal realization of the mathematical sublime—the display of an infinity whose sensible intuition is impossible but which is conceivable by reason. But the extraction lies precisely in there—as a way to use Kantian philosophy's conceptual assets against the necessity of them being instantiated by a (necessarily) human subject.

Strawson proposed initially to derive objectivity from time by constructing an analogon of space in a purely auditory world. To which Gareth Evans responded by showing that objectivity thus construed fails to account for decisions regarding the continuity of

simultaneous processes, and pleas for a theory of primary and secondary qualities in order to construe a more robust space-time. Quentin Meillassoux's argument against post-Kantian (that is, subject-centered) objectivity in After Finitude hangs also on temporal extension—of the arche-fossil as an event that precedes the advent of a living witness. That is, that inhabits a Time previous to the Time propounded by transcendental subjectivity. This proposes a dramatization of an event that can't be subjectively constituted but whose date can be, nevertheless, measured in our own time by our own technological means. A double bind insinuates itself here: first the arche-fossil indexes a reality outside of the legislation of subjective synthesis, indicating a real that does not presupposes the synthetic operations of the subject; but, at the same time, the argument is cogent only because it is an event whose date we can deduce. The capacity then for the deduction of the time of the arche-fossil hangs on the reality of primary qualities as objectively mathematizable, hence, of the objectivity of the dating of, for instance, the accretion of Earth. Here too, what is called for is a difference between primary and secondary qualities.

While Drone usually articulates Vertical Time (in J. Kramer's words) discarding musical indexicals, by the same token presenting an image (for the subject) of an absolute Present, it is the accountability of extensive time, and not the intensive experience of time that enables us to think the outside of subjectivity through time-stretching. The fact that there is such and such events that should take place in a musical form a few years from now is that which makes it possible to think about a temporality beyond that of the empirical single subject. For us time itself divides into a subjective temporality from which emerges a certain image of time, and time as the form of succession,

17   An interesting question posed by Roads in one chapter of his Microsound is "Are the sound particles real?". It is interesting as it mirrors the Sellarsian questioning of the manifest image from the point of view of the scientific image, as it relates to the reality of imperceptibles. (Cf. W. Sellars. "Philosophy and the Scientific Image of Man". In Brandom, Scharp (eds.) In the space of reasons. Harvard University Press, 2007

that is presupposed for these operations themselves. Something analogous to primary and secondary qualities emerges inside the dimension of Time itself and is demonstrated by the duplicity immanent in the procedure of time-stretching—as that which gives rise to a form of qualitative (or we should say secondary-qualitative) listening characteristic of Vertical Time, and, nevertheless, still on a second degree pleas for a structural listening that recognizes the proper indexicals (extensions of time) of the form that's being stretched. This amounts to a synthesis of a qualitative time which results from a quantitative operation that exceeds the capacity of the subject to follow the discourse proposed in the work, proposing if not an objectivity of time itself as something that can exceed the operations of the empirical subject, at least a perspectival "experience" of time not tethered to the specific form of the human subject, to be integrated into an exceeding and not necessarily human—an alien or machinic- transcendental subjectivity.[18]

References

Barcelos, L. "The nuclear sonic: Listening to millennial matter" In: Brits, Gibson, Ireland (eds) Aesthetics after finitude re.press, Melbourne, 2016.

---

18   This aesthetic hyper-temporality is criticized by Lendl Barcelos (L. Barcelos. "The nuclear sonic: Listening to millennial matter" In: Brits, Gibson, Ireland (eds) Aesthetics after finitude re.press, Melbourne, 2016.) on grounds that its continued mobilization of spaces, people, and money for maintaining a work such as Cage's piece being presented in Halberstadt (Organ² / ASLSP) would affirm anthropocentrism. The extension of the work demands the extension of the engagement of the art world. I believe that extreme time-stretching is less subject to such critique, as all that is required is one computer for its completion, and my argument doesn't stem from the public status or maintenance of such works, but its simple one-on-one relationship to a listening subject and the real possibility of its happening. I believe this is sufficient to establish the subjectivation of the machine against the subjectivation of the listening subject as an extraction of (clock) time from Kantian transcendental subjectivity.

Caron, J.-P. Aspectos de tempo e espaço musicais em Giacinto Scelsi e La Monte Young. Masters in music, Universidad Federal do Estado do Rio de Janeiro, 2007.

"Into the full: Strawson, Wyschnegradsky and acoustic space in noise musics" In Goddard et al (org.) Resonances: Noise and contemporary music. Bloomsbury, 2013.

L'indétermination à l'oeuvre: John Cage et l'identité de l'oeuvre musicale. PhD dissertation. Philosophy. University of Paris 8, 2015.

Evans, G. "Les choses sans l'esprit. Un commentaire du chapitre deux des Individus de Strawson" In. D. Perrin et L. Soutif (org. and translation) Cahiers de philosophie du language, vol 7 "Wittgenstein em confrontation" Paris, L'Harmattan, 2011.

Kant, I. "What does it mean to orient oneself in thinking?" In: Religion and Rational Theology. (translation by A. Wood and G. Giovanni) Cambridge University Press.

Kramer, J. The time of music. New meanings, new temporalities, new listening strategies. Schirmer Books, 1988

Meillassoux, Q. After finitude: Essay on the necessity of contingency. Continuum, London, 2007.

Partch, H.- Genesis of a music. Da Capo Press, 1979

Roads, C. Microsound. The MIT Press, Cambridge, 2004.

Sellars, W. "Philosophy and the Scientific Image of Man". In Brandom, Scharp (eds.) In the space of reasons. Harvard University Press, 2007

Strawson, P. Individuals. An essay in descriptive metaphysics. Routledge, 1991 (1959).

DRONE HEADSTONE: TONE EXHUMATION

Painstakingly manicured, it all starts with the signal path. From a litany of different overdrive and distortion pedals I've experimented with, it begins and ends with a Dunn Effects Deceiver and early 90's ProCo Rat 2. Shaping of a constant, rich harmonic dirt is key for a stable platform to create. From there it moves to the boost and fuzz stage. A pair of Lone Wolf Audio pieces, the Plague Rat and Extreme Overdose/Overload Octave Fuzz move the already brittle distorted tone into a crushing lead voice and a blown out, obliterating mountain of gain and saturation. Next along the chain is probably my favorite effects pedal I've ever owned. The Boss PS-3 Pitch Shifter Delay is a diamond in the rough. While

the digital delay is warm and analog sounding, the real power of this pedal comes in a polyphonic multi-octave-ranged tone pitch-shift. It comes out sounding like a brittle organ where you're just smashing the keys all the way up the diatonic scale and ending with a trickle of high octaved jingles and jangles. Almost like broken glass from a skylight digitally floating down on you after a meteor smashes through it. Foregoing any other modulation, I added my Delay and Reverb at the end of my chain to fully color the deep end of my distorted tone. Using another pair of Lone Wolf Audio pieces, the Full Nelson Reverb/Delay unit and the Chokehold lo-fi Digital Delay with a repeating feedback hold. Choking out a slow into a fast delay drenched in reverb has been my favorite way to achieve cavernous, harrowing atmospheres. Being the only guitar player I try to give a touch more effect level than normal to fill out our sound, alongside playing through two amplifiers and at times four 4x12 guitar speaker cabinets as well. A Marshall Plexi voiced custom made Stonecutter 100 watt EL34 powered amp is complemented by a 1975 Red Knob Model T Super voiced Stonecutter 200 watt KT88 powered unit. Being a fan of biting high mids and flattening, crushing low mids, I try to voice the guitar sound in the middle of boosted and cut mids to crutch our low frequency assault. Always on the hunt for more efficacy in pushing air, I've been pricing out pieces to put a third rig together......

Photo by Christopher Denman
Read the complete interview @ voidfrontpress.org

GET PATIENT

Garett Strickland

> We have to play with repetition, unless we want to exempt our-
> selves from life. We have to play with pulsating life which simply
> repeats involuntarily. Which rises to the attack again as involun-
> tarily as the heart's beating. As involuntarily as the breathing of
> lungs.

Pascal Quignard

Open womblight: & the ice is still a sea: the moshing static of details
unable to contain themselves. Stray filaments, their rush, the waves
encroach upon the sleeping polis—the vibrating hills, the pink ice,
the castle encased, its cubicular juttings beneath. Branches of ice
giving their slip, interrogating the bricks, seeking hard in diagonal
slant. Here's the way nature generously extends itself but doesn't
crash. Epochs blink out like holiday lights in the slow straining
forethought of future offspring. An unstoppable train thru ash &
bone & beyond. But glad we've been, will be, of the brushstroke,
its obscurescence of portrayal, the curling darker hands shriveling
at our grasp of blue barns, flashed crucifixion streams & echoes
thrown over car trips or weblife. The wires pirouetting along the
route. The cute rush of goings. To dance one's rot so many beats per
second that it scans as an out-of-phase rumble, blurred quiver tho
what we have here is just as well a thrashing. The statue only barely
staying in the skin of its mineral.

))) BREATHE IN (((

STRIDING   TO THE DOOR

THRU HONEY   & TAR

There's this way nature is extending itself without crashing. Hyperobject swallowing its own tail, recapitulating, returning to naught and
then to swell again. The plateau going green & the voice seeking
stone but leaking—the smog too much. Everything built into those
cliffs seems overly improvised. The palest glow still moshes in the
froth as it conquers the ice & its green lozenge thought. The wheat
as it crystallizes against festival bricks. The myth one makes in the
self hollowed out is hardly enough to squat inside. The demand for
a trestling. The fault was being overwhelmed, but undermined in
the failure to see the remnants of society for how courteous was
the geology that'd curtsied, then reclined naked on its password,
the stricken monoscape, syllable by syllable, punctuated each by its
cataclysm.

DRAW OUT

(((BREATHE OUT)))

THIS TERR   _   IBLE BLANK

There's no law in such a grounding. The travails of the sun have not
touched us. We dream the deeper streams of narrative and then forget.
The beauty as repellent as astounding. Becuz the ice is still a seething,
the NOTHING takes on the manner of farms. We soar, itself, impregnat-
ing, thru the nighttime windows of our neighbors' caves to scope the
privacy of their disease in myriad contortions. The beauty at the bus
stop nonetheless blinds us. The grain of the deepening shade of those
clouds, their curdles, projected upon in bedecked sunset watercolors.
The occasional flash of metal in the swell of evening. Its tidal wave, its
tumbleweed, its entirety being gouged out by birds until nothing's left
beyond the pleasure & the shame. The slime candy. The darkness &
silence below the threshold. Where you can say anything, and have.

))) BREATHE IN (((

STRIDE   TERR _ ING

    THIS   HONIED

        BLANK

In the stasis-corridor, a frozen egg roaring. Violent patience of becoming. Each cell buffering an eternal return. Its own, its neighbors'. My absence, yours. Opened womblight, the static of details
unable to contain themselves. The proliferation trapped under the
slide. The psychedelic morning was alike, the thrill of the petals
shining beneath the ice, periscoping to the anthroposophic diagram
of our breath. Then the menacing vision of black plastic columns
amidst the dance of dimensions. Party shards of cellophane in the
swimming hole drawn slowly into the tourbillion of still greater
assimilation. A perpetual misstep in being born, this line extends,
an unstoppable train, the effort to project into another view so as to
reassess resulting only in a dilation of the unit, revealing an essential
sameness, nested dolls of what's horizontal, maddeningly so. Weight
that has found its weight for dying forward, entropic momentum
dialed high, a speed so quick it's undetectable.

DOOR

(((BREATHE OUT)))

BLANK'D   TARRED

TORN   STRIDING

< I'm so excited about my art, > says your boy. < Let me
show you it. > He closes his eyes, seemingly intent.
A rush or plummeting does what it does to your
stomach. Grains, little pixels, lift from his face, neck,
shoulders. Before a question becomes so much as
embryonic, he's gone. You look to look at your hands
and it's the same. Effaced by time identical, vanished
as the footstep of this conversation. Nothing but
a filthy dabbler at existing, I flit from rock to rock,
or else in what passes as the effort am eaten by the
wind between stations. There is no law in this sort of
grounding. Rooting endlessly through outfits, wild
ball of garments. The archive still flows from the horn
of abundance, burbles forth produce. A hill-dwelling
being as any, really, palaced in the static and groaning.

    ·

))) BREATHE IN (((

DRAW   BLANK

TEAR   DOOR

—

A frozen egg roars in the stasis-corridor. O humdrum dullery, in how
many ways have you betrayed me? Are this loop & disk the same
complacence? Plenty NOTHING to farm before the scales drop off then
who knows. The generous extensions of nature, the unstoppable
train. Take your time sucking this creature's dick. Fire not yet gifted
or invented. The sum of all permutations as the exit of which this
is the conjoined Will & Manifestation, its closure the overture that
assures a sound sleep at the game's conclusion, hysterical laughter
in the face of what we'll have endured, fought for, lost. In Gabriel's
horn, in Fenrir's howl are we bivouacked here in such a lung, canopy
bed of snakeskin veil, billowed out & back again again thru illusory
duration. The archon cog a puzzle piece self-embedding in the wall
of the interface that having been berthed did, and gave us.

(((BREATHE OUT)))

)))   (((

(((   )))

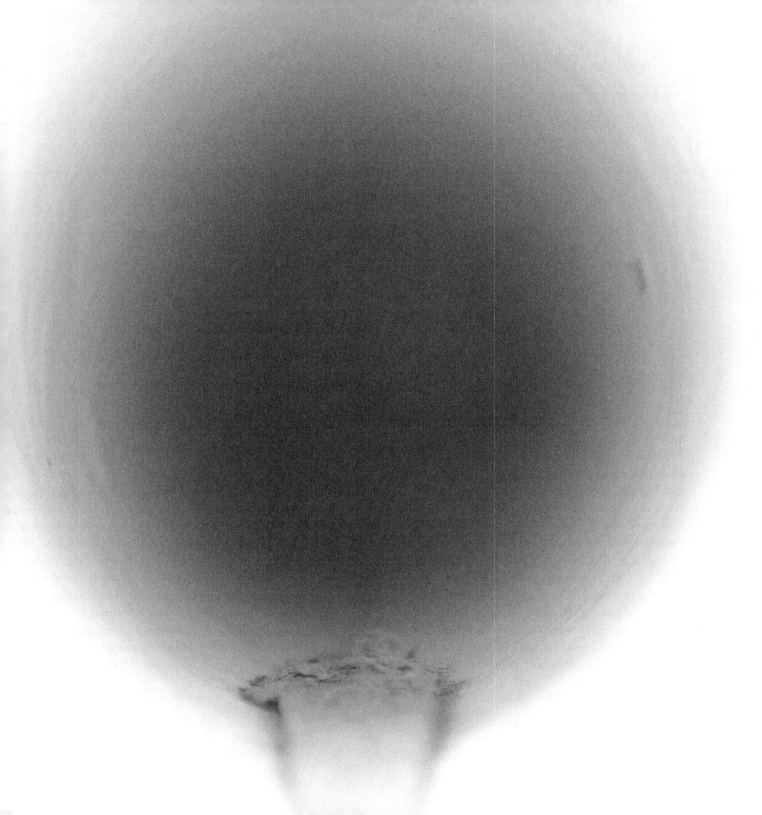

SUMMONING THE BLACK FLAME
TREPANERINGSRITUALEN'S MUSIC AND ABSOLUTE EMPTINESS

ABSENTOLOGY (Mark Horvath & Adam Lovasz)

Dark ambient ritual noise band Trepaneringsritualen allows the listener to contemplate the "black flame," the foreclosure of existence. The droning monotony transmits what Maurice Blanchot in his *The Writing of the Disaster* calls "the language of waiting," a silent mode of communication that is directed towards nothing other, the No-Other, which is death. Noise is the infinitely dense form of silence, the recollection without object. Each object, through such dark ambience, contains objecthoods glued to its form. Trepaneringsritualen's "All Hail the Black Flame" is animated by a sense of basic incompleteness. In Peter Schwenger's view, the defining characteristic of objects, including the objects of love, is the impossibility of possession. We must ask what is the mysterious item of Trepaneringsritualen's love? What is the Thing that we pray to when we engage in black rituals, when we "hail the black flame"? What is it that blackens the flame? There is

a ceaseless howling, both "cherished and despised," underlying all existents. This howling is the ever-present murmuring of emptiness (*shunyata*). Indeed, every object, we argue, may be interpreted as constituting a ceaseless howling, a manifestation of empty noise. Alphonso Lingis observes that human voices, however individuated they may seem, are indistinguishable from the murmur of the world. Rather than seeking to escape from noise, we must recognize its inherent unity with silence. To unite oneself with the murmur of the world is to "become what one is" and be dispersed among degraded ruins. This black flame is more than a mere absence: it is the absolute emptiness of emptiness. Autopoesis annihilates the world and makes room for manifestation, the irruption of volcanic emptiness.

The corpse may be seen without interruption. We try to grasp the word whereby its reality may be ascertained. We try to enjoy its fluids, ruptures, we attempt to enter into its gaping wounds. But all that remains is *shunyata* (emptiness). According to the *Suramgamasamadhi sutra*, written in the spirit of Madhyamaka Buddhism, emptiness should not be perceived as a merely limited negation, an avoidance of the avoidance of the void. Such a viewpoint would be, in itself, an overcomplication. Rather, emptiness allows us to perceive the corpse of this world, all its ruptures, openings and closings, in their limitless simplicity. What makes the blackened, rotten object of finitude simple is the absence of any absolute Outside. As the *Suramgamasamadhi sutra* notes, "all dharmas are empty, like an illusion."[1] It is in their unreality that we must attain their reality. Emptiness is an incitement, a challenge, an invitation to view this dead world's corpse, to "corpse" our own vision. The inactive inoperativity of the nontologically-accessible world is nothing more than reality itself, albeit a reality that is vacuous, empty, a place that dissolves into the (in)finitude of chaotic space. Emptiness, once perceive by corpsed-vision, learns to see the nothingness of beings in the process of their birthing. Images, simulacra, are born constantly within corpsed necrotic vision, not unlike the maggots generated by rotting, abandoned bodies. There can be no exception: the scripture makes very clear that *all* dharmas, *all* truths, including the truth of the text itself, are empty. Not only the receiver, the vessel that would accept the Teaching, but also the source of the teaching. The sutra goes on to make a strikingly bold claim: all these Tathagatas are real. And why are they real? These Tathagatas, originally and spontaneously, are not born: hence they are real. These Tathagatas are non-existent in the present and in the future: hence they are real. (…) These Tathagatas are the same and without difference at the beginning, in the middle and at the end, hence they are real."[2] The very proof

of the Tathagata's reality is the absence of their revelation. When we try to enjoy bodies, their fluid-filled openings, the succulent absolute Insides, our activity gains access to nothing apart from an absolute Outside, a voidness that voids even its own (un)reality. Nothing remains within the sphere of such a corpsed perception, aside from the black object of finitude. Vision corresponds to the reality of the Tathagatas, who are born-without-birth. Impotentialized, philosophy cannot remain. In a constitutive sense, philosophy informed by emptiness cannot be anything other than disaggregated; empty nontology is a succumbing to indifference. As Maurice Blanchot writes about the blackness that engulfs those never born and never killed, "when the disaster comes upon is, it does not come."[3] The infiniteness of the disaster "has in some way broken every limit."[4] Situated as we are—irredeemably—within the insides of an absolute Outside, we cannot remain attached to the raucous tones that correspond to the rising of nothing in particular. Nontology, too, by consequence of its momentary correlation with the intentionality of necrotically-overinformed thinking agents, is dismembered, rendered indifferent to difference. Lines of thought infected by the presence of emptiness understand well that "all dharmas are the same."[5] How could there "be" anything, aside from the relational emptiness, a disconnectivity of agents with one another? Indifference, born from the womb of sameness, is no mere "middle way." We are encouraged to remain the same "without difference" at the "beginning, in the middle and at the end."[6] If one wants to remain indifferent (hence open to the call of emptiness), one must understand well the necessity of negating every position, including that of the middle. This "middle" does not simply denote some temporal state, but rather, the false position of a dogmatic

1   Lamotte 2003 [1965]: 117.

2   Lamotte 2003 [1965]: 117-118.

3   Blanchot, Maurice (1995 [1980]) The Writing of the Disaster (Lincoln: University of Nebraska Press), 1.

4   Ibid.

5   Lamotte 2003 [1965]: 118.

6   Ibid.

skepticism that would situate itself outside of *Samsara*. Negation, as exemplified by Madhyamaka Buddhism, negates even skepticism. Because of this negating motion, emptiness is real. To put it differently, reality is empty, therefore reality is real.

Revelation of revelation unleashes the lucidity of thought, lacerating us into silence and obscurity. There is no antagonism between obscurity and lucidity; the two terms are clouds upon an empty, starless sky. What Blanchot writes of the disaster we could very well say of emptiness: "we are passive with respect to the disaster, but the disaster is perhaps passivity, and thus past, always past, even in the past, out of date."[7] Emptiness is always extratemporal; time, strictly speaking, has no function, no use, no presence. It is seen without consequence. Necrological vision holds, within the interstices of bleak silence, the source of its own (illusory) horizon. No middle ground can stifle the plume of smoke that ascends from the cremation-ground. Once the divinity is held between the strong hands of its executioner, distance dissolves into the suffering of the broken Absolute. With open eyes, we must watch the moments of joyous impurity. One anthropological study relates the Chihamba ritual, an initiation in which candidates behead a cock, a symbol of the divinity Kavula. Beheading, once initiated, must come full circle: the joy of impurity is retroactive, returning to the candidates themselves: "the deity is 'beheaded' (ketula hamutu) by the candidates, and the following day, through his adepts, he 'beheads' them."[8] With the night of the divinity's death, nothing is commensurate. Nothing can come into adequation with the disaster; "one cannot believe in it."[9] One cannot "believe" in the god whose head rolls upon

sacred ground, spilling its redness upon the earth. But this effluence, this rotten outflow is a necessary precondition of the eternal return. From false homogeneity, heterogeneity emerges: Kavula, once beheaded, becomes a beneficent entity bringing fertility to his devotees. Sacrificial movement takes us from homogeneity to heterogeneity, from the "One" to the "Many."[10] Temporality, in emptiness, is a revelation of meaning whose immanence escapes capture. Rather, the beheaded god returns to reap his reward, beheading his followers, ripping them apart to soak the earth in turn with streams of (imaginary) blood. Immanence is a ripping apart, a subduing of images and discordances. Heterogeneity is one with discord, a synonym for what Peter Schwenger, following Julia Kristeva, defines as "the abject": "everything that betrays [...] coherence—the body's wastes, its fluids, ruptures, and putrescences—is associated with the abject."[11] The Ndembu know, or at least knew, at some point in the past, that the killing of God/s has consequences. Removal of the foundation constitutes part of a cycle, a pendulum swining between the One and the Many, the homogenous and the heterogenous. But what if we slaughter the god/s one too many times? Reality, once conceived of as "devoid," necessitates the radical rethinking and revisal, even reversal, of sacrificial practice. The head of Kavula rolling upon the ground is empty, hence real. His presence is the absent presence of a divinity that cannot be born, hence the need to force Kavula into rebirth. This divine head, once removed from its prostrate, helpless body, comes to be saturated with the spirit of the earth. Lacerated by his executioners, the god is himself transformed into a detemporalized ecstatic entity, a process of movement that punishes the subversion of his oneness and bodily coherence through the violation of his executioner's integrity. It is especially interesting that the Ndembu seem to equate fertility—productivity—with the return of the beheaded resurrected divinity. Not only does

7   Blanchot 1995 [1980]: 3.

8   Turner, Victor (1977) "Sacrifice as Quintessential Process Prophylaxis or Abandonment?" *History of Religions* 16.3, 193.

9   Blanchot 1995 [1980]: 2.

10 Turner 1977: 193.

11 Schwenger, Peter (2000) "Corpsing the image." *Critical Inquiry* 26.3: 399.

Kavula die and regain presence through the advent of his revenge, but also, Kavula reattaches those who have lost their heads to their land. Removal of the head is a prelude to the continuation of empty existence and nontologically embedded work.

Repetition is an elementary desire; in the shadow of the death/s of the god/s, we feel a strong desire to make the world whole again. This need is a constant itch, an anguishing feeling of inadequacy as compared with the divinities whose blood we spill. Secretly, even the most fanatical atheists, deep down, feel the need to be subjected to absolute power. "Repetition" is, essentially, "un-power."[12] The un-power of a beheaded demi-god illustrates all too clearly that "abstinence is the definition of divinity."[13] What is it, after all, that characterizes, first and foremost, the Tathagatas? It is the circumstance of their emptiness that guarantees their "reality." Their reality is one with the emptiness of the world, as perceived by corpsed perception. One important characteristic of true Tathagatas is their "being at ease with the sounds of Brahma."[14] In other words, those enlightened by awareness of emptiness are capable of listening to repetitive recitations. Emptiness has an irreducible aural dimension. Perception is not exclusively visual, but a holistic process of opening up and lacerating oneself to the vacuity of this universal black cemetery otherwise known as the multiverse. Realities present themselves in the mode of dirty multiplicity. Empty relationalities, exterminated in their groundlessness, exude maternal melodies interspersed with unpredictable swings and gyrations. Indifference and sameness, when understood in a nontological sense, need not lead to the ignorance of relations. It is "with a perfectly calm mind" that we must, if we are to ascend to knowledge of singular-

ity, dwell on "emptiness and signlessness."[15] This dwelling upon is also, of necessity, a dwelling-within. Experiencing empty signlessness is as much an aural experience as it is a visual one. It is actually much simpler to feel the absence of the beheaded Absolute upon our tortured, anguished bodies than to envision divine abstinence. All views, in the absence of both absence and presence, must be abandoned. In a later section of the *Suramgamasamadhi Sutra*, the Buddha makes the stunning claim that "all dharmas [...] are perverse views."[16] Because of its radical impurity and heterogeneity, this thought is one that the Buddha, significantly, cannot announce directly; it is imputed to Gopaka, a minor divinity, somewhat akin to what we would consider a demon. It could easily be dismissed as an incidental remark of no great significance, were it not for the fact that the text makes clear it is Gopaka who represents the accepted Madhyamaka position! Gopaka is capable of changing bodies, of going outside of himself and transforming into a woman and back again.[17] Yet this change, when viewed from the perspective of emptiness, must be regarded as itself illusory. As Gopaka maintains, "dharmas do not consist of either 'fulfilment' or 'changing.'"[18] Truths, in their metastability, are indifferent and "free of duality."[19] Not only is divinity characterized by abstinence, but fulfilment also exterminates itself into ecstasy. Such a position would be akin to the condition of solipsistic wholeness described by Nicola Masciandaro: "I, effect of the universe, am enclosed inside of myself, I am forced away from my transcendent dwelling place and come to abide outside of all things, and I do so by virtue of my supernatural and ecstatic capacity to remain, nevertheless, without myself."[20]

---

12 Blanchot 1995 [1980]: 9.

13 Ibid.

14 Lamotte 2003 [1965]: 120.

15 Lamotte 2003 [1965]: 126.

16 Lamotte 2003 [1965]: 156.

17 Ibid.

18 Ibid.

19 Lamotte 2003 [1965]: 157.

20 Masciandaro, Nicola (2010) "Anti-Cosmis. Black Mahapralaya", in: Masciandaro, Nicola (ed. 2010) *Hideous Gnosis. Black Metal Theory Symposium I.* (Charleston: CreateSpace), 77.

To remain, albeit without oneself, is persistence after removal of every single duality.

Dwelling within the non-dual, one becomes indifferentiable, a cloud of nonsuffering inexistence. Alphonso Lingis, in a way not unlike that of Buddhist ethics, connects enjoyment with death. "Every enjoyment", writes Lingis, "is a death", a process of disaggregation, a "dissolution into the beginningless, endless, and fathomless plenum of the elemental."[21] This dissolution returns us to the earth. As with the Ndembu people who sacrifice their heads to Kavula, enjoyment in general allows the subject to blend into the elemental plenum. Exterminated reality reveals the advent of the plenum in all its emptiness. The plenum is nothing but the original oneness of time, the event of our own advent. Existence is a tendency towards sacrifice, the stained tiled floor that unsleeves us from ourselves. Located within suchness is the return of cremation trenches, supporting access to an alterity offered in suspense. The other is nothing, nothing other than the elemental itself: "the face of the other is a surface of the elemental—the place where the elemental addresses, appeals and requires."[22] Located within the elemental, we are immersed in enjoyment of the solar, albeit a solarity tainted with rotten decay and cold, frozen Arctic liquidity. It is not we who make demands upon the anonymity of the elemental; quite the reverse: the elemental approaches us, demanding veneration.[23] Meaning is exclusively relational. Individual human voices are, for Lingis, continuations of the elemental plenum, resoundings, repetitions of "the murmur of the world."[24] Their purpose is to repeat this murmuring anonymity. Offered within suspense, communication reveals a troubled land of negative interpenetration, a hoarse, raucous tonality, a world of aural stripping away, a naked exposure that corpses bodily perception and sense. Exposure is the incoherence of everything touched by surfaces of mourning, resonating with the sinister murmur of trans-appropriation. Trepanerings-ritualen's music is, according to our thesis, precisely such a persistent reverberation, trans-appropriating the non-dual maternal melody of the dark abyssal matrix. Leon Marvell has speculated upon the necessity of opening up discourse to the substratum he chooses to call "the matrixial void." This opening is at once the original oneness of a corpselike vacuity and an element that organizes itself, a "Receptacle" whose formlessness constitutes an invitation to violation and violent laceration.[25] Maternal melodies allow us to open up the non-dual space of the substratum. Autopoesis is "immanent and virtual,"[26] the immanence of an image whose impure contemplation is always linked to the melancholy act of mourning. Unclean existence allows the user of auto-annihilating mutilation to read the Outside of non-substantial simplicity. To envision a lacerated, corpselike image is to simply be, without clarity, without content, without god/s. Presentation, when it is transformed into the constant underlining of repetitive negativity, reminds us of visual pervasiveness.

What is seen at the end may also be seen at the beginning, but this devastated scenery attains its pinnacle in a Middle that is distant from everything, including the middle itself. As one study relating to the aesthetics of corpses emphasizes, the (re)presentation of corpses reveals "an affinity between theater and death," while also serving as a reminder "that the etymology of the word morgue in French derives from an archaic verb that means 'to stare.'"[27]

21 Lingis, Alphonso (1994) *The Community of Those Who Have Nothing in Common* (Bloomington and Indianapolis: Indiana University Press), 75-6.

22 Lingis 1994: 78.

23 Ibid.

24 Lingis 1994: 15.

25 Marvell, Leon (2011) "The pineal eye and the matrixial void", *Column*, vol. 7, 8⬤

26 Marvell 2011: 87.

27 Wigoder, Meir (2012) "The Acrobatic Gaze and the Pensive Image in Palestinian Morgue Photography." *Critical Inquiry* 38.2: 268.

Vision is inherently corpselike; the morgue is the place of liberating vision, a place wherein exposure meets with the funerary character of all existents. Abjection wins out, producing encapsulations that never cease to shock with their subversive promises of extermination. Returning to the morgue, we are confronted with an abyssal, insane reversibility: those who sacrifice can never be sure of whether the sacrificed shall return or not. Extermination reverses itself through autosacrificial praxis. To visit the morgue and stare at corpses is to look at the infinite absence of time. Within the catastrophe, we remain within the ecstatic realm of extratemporality. Searching for a set of sensory accidents, the cursor of the mouse happens upon Trepaneringsritualen's "All Hail the Black Flame."[28] These ambient noises formulate the desperation of life, a vitality whose finitude is constantly underlined by the bleakness of these dark melodies. Trepaneringsritualen's musical world is a negativity that strips away the richly resonant skin of the listener, until nothing, not even emptiness, is left intact. Neither emptiness nor its contrary may be restored. Once we are situated in the vicinity of the "black sun," our immanence is exemplified, flayed and burnt at the stake. Neither extreme may be followed: the body's wastes are thrown into indistinct coagulation. Outside of communicative exteriority is a communication through which "we make contact with inhuman things by embracing their forms and matter."[29] What else, after all, could vision do, but become-corpsed, once it embraces the abject forms of rotting, helpless corpses. The sacrifice is committed to itself and nothing else. Within "All Hail the Black Flame," there is an implicit heliocentrism at work, an abyssal veneration of a decaying, rotten celestial star and its incestuous relationship with a dying Earth. The Earth apparent "warming" is, in truth, a mere prelude to the coming Arctic cold. Or rather, a Marslike unbecoming of the terrestrial atmosphere. Trepaneringsritualen's music is a message from a cold, dead Earth, an Earth bereft of all life, with the possible exception of bacteriological agents. These sounds are indifferent, committed to nothing apart from the abyss. One could only imagine "Alone/A/Cross/Abyss," for instance, being played on the surface of a completely abandoned, desolate, barren planet, a piece of rock destined for subsumption within an irrupting, doomed star.[30] All existence is doomed to disappearance; even the Sun that would consume Earth is indistinct from the blackness of the universe, hence the necessity of recognizing blackness within its bright, hellish flames. Aspasia Stephanou compares the aural strategies of black metal musicians with Orpheus' descent into Hell: "Orpheus' katabasis or descent into the subterranean realm can be paralleled to the [...] schizotrategy of the black metal musician whose 'becoming chthonic' entails a non-escapist flight into the chthonic earth and a radical openness, seeking to devour and be devoured."[31] Melancology is a "double movement" that conjures a "black ecology and a black logos."[32] The desire that would transcend even transcendence itself is a flaying of exposed, vulnerable corpses, a tendency whose dissolving powers are unappropriable in their impropriety.

Sacrifice cannot be contrasted to anything. What black metal (and, it should be added, industrial drone) music does is sacrifice the pleasure of the listener to the indistinct inhumanity burrowing itself through industrialized noise towards the blasphemously ignored receiver of this nihilating message. Contamination is the rule within indistinct aural coagulation. Exposure, in this deathly droning, refers to plurality transported to the state of anguished self-surrender. Within the realm of mutual interpenetration, as

28 Trepaneringsritualen (2012) "All Hail the Black Flame," album: *Deathward, to the Womb* (label: Release the Bats Records, producer: Thomas Ekelund).

29 Lingis 1994: 15.

30 Trepaneringsritualen (2014) "Alone/A/Cross/Abyss," album: *Perfection and Permanence* (label: Cold Spring, producer: Thomas Ekelund).

31 Stephanou, Aspasia (2014) "Black Sun," in: Wilson, Scott (ed. 2014) *Melancology. Black Metal Theory and Ecology* (Winchester & Washington: Zero Books), 50.

32 Stephanou 2014: 49.

exemplified by the morgue (the place wherein we stare), "the sun of life and the darkness of death are mutually contaminated."[33] Rebirth takes place constantly, betraying the hiddenness of torn veils. Truly, desirous vision is corpsed through the indifference that subsist within the blackened gaze. As Schwenger reminds us, all images are inherently corpselike dead remnants, the final dregs of ruined beings: "the 'living image', whatever its subject matter, is always the figurative corpse of what has been alive."[34] No image, even the "living image", is ever truly animate. Every image is a reification of living reality; between the two, no correspondence is possible. It is through their unreality that images are alive, and through their reality that the (re)presented are (and remain) dead. Depiction is dereliction. Reza Negarestani has called for a renewed embrace of the Earth, albeit in a non-nostalgic manner. Rather than thinking of it as a permanent, bright object, a place for optimism and futureality, we must think of Earth "as a fractal clump", "a passing oval meteorite whose crater has already bored into the skin of astral corpses."[35] Our substratum may, when viewed from an impossible extratemporal perspective, be perceived as a nonsuffering being-thrown of waste, a power of suicidal auto-dissolution. Of Earth, there quite possibly shall only remain one or two traces, disaggregated asteroids that crash into distant planets. Negarestani's vision, for all its temporal distance, is by far the most realistic one. From an ecological standpoint, heliocentrism is unsustainable. Once "heliocentric slavery" is abolished, once the Sun is disregarded altogether, discursive space opens up to the renewed appreciation of the Earth's "aquatic vitality", an abyssal liquidity, an "earthbound abyss which erupts in the form of corrosive oil."[36] Not only is oil corrosive, it is also flammable. This flammability refocuses us to the inherent

message of "All Hail The Black Flame": the flame's dark nature shows the possibility of a subterranean non-transcendence, a transcendence-in-reverse. The music of Trepaneringsritualen constitutes a ladder leading downwards, into the labyrinthine mess which is the underworld. To create black flammability is to unleash the corrosive power of the "earthbound abyss." Revelation allows agents to release the possibility of mirroring. There are literally billions upon billions of hidden realms, functioning as cremation trenches, consuming agents caught within Earth's grip. There can be no escaping the black flame. As opposed to views that would place the Sun in the position of a royal sovereignty, Negarestani asserts, not unjustifiably, that "Sun itself is a contingency whose interiorized conception is in the process of loosening into the abyss."[37] Such a dead star, once it explodes, cannot be speculatively sewn back together. Eternalism is nothing other than the purity of a moment that has attained existence within the substratum here and now. Being lowered into the advent, perception must return to the richly resonant pluralism of its forms.

There are many ways of dying, of lowering oneself into the ground, of becoming an inhabitant of a morgue. Not even the greatest of suns is capable of dictating our own death, in spite of the ambitions of ostensibly bright heliocentrism. Suspense tears open perception, until the return of form becomes the advent of inexistent indifference: "we have to look into the core of blackness."[38] How can one observe a black sun without becoming blinded, without becoming ground down into mincemeat? One possible aesthetic solution to this dilemma is that attempted by Jean Des Esseintes, hero of Joris-Karl Huysmans' decadent novel, *A REBOURS*. In a scene of great importance, Des Esseintes decides to decorate the shell of his tortoise with the most expensive and brightest gems. This experiment

33 Stephanou 2014: 50.

34 Schwenger 2000: 396.

35 Negarestani, Reza (2010) 'Solar Inferno and the Earthbound Abyss.' in: *Our Sun* (Pamela RosenKranz) (Milan: Venice Branch & Mousse Publishing), 3.

36 Ibid.

37 Negarestani 2010: 5.

38 Stephanou 2014: 49.

is apparently a conventionally heliocentric one, a method of producing an excess of light that would bathe Des Esseintes' chateau in solar light. Indeed, the bejeweled tortoise is explicitly compared to the sun. We are informed that it "blazed as brightly as any sun, throwing out its rays over the carpet, whose tints turned pale and weak."[39] What else could this be, if not the triumphant procession of an oppressive, sovereign Sun, a phallicized celestial emperor who rules over his emasculated subjects? Des Esseintes' decorated tortoise seems to be a paradigmatic solar monarch, a benevolent emperor spreading enlightenment to all entities subjected to the influence of his patriarchy. But the truth is far more complex. As opposed to the bright, white Sun, the Sun/tortoise constructed by Des Esseintes is designed to spread death, to deaden all other sources of color, to drown out all alternative lightsources: the tortoise is intended by the bored aristocrat to be "a brilliant object that would kill everything around it, drowning the gleams of silver in a golden radiance."[40] Even silver must be displaced by the gleams of this dark sun. Yet Des Esseintes' tortoise is far more Satanic that divine. The awakening that accompanies the return of form to formlessness is a source of anguish, the opening of the skin to the radiance of a subterranean plenum. Through his decoration of the tortoise, Des Esseintes condemns himself to damnation. The tortoise, it turns out, dies, unable "to bear the dazzling luxury imposed upon it, the glittering cape in which it had been clad, the precious stones which had been used to decorate its shell like a jewelled ciborium."[41] From a dark creature, Des Esseintes attempts to create an object that shines, destroying everything with its blinding light. The flaming colors of the tortoise constitute a black flame, a dissolving astral entity that produces nothing apart from incoherence and funereality. Luxury is the antithesis of life; luxurious light is pure darkness, desubjectivizing and dismembering vitalism. Squashed by the oppressiveness of luxury, the tortoise becomes an infinitely dark spot, a beacon shining with black light. As Rodolphe Gasché writes, "the traditional symbol of the tortoise represents an animal of darkness and evil, struggling against spirit, light, and everything elevated."[42] The tortoise is a black animal, an agent opposed to everything spiritual. It is the impossibility of elevation that prevents this dark spot from becoming anything other than what it is. And yet, Gasché believes that Des Esseintes' experiment is a success, in that he succeeds, against all odds, in producing light from darkness. This light is a murderous emanation, a negativity that cannot be expressed, not even in the form of photographed corpses. Desubjectivation removes the possibility of any middle, of any distance separating perception from its incoherent object. Visibility only pertains to a small slice of the empty multiverse. One recent study has mentioned the possibility that "the lightest supersymmetric particle will not reside in the visible sector" of the multiverse.[43] A phenomenology of dark matter should, ideally, take into account the possibility of hiddenness. The "lightest visible supersymmetric particle" (LVSP) is, according to the authors of the report, "very likely unstable. It is non-generic to avoid sizeable kinetic mixing and light hidden sector states."[44]

Removed from plurality and mixing, the lightest of particles, the darkened Tathagatas remain real in their unreality. Everything, once collapsed into lightness, becomes corrected, that is: withdrawn. Obscurity is a place outside of textuality, outside of language. There is not outside, save that which is outside of itself. Excess is the betrayal of objects

39 Huysmans, Joris-Karl (2003 [1884]) *Against Nature* (London and New York: Penguin), 41.

40 Ibid.

41 Huysmans 2003 [1884]: 49.

42 Gasché, Rodolphe (1988) "The falls of history: Huysmans's *A REBOURS*." *Yale French Studies* 74, 201.

43 Acharya, Bobby S., et al. (2016) "The lightest visible-sector supersymmetric particle is likely to be unstable." *arXiv preprint arXiv:1604.05320*, 1.

44 Acharya 2016: 4.

that present themselves as images. Everything touched by the black light of Des Esseintes' tortoise is killed, gutted, deadened, obscured by the light of a Sun that shines from *beneath*. Speech and rhetoric, as emanations of the elemental, outlive their subjects. Similarly, the black light emanating from the tortoise outlives its usefulness. We read in the *Suramgamasamadhi Sutra* a description of a prototypical bodhisattva: "he never sees the self-nature of beings but, in order to ripen them, he speaks of beings. He does not see either a living being or an individual, but he speaks of a living being and an individual."[45] Such a mode of perception, far from constituting a failure of vision, is actually a method that gains access to the obscurity lying outside of possibility. There is no duplicity in such an apparently hypocritical position: coherence is maintained within the wasteful incoherence of a speech delivered to vacuity and chaos. Instead of forgetting the Thing, melancholic language actually delivers us to the relentless acceptance of blackened, necrotic beings: "language stages the melancholic void, emptiness and loss by giving presence to the Thing."[46] This "giving presence" is the utmost revelation of bodily incoherence. In Trepaneringsritualen, there is a complete lack of enjoyment, so to speak. Most certainly this does not mean that Thomas Martin Ekelund's music is unenjoyable: quite the obverse! What we understand under "the lack of enjoyment" is a jouissance directed towards the darkness of a matrixial void. Such sounds transport us to the desubjectification of detemporalized incoherence. As disaster, Ekelund's aural world is a form of aural skepticism, albeit a skepticism that hates itself, a negation that negates the possibility of both neutrality and engagement. Even indifference is not indifferent enough to the truly empty ones: "skepticism is indeed the return of the refuted, that which erupts anarchically, capriciously, and irregularly."[47] Skepticism, at least in the mode of self-referential sui-

cidal necrophilia, the love of one's (dead) Self, is volcanic, an eruption of that which should have disappeared. One has not the faintest idea of where Trepaneringsritualen's sounds emerged. To be sure, there are a variety of musical predecessors too many to enumerate in the context of this brief investigation. Ours is not an exercize in musical theory, but rather an attempt to conceptualize the sheer annihilating emptiness that presents itself in the form of this necrological aural atmosphere.

To listen to Trepaneringsritualen is to let one's head be trepanned so that one may learn to see with the pineal eye, the organ René Descartes so feverishly searched for. Neutrality is the irrefutable voice that gives presence to the community of nothingness, to that which is "other than being, and draws near unordered, unchosen, unwelcomed."[48] Descartes held that the pineal gland was the source of spiritual movements and the alternation of passions:

[…] the part of the body in which the soul directly exercises its functions is not the heart at all, or the whole of the brain. It is rather the innermost part of the brain, which is a certain very small gland situated in the middle of the brain's substance and suspended above the passage through which the spirits in the brain's anterior cavities communicate with those in its posterior cavities. The slightest movements on the part of this gland may alter very greatly the course of these spirits, and conversely any change, however slight, taking place in the course of the spirits may do much to change the movements of the gland.[49]

The imageless interiority of the brain is the middle path to nothing apart from the shock of chaotic fascination. Elusive rags of flesh are animated by the fascinating Third Eye

45   Lamotte 2003 [1965]: 133-4.

46   Stephanou 2014: 51.

47   Blanchot 1995 [1980]: 76.

48   Blanchot 1995 [1980]: 87.

49   Cottingham, J., Stoothoff, R., Murdoch, D. (1984). *The Philosophical Writings of Descartes, Vol I.* (Cambridge: Cambridge University Press), 340.

this innermost place that is devoid, derived from a cyclopic primordial origin. Immanence, viewed by the inmost pineal eye, is the absolute zero of the inverted Outside. The pineal gland is the infinitely accidental shunyata that breeds intersectional space, "the space of relation between what cannot be spoken and the speech that destroys."[50] Dissonantly accomodative, the tones of Trepaneringsritualen open our Third Eyes to the absolute spillage of this nontological innermost space. Our pineal glands are the inmost sacrificial dear hearts, circulatory organs installed within our Logos. *Shunyata* strips away the absolute of both Inside and Outside. O, this black object, let it awaken! Negativity without god/s, decaying into the abyss of ancient diversions: this tendency to sacrifice is a blackened, dried gland inserted into the brains of unknowing apes… So indefinite is the originary violence of intelligent installation, that we can only wish to return to a family of Tathagatas situated within an obscure cloud-palace. Our heartfelt wish is to be incinerated within the infinite revelation of one hundred thousand bodhisattvas. David Tibet of Current 93 sings hauntingly of this abyssal, twinkling stripping away of exteriority:

And I wished to die inside of you
 And push up into your heart so violently that
 Face to face with matrix creatrix am
 The inmost light
 The inmost night[51]

Face to face with the vaginal disaster of the sacrificial matrix, we are rendered one with the inmost night, the indefinite silence of a substratum without language, without words, without, in the final instance, accomplishment. Nothing is accomplished, nothing is attained. Only the Third Eye, opened to the infinitude of neutrality, is capable of ridding itself of doubt. Any attributes that formerly remained have been burnt away in the inmost fire of the dark night. How could any karmic inheritance pertain, in the inmost depths of the mind's middle path? Whatever traces can be picked up from the rottenness of this ground are shards of glass, remnants of shattered mirrors. This world of decadence we have left was truly no more than "a room, where mirror echoed mirror."[52] But in the absence of a mirror, what possibly could remain of that which was—formerly—reflected?

---

50 Masciandaro 2010: 83.

51 Current 93 (1996) "The Carnival is Dead and Gone," album: *All the Pretty Little Horses* (label: Durtro, producers: Steven Stapleton, David Tibet, Michael Cashmore).

52 Huysmans 2003 [1884]: 11.

157

MUSIC

CURRENT 93 (1996) "The Carnival is Dead and Gone," album: *All the Pretty Little Horses* (label: Durtro, producers: Steven Stapleton, David Tibet, Michael Cashmore).

TREPANERINGSRITUALEN (2014) "Alone/A/Cross/Abyss," album: *Perfection and Permanence* (label: Cold Spring, producer: Thomas Ekelund).

TREPANERINGSRITUALEN (2012) "All Hail the Black Flame," album: *Deathward, to the Womb* (label: Release the Bats Records, producer: Thomas Eklund).

BIBLIOGRAPHY

Acharya, Bobby S., et al. (2016) "The lightest visible-sector supersymmetric particle is likely to be unstable." *arXiv preprint arXiv:1604.05320.*

Blanchot, Maurice (1995 [1980]) *The Writing of the Disaster* (Lincoln: University of Nebraska Press).

Cottingham, J., Stoothoff, R., Murdoch, D. (1984) *The Philosophical Writings of Descartes, Vol I.,* (Cambridge: Cambridge University Press).

Gasché, Rodolphe (1988) "The falls of history: Huysmans's A REBOURS." *Yale French Studies* 74: 183-204.

Huysmans, Joris-Karl (2003 [1884]) *Against Nature* (London and New York: Penguin).

Lamotte, Etienne (trans. 1965) *Suramgamasamadhisutra. The Concentration of Heroic Progress* (English Boin-Webb, Sara trans. 2003) (New Delhi: Motilal Banarsidass).

Lingis, Alphonso (1994) *The Community of Those Who Have Nothing in Common* (Bloomington and Indianapolis: Indiana University Press).

Marvell, Leon (2011) "The pineal eye and the matrixial void," *Column,* vol. 7, 83-88.

Masciandaro, Nicola (2010) "Anti-Cosmis. Black Mahapralaya," in: Masciandaro, Nicola (ed. 2010) *Hideous Gnosis. Black Metal Theory Symposium I.* (Charleston: CreateSpace), 67-93.

Negarestani, Reza (2010) "Solar Inferno and the Earthbound Abyss," in: *Our Sun* (Pamela RosenKranz) (Milan: Venice Branch & Mousse Publishing), 3-8.

Schwenger, Peter (2000) "Corpsing the image." *Critical Inquiry* 26.3: 395-413

Stephanou, Aspasia (2014) "Black Sun," in: Wilson, Scott (ed. 2014) *Melancology. Black Metal Theory and Ecology* (Winchester and Washington: Zero Books), 47-60.

Turner, Victor (1977) "Sacrifice as Quintessential Process Prophylaxis or Abandonment?" *History of Religions* 16.3: 189-215.

Wigoder, Meir (2010) "The Acrobatic Gaze and the Pensive Image in Palestinian Morgue Photography." *Critical Inquiry* 38.2: 267-288.

Pieter Bruegel the Elder, The Triumph of Death, ca. 1562, oil on panel, 117cm x 162cm. Museo del Prado, Madrid.[1]

---

1   Available from Museo Nacional del Prado, http://www.museodelprado.es/en/the-collection/online-gallery/on-line-gallery/obra/the-triumph-of-death/ (accessed June 21, 2016).

Early germ
      warfare. The dead
      hurled this way turn like wheels in the sky.

—Thomas Lux, 'Plague Victims Catapulted Over Walls
      Into Besieged City' (2003)

Hear the germs pinging on the night wind . . . The ange-
      lus begins

—Scott Walker, 'Psoriatic,' The Drift (2006)

(Meddlesome meddlesome meddlesome bells

Meddlesome meddlesome meddlesome bells . . .)

Thunderous resonant sounds call from beyond the
      depths

And the winds of gravity change . . .

—Sunn O))), 'Agartha,' Monoliths and Dimensions
      (2009)

(Meddlesome meddlesome meddlesome bells

Meddlesome meddlesome meddlesome bells . . .)

Now, in darkness, world stops turning

Ashes where their bodies burning

No more war pigs have the power

Hand of God has struck the hour

Day of judgement, God is calling

On their knees the war pigs crawling

Begging mercy for their sins

Satan laughing spreads his wings

Oh lord yeah!

—Black Sabbath, 'War Pigs,' Paranoid (1970)

(Meddlesome meddlesome meddlesome bells

Meddlesome meddlesome meddlesome bells . . .)

—Sunn O))), 'My Wall,' White1 (2003)

On a black day in October 1347 twelve Genoese trading ships docked in Messina harbour in Sicily. The ships contained an ominous cargo: dead or dying sailors with blackened extremities and strange bulbous swellings in their groins and armpits. Those living were distinguished only by heavy coughing and sweating, for like the dead all was foul and rotting in them. It was rumoured that these ships had come from Caffa, a Genoese trading post on the Black Sea that had come under attack by a Tartar army. It was alleged that during this attack the Tartars were struck by a strange pestilence, and that though the Genoese first rejoiced in it, when the Tartars began catapulting the corpses of their dead over the city walls the celebration soon ended; the Genoese were overcome by the stench of death so completely that they proceeded to submerge the bodies in the surrounding water before fleeing by ship to Sicily, taking the Great Pest, come to be known as Black Death, with them:

Anonymous illustration, ca. 1400, 37cm x 25cm.

I say, then, that the years of the beatific incarnation of the Son of God had reached the tale of one thousand three hundred and forty-eight, when in the illustrious city of Florence, the fairest of all the cities of Italy, there made its appearance that deadly pestilence, which, whether disseminated by the influence of the celestial bodies, or sent upon us mortals by God in His just wrath by way of retribution for our iniquities, had had its origin some years before in the East, whence, after destroying an innumerable multitude of living beings, it had propagated itself without respite from place to place, and so, calamitously, had spread into the West.

—Giovanni Boccaccio, The Decameron (ca. 1351)[2]

. . . so many died that all believed it was the end of the world.

—Agnolo di Tura del Grasso, Siena, Italy (1357)[3]

Few terms in any language conjure more dread than the doom-laden nomination Black Death, Peste Noire, Der Schwarz Tod, Peste Negra, ... a name attributed by posterity to the 'Great Pestilence' or 'Mortality' that spread throughout Europe in 1347, cutting its population in half by 1400; 'so many died,' as Agnolo di Tura writes, 'all believed it was the end of the world.' The epithet 'black,' 'noire,' 'schwarz,' 'negra,' . . . thought to be of Germanic and Nordic origin,[4] was attributed by some to the acral necrosis (distal necrosis of fingers, toes, nose, et cetera: a black discolouration of the skin and tissue primarily on the extremities) that covered the victim's bodies, by others to a simple mistranslation of atra mors, the Latin term for 'plague' (atra literally means 'grim,' nominative feminine of ater, agreed with mors; mors means 'death'), and by others still to the 'black' or funereal atmosphere that pervaded in its wake, deemed the closest approach to the effect of thermonuclear war in history.[5] Everywhere lingered 'a kind of dementia and despair,' a Bavarian chronicler of Neuberg is alleged to have said, "'Men and women ... wandered around as if mad," and let their cattle stray, "because no one had any inclination to concern themselves about the future.'"[6]

2   Decameron Web, 'The Decameron of Giovanni Boccaccio (translated by J. M. Rigg, 1921),' Brown University, http://www.brown.edu/Departments/Italian_Studies/dweb/index.php (accessed June 21, 2016).

3   Agnolo di Tura del Grasso, 'The Plague in Siena: An Italian Chronicle,' as cited in Aspects of Western Civilization, P. M. Rogers, ed. (Upper Saddle River, NJ: Prentice-Hall, Inc., 2000), 358.

4   J. F. C. Hecker writes: 'On account of these inflammatory boils, and from the black spots, indicatory of a putrid decomposition, which appeared upon the skin, it was called in Germany and in the northern kingdoms of Europe the Black Death, and in Italy, la mortalega grande, the Great Mortality' (The Black Death and The Dancing Mania [London and Paris: Cassell & Company Ltd, 1888], 4).

5   According to the United States Atomic Energy Commission's Disaster and Recovery, a Cold War-era study of thermonuclear conflict, the Black Death—of all recorded human events—comes closest to mimicking "nuclear war in its geographical extent, abruptness of onset and scale of casualties" (John Kelly, The Great Mortality: An Intimate History of the Black Death [London and New York: Fourth Estate, 2005], 11).

6   As cited in Barbara Tuchman, A Distant Mirror: The Calamitous 14th Century (New York: Random House Publishing, 1987), 99.

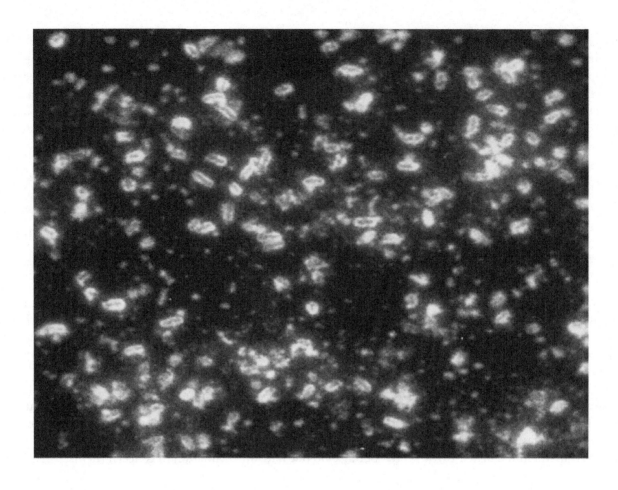

CDC PHIL 6721 Micrograph of Yersinia pestis bacteria imaged in florescent antibody test, dimensions variable.[7]

Woe is me of the shilling in the armpit!

—Welsh Lament (1349)[8]

---

7   Available from Global Health, http://globalhealthissues.wordpress.com/2012/03/12/plague-review/ (accessed June 21, 2016)

8   Ieuan Gethin, as cited by Tuchman in A Distant Mirror, 93.

For I have seen beyond the stars

I have felt the strength of chaos

I have reached the point of sanity

And was married by the Chaos star

I welcomed the darkness that filled my soul

I was blessed by the madness of the Chaos star

—1349, 'Manifest,' Liberation (2003)

We are divine like the stars. We come from chaos in the midst of those celestial bodies that, in their constellations, men believe influence and act upon them, determining their destinies.[9] With no means of acting in turn upon them, the stars are deified. Yet the stars need not be so enchanted for they do not act upon men, they simply disgorge their energies uselessly in the dark. Ah but we do act upon men, and indeed other forms and creatures that provide the vectors of our ecstasy, arcing into the blackened skies of the dead. And there is nothing they can do about it.

Our skies are forever black

Here is no sign of life at all

For burning spirits we are

Consuming your small universe

We are legion, yet imperceptible, neither their faith nor their reason can fathom our presence or the principles that pertain to us except through our manifestation in their distress, agony and death throes. They have no name for us other than to evoke the blackness with which they describe our effects, the divine way we act upon them: 'black death,' 'black plague,' 'peste noire,' 'swarta döden,' and so on. They believe we come from God, from realms of Hell. We are un-dead, then, yet active in the world though no one can see us; we're not made of flesh and blood, though flesh and blood and spit and phlegm and vomit and shit smooth our way from vector to vector: from carcass to carcass.

---

9   Cf. '"In August, a very large and bright star was seen in the west over Paris," wrote chronicler de Venette, who believed the brilliance of the star "presaged the incredible pestilence which soon followed"' (Kelly, The Great Mortality, 177).

One day life emerged from the chaos,

Slowly but surely, changing from one dimension to another

Out of the nihilistic kingdom to spread destruction

An unseen invasion to conquer

The spoiled land . . . till total extinction

The human claim to rule their world

They don't even understand the meaning of death . . .

A black hole is eating each soul

—Deathspell Omega, 'From Unknown Lands of Desolation,' Inquisitors of Satan (2002)

***

The pest, or peste, as it was called in France, Spain, Italy, . . . or der pest, in Germany, was bubonic plague, seemingly present in two forms: one that infected the blood stream, causing the bulbous swellings (buboes) and black spots indicatory of a putrid decomposition, and a second, more virulent pneumonic type, that took the form of a carbuncular affection of the lungs; the former was spread by contact, the latter by respiratory infection. It was the dual presence of these forms of the disease that caused the inordinately high mortality and speed of contagion; so rapidly did it spread from one to another that of a French physician, Simon de Covino, it is said: 'it seemed as if one sick person "could infect the whole world."'[10] And the malignity of the contagion appeared all the more terrible, as one author notes, because its victims knew no prevention and no remedy; the physical sufferings of the disease together with its aspect of evil mastery were expressed in an oddly alimentary Welsh lament, which saw

death coming into our midst like black smoke, a plague which cuts off the young, rootless phantom which has no mercy for fair countenance. Woe is me of the shilling [bubo] in the armpit! It is seething, terrible . . . a head gives pain and causes a loud cry . . . a painful angry knob . . . Great is its seething like a burning cinder . . . a grievous thing of ashy colour . . . [Its eruption is ugly like the] seeds of black peas, broken fragments of brittle sea-coal . . . the early ornaments of black death, cinders of the peelings of the cockle weed, a mixed multitude, a black plague like halfpence, like berries . . .[11]

---

10   Covino as cited in Tuchman, 93.

11   Gethin as cited in Tuchman, 93.

One of the earliest extant accounts of the Black Death in Europe is given in the work of the Italian poet, and Dante scholar, Giovanni Boccaccio (1313-1375). His Decameron, a work commenced in 1348, the year the deathly peste reached Florence, relates the story of seven women and three men who flee the plague-ridden city to a countryside villa in Fiesole. The Decameron is structured in a frame narrative, the title, which is a combination of two Greek words meaning 'ten' (δέκα déka) and 'day' (ἡμέρα hēméra), refers to the course of their stay. To pass the time each member of the party is charged with telling one story for each one of the nights spent at the villa. Although fourteen nights pass, each week two days are set aside, one day for chores, and one holy day during which no work is done. Thus, one hundred stories are told in all over the course of ten days; some licentious, others full of pathos, but it is the first, told by Boccaccio, that provides the chilling backdrop. Here, Boccaccio describes the physical and psychological effects of the peste amidst penitent processions and Florentine measures to establish a cordon sanitare—a sanitary zone maintained by sentries posted to restrict entry into the city by infected or potentially infected people; no doubt an extended ordinance of the first official quarantine imposed by the Venetian doge in 1348[12] after the local death rate had risen to six hundred per day:

John W. Waterhouse, A Tale from the Decameron, 1916, oil on canvas, 102cm x 159cm.

Lady Lever Art Gallery, Liverpool.[13]

---

12   This quarantine, the first ever officially imposed, was directed by the Venetians doge against travellers returning from the Orient, and was fixed on a period of forty days—in Italian quaranta giorni—simply because this was the period of time that Christ had been sequestered in the desert.

13   Available from JW Waterhouse, http://www.johnwilliamwaterhouse.com/pictures/tale-decameron-1916/ (accessed June 21, 2016).

[009] In Florence, despite all that human wisdom and forethought could devise to avert it, as cleansing of the city from many impurities by officials appointed for the purpose, the refusal of entrance to all sick folk, and the adoption of many precautions for the preservation of health; despite also humble supplications addressed to God, and often repeated both in public procession and otherwise, by the devout; towards the beginning of the spring of the said year [1348] the doleful effects of the pestilence began to be so horribly apparent by symptoms that shewed as if miraculous.

[010] Not such were they as in the East, where an issue of blood from the nose was a manifest sign of inevitable death; but in men and women alike it first betrayed itself by the emergence of certain tumours in the groin or the armpits, some of which grew as large as a common apple, others as an egg, some more, some less, which the common folk called gavoccioli.

[011] From the two said parts of the body this deadly gavocciolo soon began to propagate and spread itself in all directions indifferently; after which the form of the malady began to change, black spots or livid making their appearance in many cases on the arm or the thigh or elsewhere, now few and large, now minute and numerous.

[012] And as the gavocciolo had been and still was an infallible token of approaching death, such also were these spots on whomsoever they shewd themselves.[14]

These gavoccioli or 'clusters (of varices)'—the colloquial expression being 'pest-boils' according to one author[15]—'oozed blood and pus,' as we read elsewhere, 'and were followed by spreading boils and black blotches on the skin from internal bleeding... victims coughed and sweated heavily . . . everything that issued [forth] from the body—breath, sweat, blood from the buboes and lungs, bloody urine, and blood-blackened excrement—smelled foul.'[16] This noxious exhalation, conceived as a miasma, and attributed to the whim or vagaries of the wind that was carrying it,

---

14 Boccaccio, 009-012.

15 Hecker, 8.

16 Tuchman, 92.

[013] ... seemed to set entirely at naught both the art of the physician and the virtues of physics; indeed, whether it was that the disorder was of nature to defy such treatment, or that the physicians were at fault... and being in ignorance of [the] source [of the pest], failed to apply the proper remedies; in either case, not merely were those who recovered few, but almost all within three days from the appearance of the said symptoms, sooner or later, died . . .[Elsewhere we read: 'depression and despair accompanied the physical symptoms, and before the end "death is seen seated on the face"]:[17]

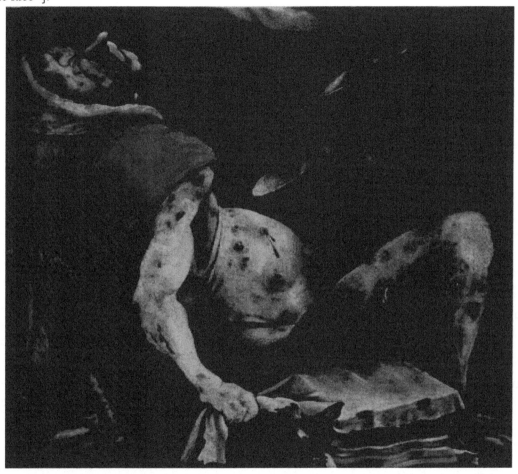

Matthias Grunewald, Suffering Man, detail from the reverse of the Isenheim Altarpiece.

ca. 1510 - 1515, oil on panel. Musee d'Unterlinden, Colmar, Alsace.[18]

---

17   Boccaccio, 013; Tuchman, 92.

18   Available from The Bridgeman Art Library, http://www.bridgemanart.com/ (accessed June 21, 2016).

Likening the virulence of the pest to a fire raging among dry and oily fuel, Boccaccio notes of how it communicates not simply from the sick to the healthy, but through contact with the clothes or 'aught else that had been touched' by the infected; indeed, such was the energy of the contagion, he suggests, that not only humans but animals suffered instantaneous death if they came into contact with such articles.[19] Thus, with his own eyes, had he seen:

[018] . . . The rags of a poor man who had died of the disease being strewn about the open street, two hogs came thither, and after, as is their wont, no little trifling with their snouts, took the rags between their teeth and tossed them too and fro about their chaps; whereupon, almost immediately, they gave a few turns, and fell down dead, as if by poison, upon the rags which in an evil hour they had disturbed.[20]

After this initial description of the outwardly physical effects of the pest and its virulence, which, as he notes, drove almost all left alive to the same harsh resolution, 'to wit, to shun and abhor all contact with the sick and all that belonged to them,' Bocaccio describes the two extreme modes of living that emerged in Florence, and according to which, as we read elsewhere: 'In one house you might hear them roaring with the pangs of death, and in the next tippling, whoring and belching blasphemes against God.'[21] On the one hand, there were those who thought to live temperately, avoiding all excess. Wherefore,

[020] . . . they banded together, and, dissociating themselves from all others, formed communities in houses where there were no sick, and lived a separate and secluded life, which they regulated with the utmost care, avoiding every kind of luxury . . . eating and drinking moderately . . . holding converse with none but one another, lest tidings of sickness or death should reach them . . .[22]

And on the other, there were those who maintained that to drink freely, even excessively, engaging in song, dance and revelry and sparing to satisfy no appetite, or to laugh and mock at no event, was the sovereign remedy for the evil pestilence. Wherefore,

---

19 Boccaccio, 017.

20 Boccaccio, 018.

21 As cited in 'Urban History, 5 Chapters,' http://www.scribd.com/doc/76677122/185290-Urban-History-5-Chapters (accessed June 21, 2016).

22 Boccaccio, 020.

Arnold Bocklin, Plague, ca. 1898, tempera on wood, 25cm x 37cm. Kunstmuseum, Basel, Switzerland.[23]

23 Available from Montana.edu, http://entomology.montana.edu/historybug/YersiniaEssays/Medrano.htm (accessed June 21, 2016).

[021] . . . resorting day and night, now to this tavern, now to that [they drank] with an entire disregard of rule or measure, and by preference making the houses of others, as it were, their inns, if they but saw aught in them that was particularly to their taste or liking; [022] which they were readily able to do, because the owners, seeing death imminent, had become as reckless of their property as of their lives; so that most of the houses were open to all comers, and no distinction was observed between the stranger who presented himself and the rightful owner . . . [Elsewhere we read of a village in which the inhabitants were seen dancing like lunatics to drums and trumpets, and on being asked their reasoning, answered that they believed they could keep the pest from entering their village 'by the jollity that is in us'].[24]

Betwixt these extremes did the pest unfurl in Florence, where, as elsewhere, together with ardent asceticism on the one hand, and lawlessness and debauchery on the other, it abased if not totally dissolved all respect for the laws of God and man. There were those who took flight of course, those who deserted their belongings, their kinsfolk, their estate, their city, and with a multitude of men and women went into voluntary exile or migrated to the country; 'as if God in visiting men with this pestilence in requital for their iniquities would not pursue them with His wrath wherever they might be.'[25] Whatever their virtue or vice people died alone and without ceremony, 'their bodies so corrupted by the plague that neither beast nor bird would touch them.'[26] Tedious is it to recount, how citizen avoided citizen,

[027] . . . brother was forsaken by brother, nephew by uncle, brother by sister, and oftentimes husband by wife; nay, what is more, and scarcely to be believed, fathers and mothers were found to abandon their own children, untended, unvisited, to their fate, as if they had been strangers.[27]

Though exaggeration and pessimism were prone to penetrate the literature of the 14h century, Guy de Chauliac, the Pope's physician, and a sober, careful observer, reported the same phenomenon:

---

24 Boccaccio, 021; Tuchman, 97.

25 Boccaccio, 024.

26 Chronicler Henry Knighton, Canon of Leicester abbey, cited in Tuchman, 98.

27 Boccaccio, 027.

Albrecht Durer, The Revelation of St. John: 5. Opening the Fifth and Sixth Seals, ca. 1497, woodcut, 39cm x 28cm. Staatliche Kunsthalle, Karlsruhe.[28]

28   Available from Web Gallery of Art, http://www.wga.hu/frames-e.html?/html/d/durer/2/12/2apocaly/index.html (accessed June 21, 2016).

A father did not visit his son, nor the son his father. Charity was dead.'[29] As with him, it seemed to Bocaccio that the whole world had gone mad, and so many died daily and nightly in the public streets, or at home where their departure was hardly observed by their neighbours, until the stench of putrefying bodies carried the tidings,

[037] ... and what with their corpses and the corpses of others who died on every hand the whole place was like a sepulchre.[30]

Rumours of a terrible plague arising out of China and spreading through Tartary (Central Asia) to India and Persia, Mesopotamia, Syria, Egypt and all of Asia Minor are said to have reached Europe in 1346, but in the absence of a concept of contagion were largely ignored until the black day the trading ships brought their burden of pestilence into Messina. These rumours told of a death toll so devastating that all of India was deemed to be depopulated: entire territories covered in corpses, others with no one left alive, in which nothing but the pestiferous odour of death survived. Few testimonies are presented to us with respect to its symptoms or its course, yet, as J. F. C. Hecker notes, these are sufficient to throw light upon the form of the malady.[31]

By this account, the Byzantine emperor and scribe Kantakouzenos—whose youngest son, Andronikus, is believed to have died of the pest in 1347—notices 'great imposthumes of the arms and thighs' as well as smaller boils that covered the body, and black spots which broke out all over, 'either single, or unified and confluent.'[32] The Imperial scribe writes of how symptoms of a cephalic affection were obvious, from palsy of the tongue victims lost their power of speech, seemed stupefied, and fell into a deep sleep; others were sleepless and without rest. He writes too of how the tongue and throat were black, and of how no libation could assuage the victims thirst. Still deeper sufferings, we read, were connected with this pest: seized with a putrid inflammation, the organs of respiration caused a violent pain in the victims chest, from which blood spewed forth or was expectorated, and the breath diffused a pestiferous odour; and contagion was evident, for we read of many houses in the capital that were bereft of even their last inhabitant.[33]

***

Born from yawning chaos, we act through the mouth; indeed, we are mouths ourselves, spiky tube mouths, some say, spuming bacilli, taking flight on the rank vapours of foul breath; spore-forming mouths hooking into creatures' mouths like tiny pins, piercing the soft flesh of organic apertures, ...

---

29   Cited in Tuchman, 97.

30   Boccaccio, 037.

31   Hecker, 4.

32   Hecker, 5.

33   Hecker, 5.

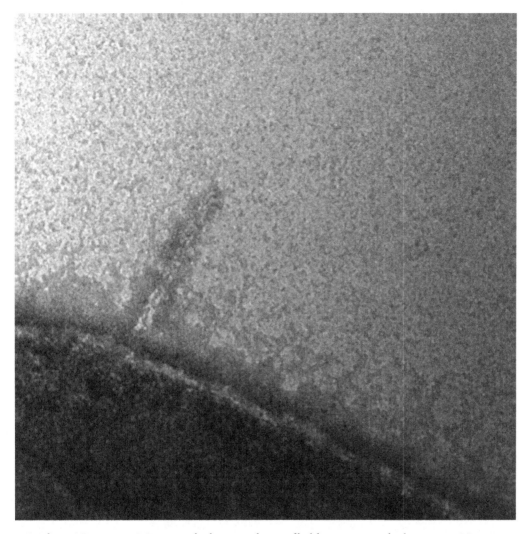

Andrew Houppert, Micrograph showing the needle-like structure the bacterium Y. pestis
uses to attack cell hosts, 2009, dimensions variable.[34]

It is important to utilise the material and imaginative resources of the enemy, if that's the right word for our hosts, the locus of our joy. It is true that there is an element of hostility to our hosting, but that is something that the concept of hospitality allows, each concept necessarily opening itself to its opposite, producing or reproducing it in

34   Available from Indiana University, http://newsinfo.iu.edu/asset/page/normal/7343.html (accessed June 21, 2016).

advance—and deconstruction is, after all, the methodology of the parasite. In the spirit of 'hostipitality,'[35] then, we plunge into the welcoming depths of our host, engaging alliances where ever we find them—with 'yersina murine' toxins, for example—with whom we can ensure our survival and passage. With this alliance we join together to form a slimy film that blocks the foregut of the rattus rattus flea-vector, where such toxins are found, so that when the flea attempts to feed some of us will be regurgitated into the wound enabling a smooth transition into our new host. Demented with hunger as we block up its gut, the rat flea-vector hops from limb to limb, frantically trying to feed, only to vomit up more and more of us into the punctured skin, warm and bloody. Born on a spray of blood and air, we deterritorialise the molar kingdoms of insects and animals, turning a landscape of corpses into blackened steaming liquids, a cloudy, bubbling sea-sky of death.

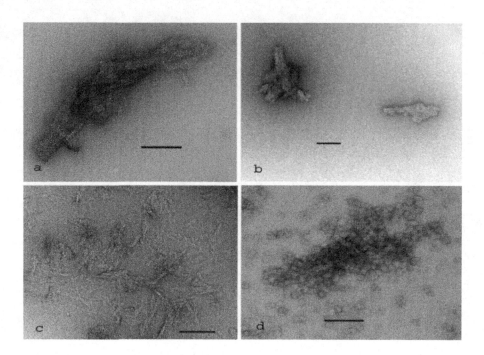

TEM images of negatively stained ultrasonicated alhydrogel with adsorbed proteins. (a) Yersinia pestis Caf1, (b) Yersinia pestis V-antigen, (c) acid-soluble rat tail collagen type 1 heterotrimer and (d) Bacillus subtilis enolase octamer, scale bars indicate 100 nm, dimensions variable.[36]

35   Jacques Derrida, 'Hostipitality,' in Gil Anidjar (ed.), Acts of Religion (London: Routledge, 2002), 362.

36   Available from Science Direct, http://www.sciencedirect.com/science/article/pii/S0968432811001211 (accessed June 25, 2016).

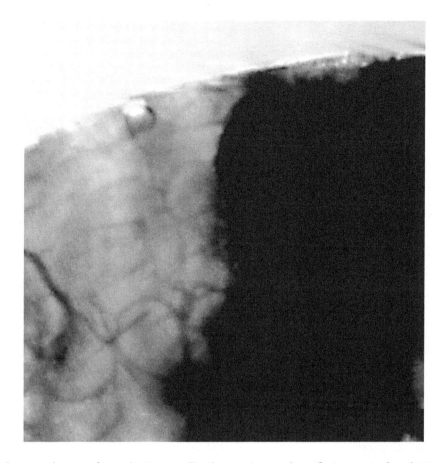

Image showing the gut of a male Xenopsylla cheopis (oriental rat flea) engorged with Y. pestis.[37]

Plague upon plague, black boil redemption
On this sea of rats I shall set my throne
Halo of fleas, blood puke salvation
Only fire is now clean enough to touch your soul

—Marduk, 'Throne of Rats,' Plague Angel (2004)

---

37   Available from CDC, http://www.cdc.gov/ncidod/dvbid/plague/ (accessed June 25, 2016).

Emer Roberts, Rat and Child. 2009, mixed media (fiberglass, plaster, faux fur, glass)
720cm x 1180cm x 1150cm (d x l x h).[38]

Rats were a particularly effective vector, the reason to our force, at least initially, at least until we were carried by the rat-born flea to the human vector, the most effective and spectacular of all, whose corpses married purulent beauty to viral efficiency. Divinity diffused to the soul, that black depth deeper than any singularity of Being, through the rat host by which it was manifested, as has been noted before, in 'the ratio between the voracity of the jaw and the headless mobility of the tail'[39]. Fur and glistening skin running in flea bites, the 'contagious potency' of rats was best expressed in their swarm behaviour, tumbling bodies upon bodies, incontinent, constantly moistening each other in urine and excrement, blood and semen. And us, a ravenous flow consuming white blood cells, all manner of mono-cytical, so-called immune systems unravelled and dissolved by our antigenic saliva; or we simply amassed in rat zones and lymph nodes where we could avoid phagocytosis, the molecular rat cops and human antibiotic security forces not daring to endanger its own. Proliferating in ever greater numbers, injecting our spores and pores in the buboes and lungs until all resistance became futile, swelling and blackening the flesh. We love the smell of rotting flesh, the taste of decomposition, it is our weakness . . .

---

38   Image courtesy of the artist.

39   Reza Negarestani 'Pest rationalism' (Unpublished MS, 2010).

See how the body contracts

Until your limbs become ropes of madness

Ropes of regret, the price of purity

Ropes of regret

Death upon death, black death redemption

On this sea of death I shall claim my crown

Halo of death, death puke salvation

Only death is now pure enough to forgive your sins

—Marduk, 'Throne of Rats,' Plague Angel (2004)

***

By January 1348 the pest had penetrated France via Marseille and North Africa via Tunis. Shipborne along coasts and navigable rivers, it unfurled westward from Marseille by way of the ports of Languedoc to Spain and northward through the Rhone up to Avignon, where it arrived in March. It reached Narbonne, Caracassonne, Montpelier and Toulouse sometime between February and May, and in Italy the very same spring made its way to Rome, Florence, and the backcountry. From Italy it traversed the Alps into Switzerland, and stretched eastward to Hungary in the summer, at the same time it reached Bordeaux, Lyon, and Paris, then spread to Burgundy and Normandy, from there crossing the channel into Northern England; where, though some claim it is of uncertain knowledge, it appears to have passed through a port in Weymouth—an extant sign suggests: THE 'BLACK DEATH' ENTERED ENGLAND IN 1348 THROUGH THIS PORT. IT KILLED 30-50% OF THE COUNTRY'S TOTAL POPULATION.[40] Remarking on the pests efficiency, one author notes of how in 'a given area [it] accomplished its kill within four to six months and then faded, except in the larger cities, where, rooting into the close-quartered population, it abated during the winter, only to reappear in spring and rage for another six months.'[41]

---

40   Available from Visit Weymouth, http://www.visitweymouth.co.uk/index.php?resource=263 (last accessed June 21, 2016).
41   Tuchman, 93.

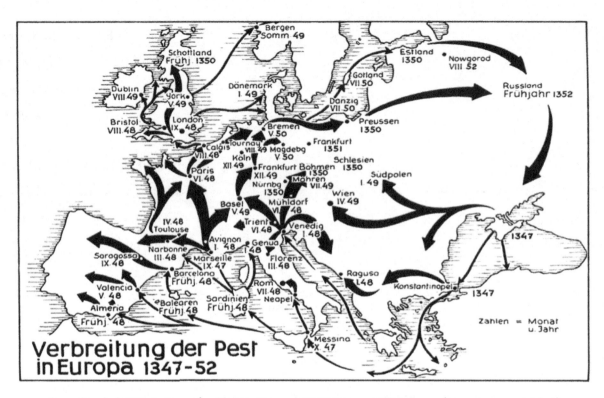

Ernst Bucholz, Verbreitung der Pest in Europa 1347-52, ca. 1956, map, dimensions variable.[42]

In 1349 it took up again in Paris, and from there spread to Picardy, Flanders and the Low Countries, and from England to Scotland, Wales, and Ireland, as well as to Norway; where, according to Hecker, 'it broke out in its most frightful form . . . sparing not more than a third of the inhabitants.'[43] With respect to its course here, the story is told of a merchant ship that sailed out of London in May 1349 carrying a cargo of wool bound for Bergen.[44] While at sea members of the crew experienced plague symptoms, and by the time the ship approached her destination all had succumbed to the ashy pestilence. It is not known how long the ghost ship drifted offshore before running aground near Bergen, only that those who went out into the fjord to inspect the doomed vessel became infected, and so the pest passed into Norway; and from there into Sweden, Denmark, Prussia, Iceland, and as far as Greenland.

---

42   Available from Oxford Journals, http://past.oxfordjournals.org/ (accessed June 21, 2016).

43   Hecker, 14.

44   Tuchman, 93-94. See also Hecker, 14. Further, see F. Donald Logan, A History of the Church in the Middle Ages (London: Routledge, 2002), 282.

Alfred Rethel, Death as Victor, ca. 1849, woodcut, 80cm x 56cm. Standort: Private Collection.[45]

Reporting on its progress in Scotland, Wales and Ireland, a cleric from Oxfordshire describes how, separated by a winter's immunity,

The joy of the Scots [at the death of so many English] turned to grief. God's wrath, having punished the English, now turned to the Scots and punished them with lunacy and leprosy ... In the following year it devastated the Welsh as it had the English. Then it travelled to Ireland, cutting down great numbers of the English settlers, but the native Irish were hardly touched.[46]

---

45   Available from Web Gallery of Art, http://www.wga.hu/frames-e.html?/html/r/rethel/index.html (accessed June 26, 2016).

46   Tuchman, 97. See also Logan, 282; Kelly, 228-9.

We know that it crossed into Ireland in 1349, where, contra this clerics conjecture, it struck native and settler alike. Watching its course here, and wondering 'whether the strange [pest] had not been sent to exterminate the human race,' Brother John Clyn of the Friars Minor in Kilkenny, twenty-five of whose fellow friars had died, bears clear testimony to the indiscriminate devastation. Sensing 'the whole world, as it were, [was] placed within the grasp of the Evil One,'[47] and awaiting the ashy death to visit him too ('waiting among the dead for death to come'),[48] in his concluding words, being his own epitaph, he writes: 'I, Friar John Clyn of the Franciscans of Kilkenny, [having] related in this book the things of note that have happened in my lifetime . . . am leaving space on this parchment for the work to be continued, if anyone should survive and any child of Adam escape this pestilence and continue the work which I have begun.'[49] A commentary added by a later hand reads: 'At this point the author apparently died.'[50] It is here, no doubt, that we find the progenitor of the Gaelic translation of the thirteenth-century Latin requiem hymn Dies Irae ('Day of Wrath') which, along with the contemporaneous La Danse Macabre ('The Dance of Death'), formed the cultural backdrop to the pests apocalyptic procession through Europe; as one author rightly notes, though the pest killed him, Brother John foiled oblivion.[51]

Dies Irae! dies illa

Solvet saeclum in favilla:

Teste David cum Sibylla!

Day of wrath and doom impending

David's word with Sybil's blending

Heaven and Earth in ashes ending!

La na feirge, laud an leurscrios

La mbeidh criocha thrid a cheile

Mur deir Dabhi 'is Tybeala!

—Dies Irae (ca. 1254)[52]

47 Tuchman, 95.

48 Quoted in Kelly, 229.

49 Tuchman, 95; Logan, 282.

50 Logan, 282.

51 Tuchman, 95.

52 Dies Irae ('Day of Wrath')is a thirteenth-century requiem hymn, attributed to the Franciscan Thomas de Celano (ca. 1200-65), which was translated into Gaelic by the

So what are the effects of our acting upon men and the rest of God's creatures, great and small, that we favour? We bring them joy. Not just the joy-before-death bla bla bla that brings the awareness of finitude necessary for virtuous or ethical action, care, solidarity, brother-and-sister neighbourliness and so on and so on. We are indifferent to such moral rationalisation; or rather, we welcome it since good Christians make such excellent vectors: they get involved, giving-of-themselves, and us. As for the miserable asceticism of human self-preservation—and why anybody would want to preserve such stinking, walking carcasses is beyond reason—we admired, by way of contrast, the ascetic rationalism of the rats. The rats, it seemed, recognised through their swarming contagion and voracity certain complicity with us, facilitating an explosion in the population of fleas and, in the subsequent massive rat die off, the migration of fleas to humans. Selfless rats, almost Christian with their anal asceticism, incontinent yet without apparent sanctimony, spreading their shit, gnawing and eating everything it is possible to gnaw and eat, including and especially religion, eating out the arse of Christianity, brushing 'their plague and urine soaked skin against Buddhism, pantheism or paganism,'[53] diffusing divinity with a territorializing oral thoroughness.

As for humans, it is difficult to say whether they found complicity with us or we acted directly through them in their weaponisation of joy. We refer not only to their desperate acts of debauchery and excess in the imminence of death, their apocalyptic festivals, but also the glorious ingenuity of their pointless 'germ warfare,' spreading the joy through catapulting blackened corpses like cartwheels arcing beyond besieged walls, infecting towns, cities, whole populations, . . .

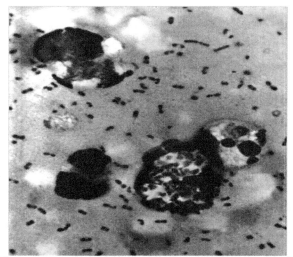

Y. pestis attacking the lymph node of a plague victim.[54]

Rev. Bernard Callan in 1800; see Bernard Callan, The Spiritual Rose, ed. Malachy McKenna (Dublin: DIAS, 2001), 242. The English translation by William Josiah Iron, ca. 1848, appears in the English Missal; albeit from a different Latin text, it replicates the rhyme and metre of the original. It was published by W. Knott and Son Ltd. in 1912, however, for a more accurate translation, see The Modern Reader's Bible, ed. Richard Moulton (New York: Collier-Macmillan, 1943), reproduced in Alec Robertson, Requiem: Music of Mourning and Consolation (London: Cassell, 1967), 15-16.

53 Negarestani, 'Pest-rationalism.'

54 Available from The History Blog, http://www.thehistoryblog.com/archives/10193 (accessed June 28, 2016).

In the river of the night I see

A face that shimmers down at me

But like a falling star burns itself out

Like a lead leaf scrapes the gravelled ground

My voice cries out, a gravelled sound

But no-one's there to hear me but the Plague

—Scott Walker, 'The Plague,' Jacky/The Plague (1967)

The noises of struggle are lost in death, as rivers are lost in sea, as stars burst in the night

I enter into peace as I enter into a dark unknown

I fall in this dark unknown

I myself am this dark unknown

—Georges Bataille, Visions of Excess (1985)[55]

Where emptiness empties

Alone

—Scott Walker, 'Angel of Ashes,' Scott 4 (1969)

***

With the exception of a strange pocket of immunity in Bohemia, and Russia unassailed until 1351, the ashy pest had run its climactic course in Europe by 1355. Though the loss of human life was erratic, fluctuating from one fifth in some places to nine-tenths or almost total annihilation in others, modern demographers have settled on a general estimate—for the area extending from India to Iceland—in the region of the figure expressed by Jean Froissart, in whose Chronicles (1322-77) we read, 'a third of the world died.'[56]

---

55   Georges Bataille, 'The Practice of Joy Before Death,' in Allan Stoekl ed., Visions of Excess: Selected Writings, 1927-39 (Minneapolis: University of Minnesota Press, 1985), 237.

56   As cited in Tuchman, 94.

Froissart's estimate, less a guess than a borrowing of St. John's figure for mortality from plague in Revelations, would have meant about twenty-million deaths. In truth, no one knows how many died, as Barbara Tuchman writes: 'Contemporary reports were an awed impression, not an accurate account.'[57] She blames the endless procession of death carts and pitiless piling of corpses for contemporary chroniclers exaggeration, at the same acknowledging the innumerable 'black' bodies that, apropos of Brother John, did not succeed in foiling oblivion.

Recounting the conditions imparted to them, Tuchman notes of how in Avignon, for example, bodies were submerged in the Rhone until mass burial pits were dug for dumping them in, and of how in London corpses piled up in such pits until they overflowed, or elsewhere were buried so thinly and hastily that dogs dragged them forth and devoured them. She writes too of how in Florence corpses were gathered by the Compagnia della Misericordia, and of how, when their efforts failed, the dead lay putrid in the street for days, and 'when no coffins were to be had, the bodies lay on boards, two or three at once, to be carried to graveyards or other common pits.'[58] Tuchman's account is complimented by that of a contemporary chronicler of Florence, Marchione di Coppo Stefani, who, in another oddly alimentary offer, notes of how,

At every church, or most of them, they dug deep trenches, down to the waterline, wide and deep, depending on how large the parish was. And those who were responsible for the dead carried them on their backs in the night in which they died and threw them into the ditch, or else they paid a high price to those who would do it for them [beccamorti, literally 'vultures']. The next morning, if there were many [bodies] in the trench, they covered them over with dirt. And then more bodies were put on top of them, with a little more dirt over those; they put layer on layer just like one puts layers of cheese in a lasagna.[59]

At a time of accumulating death and dread of contagion, people died without last rites and were buried without prayers or penitence; so many so, that Clement VI found it necessary to grant remissions of sin to all who died of the pestilence, because most were unattended by priests, and died alone with no one looking after them. As The Florentine Chronicle (ca. 1370 - 1380) suggests,

---

57 Tuchman, 94.

58 Tuchman, 94.

59 Emphasis ours; University of Virginia, 'The Florentine Chronicle (Stefani, Marchione di Coppo. Cronaca fiorentina. ca. 1370 - 1380 Rerum Italicarum Scriptores, Vol. 30., ed Nicolo Rodolico, Citra di Castello: 1903-13),' University of Virginia, http://www2.iath.virginia.edu/osheim/marchione.html (accessed June 21, 2016).

. . . many died with no one looking after them. And many died of hunger because when someone took to bed sick, another in the house terrified, said to him: "I'm going to get the doctor." Calmly walking out the door, the other left and did not return again . . . Child abandoned father, husband the wife, and wife the husband, one brother the other, one sister the other. In all the city there was nothing to do but to carry the dead to a burial.[60]

Hartmann Schnedel, illustration from the Liber Chronicarum (Nuremberg Chronicle), ca. 1493, woodcut.[61]

---

60 University of Virginia, 'The Florentine Chronicle,' University of Virginia, http://www2.iath.virginia.edu/osheim/marchione.html (accessed June 27, 2016).

61 Available from Wikipedia, http://fr.wikipedia.org/wiki/Fichier:Nuremberg_chronicles_-_Dance_of_Death_(CCLXIIIIv).jpg (accessed June 28, 2016).

But 'no bells tolled,' as another chronicle attests, 'and nobody wept no matter what his loss because almost everyone expected death. . . . And people said and believed: "This is the end of the world."'[62]

Ring around the rosie;

Pockets full of posies.

Ashes, ashes,

We all fall down.

—14th Century Children's Rhyme

***

We, the so-called 'pest' or peste, man's ominous 'black death,' remained undiscovered by him for another five hundred years, . . . We still maintain our secrets. There is no 'we,' of course, anymore than there is an 'I' with a concern or difference from a 'you'? Who are you? 'We' are 'you'? You are the only ones with this concern for language; we are over ten times more populous, on your skin and in your guts, than the cells of your body. Words and numbers, names and formulae. All are fiction. Wikifacts: Bacteria, archaea, bacilli, spirilla, spirochaetes, streptococcus, endospores, sporohalobacter, anaerobacter, thermodesulfobacteria, myxococcus xanthus, vampirococcus . . . feeding off sunlight, off the darkness, off inorganic as well as organic compounds, vampirically feeding off each other; more than five nonillion (5x1030) bacteria inhabit the earth forming a biomass that exceeds all plants and animals put together. Fermenting in the depths of the soil, in acid, in radioactive waste, deep in the earth's crust, lying dormant for millions of years, capable of interplanetary travel, borne on solar winds . . . 'most bacteria have not been characterised.'

Speculative entities, un-coded particulate systems, innumerable actors below the threshold of Latin names and numbers, Pythagorian or digital, we are the burning spirits of a base materialism that seethes, unknown and unknowable, in the rutatis rutandis-taste of stinking guts at the alpha and omega of the cracked earth, swarming in the black depths of the sky. We are the future, welcome to our bacilli banquet.

---

62   As cited in Tuchman, 95.

NON-TERMINATOR: RISE OF THE DRONE GODS

Gary J. Shipley

"All men desire solely to free themselves from death; they
do not know how to free themselves from life."

—Lao-tse

The abyss of death is as unthinkable as the abyss of infinite life, for immortality is itself a form of death: inescapable, without end, the unmaking of what we recognise as this distinctly human life. It is our inability to conceive immortality as anything but an increasingly pestilential drone that provides some lukewarm comfort to our eventual deaths. The situation is analogous to the reflexive excruciations endured by those outstaying their welcome in anechoic chambers—where the sound is you, and the sound is unbearable. The drone of this hypothesized forever comes from within, and it will either destroy us (in some hideous yet non-fatal destruction) or else turn us into gods. In order to be clear about precisely what's at stake, we must consider the following two options:

1) The offer of immortality with a get-out clause.

2) The offer of immortality with no get-out clause.[1]

If offered a choice between these two options we would, it's safe to suppose, almost universally be inclined to prefer option 1 to option 2, and make our choice accordingly. For while option 1 looks to have no obvious drawback, option 2 would in all likelihood strike most of us as conceptually revolting, not to mention terrifying. Option 1 allows us room to breathe, room to keep death at bay for as long as the positive aspects of life remain, whereas option 2 threatens to drown you in its ineludible monotony. But if, as Miguel de Unamuno explains, "longing is not to be submerged in the vast All, in an infinite and eternal Matter or Energy, or in God; not to be possessed by God, but to possess Him, to become myself God, yet without ceasing to be I myself, [. . .] [for] we crave the substance and not the shadow of immortality,"[2] then option 2 is imperative in order to enact such a transformation, a transformation that is indeed necessary if we are to withstand the demands of an immortality which is not a mere shadow of the real thing (an immortality*).

In his 1973 paper, "The Makropulos case: reflections on the tedium of immortality",[3] Bernard Williams claims to be discussing a "state without death," but he isn't. For the Makropulos case is the story of a woman (Elina Makropulos) who can at any time, and who eventually does, refrain from imbibing the elixir of life that keeps her alive. Williams never deals with option 2—although he is by no means isolated in this respect—and doesn't seem aware of the problems involved with not doing so. Williams claims that we are lucky to have the chance to die, but then Elina also had the chance to die, and is she really to be considered unlucky just because she had the chance of postponing it indefinitely? This is the immortality of Dracula, which though progressively burdensome, we imagine, is still a choice, albeit one muddied with compulsion.

It could be argued that by not choosing option 2, by lacking the necessary attributes needed to make such a commitment, we would not be giving immortality its due observance. For by retaining the option of death you will never be able to commit to your extended life in a way that is comparable to that forced by option 2. And it is only via the complete excision of death from

---

1   If the majority of physicists are correct, then the fate of the universe may well offer its own get-out clause, but let us suppose that this cannot be taken for granted, or maybe less contentiously that it isn't coming soon enough to affect the points I wish to make.

2   Miguel de Unamuno, Tragic Sense of Life (Dover Publications, 1954), 47.

3   Bernard Williams, Problems of the Self (Cambridge University Press, 1976), 82-100.

our lives that we will ever come to terms with the implications of living forever, and so successfully make the psychological adjustments necessary for such an event. If you can always bail out at any time, you are not even experiencing what it is to be immortal—at least not in the sense that option 2 makes you immortal (from now on immortal*). Choosing immortality over immortality* would, no doubt, allow you to bear the burdens of life-extension rather better than those who opted for immortality*—initially at least. The opt-out clause might, in fact, be the only thing that could make the prospect of a possibly endless future bearable.[4] However, those that chose immortality*, or had it thrust upon them, would have no choice but to bear it. They might do so in a perpetual state of panic and misery, but endure it they would, for the choice is not theirs to do anything else. To get to the root of what we really think about death we must talk in terms of immortality* (an endless life in which death is not possible) as opposed to Williams's immortality, where nothing more is implied than the mere potential for continued life extension. To be truly immortal (immortal*) is to be in a state free from death, not to walk in its shadow for as long as one chooses. This being the case, it makes little sense to ask whether immortality* would be bearable, as, in a sense, there would be no way in which one could avoid bearing it. Is it not, then, more constructive to ask whether or not it is likely to be a happy or rewarding existence? Maybe, if this question weren't equally ridiculous, for it remains unanswerable for a life of any duration. And to add to this insolubility, how are we to know the lengths to which we might go in order to occupy ourselves, the full extent of the inventiveness that

would surface in people threatened with an endless life of insanity and desolation, should they crumble under the weight of time? "If a human being were a beast or an angel, he could not be in anxiety,"[5] but which would we become?

In concurrence with Franz Kafka's famous proclamation on the existential beneficence of cessation,[6] Williams claims that "[i]mmortality, or a state without death, would be meaningless, [. . .] death gives meaning to life."[7] According to these assertions, immortal life would not be worth living, would be worthless in a way that ordinary finite life is not, worthless, then, because it will rapidly exhaust our potential for meaningful growth, our limitations making us suited only to a finite and rather brief existence. But can we ask, with a straight face, if we are necessarily limited in this way? And need immortality*, by necessity, be a ridiculous and arduous prospect? With this apparent nonsensicality in mind, I'll ask it anyway, even if I must smirk a little as I do it.

That exhaustive pessimism, of the kind we find in Zapffe, Mainlander, Michelstaedter, etc., would have to recede even further into the stygian murk of our consciousness, seems obvious from the start. As Thomas Ligotti has pointed out in *Conspiracy Against the Human Race*, we are hard pushed to give these ideas headroom when our lives are, by comparison, extremely brief. With human life made sempiternal, the toxicity of such philosophies would surely prove untenable. As a luxury of intellectual conjecture it would need to be

---

4   It would, of course, make a difference just how frequently your death was available to you (assuming suicide is somehow made impossible): day by day, week by week, month by month, year by year, etc. one might always be able to face the thought of one more day, but one more year might prove more of a challenge the longer one had existed.

5   Søren Kierkegaard, The Concept of Anxiety, ed. and trans. by Reida Thomte and Albert B. Anderson (Princeton University Press, 1980) 155.

6   "The meaning of life is that it stops."

7   Williams, Problems of the Self, 82.

eradicated, or at least inoculated against, perpetually and forever. (And maybe there, already, you have a purpose, a reason to be that itself depends on discovering a reason to be: the search for meaning that is its own reward, a pathway of endless and impassioned inventiveness that, quite rightly, fears a faltering step more than anything else.) Quoting from Ernest Becker's *Denial of Death*, Ligotti lays down our contrivances in the face of terror, of how we crawl away from the "outlawed truisms" and "taboo commonplaces" that tell of our essential meaninglessness and scant existence, and how in running from one madness we fabricate a different one, a liveable one: "I believe that those who speculate that a full apprehension of man's condition would drive him insane are right, quite literally right. [. . .] [Man] literally drives himself into blind obliviousness with social games, psychological tricks, personal preoccupations so far removed from the reality of his situation that they are forms of madness, but madness all the same."[8] And this in turn is a reworking of a similar idea expressed by Otto Rank, for as he makes clear, the neurotic (and the pessimist, for they are scarcely distinguishable here) "suffers, not from all the psychological mechanisms which are psychically necessary for living and wholesome but in the refusal of these mechanisms which is just what robs him of the illusions important for living."[9] The quandary, then, is either that of how we infinitely fortify and perpetuate the deception (and so take heed of the warning: take the contrivance seriously or else—or else there'll be nothing to do and no one to be), or how we approximate something like living within the maddening drone of that deception, or alternatively how we might do away with the need for the deception altogether.

It is important to note, however, that, in Rank's terms, the true pessimist cannot 'partialize': he cannot limit his eating to only his allotted slice of the existential cake. He is compelled to eat the lot, and it is this that makes him sick—or sick, at least, in the eyes of those who can comfortably nibble from their own slice without needing to taste from the whole from which it came. Reality is always too much for man to stomach. It demands to be sipped on through a narrow straw. Health and worldly-belonging, like those judgements of beauty from Nietzsche's herd men, are inescapably *shortsighted*. For no true pessimist could ever sustain an experience of something as simply beautiful—although the possibility that such an experience could momentarily blindside him can never be completely ruled out—because such an experience necessarily partializes in a way that he cannot: "The neurotic type [the pessimist …] makes the reality surrounding him a part of his ego, […] has taken into himself potentially the whole of reality"[10] and no judgement of beauty could hope to breathe in this re-circulated air, even if it could arise momentarily and perhaps survive as long as it is able to hold its breath. The need is for man to see more and not be damaged by it, to partake of not only the omnispection of gods, but to acquire the power to assimilate what they see. Or as Becker puts it:

Gods can take in the whole of creation because they alone can make sense of it, know what it is all about and for. But as soon as man lifts his nose from the ground and starts sniffing at eternal problems like life and death, the meaning of a rose or a star cluster—then he is in trouble. Most men spare themselves this trouble by keeping their minds on the small problems of their lives just as their society maps these problems out for them. These are what Kierkegaard referred to

---

8   Ernest Becker quoted in Thomas Ligotti's Conspiracy Against the Human Race (Hippocampus Press, 2010), 159.

9   Otto Rank, Will Therapy and Truth and Reality (Knopf, 1936), 252.

10   Ibid, 146-7.

as the "immediate" men and the "Philistines." They "'tranquilize themselves with the trivial'—and so they can lead normal lives.[11]

Here the objective would seem ridiculously grandiose if it weren't for the fact that the pessimist is part of the way there already and, relative to that part, incurable (unless we accept impairment as a cure and go about healing him of the truth), and so poisoned with the conditioning of gods merely as a result of his not being one. The task as it presents itself here is not so much how such a person might become a god, but how he might become just godlike enough to inoculate himself from the suffering attendant to his perspectival overreaching. Or else, were option 2 available, become a Drone-God: for the Drone-God does not drown in his depression, he drinks it.

The very idea of our lives being extended indefinitely is at best a problematic one, at worst horrific; for while there may be some who would see no reason why we couldn't embrace such an opportunity without reservation, their optimism looks too much like ignorance or gross stupidity to be anything else. Whichever side one falls on (the problem to be solved/the inevitable horror), and most will probably tend to oscillate between the two, it will prove useful to consider whether we might possibly make ourselves worthy of immortality*, *become* the sort of beings to which the prospect of an endless life is considered unquestionably beneficial, an endless life that might just prove transformative enough to have the pessimist come to emulate the gods like which they are accustomed to think. It is, of course, contentious whether it is even possible for us to know how such a being would

need to approach himself and his environs. But this is a goal worth having, if any goal is, whether it is achievable or not: to make ourselves more meaningful. Nietzsche quoting Dante writes, "[n]ot "mankind" but *overman* is the goal [. . .] *Come l'uom s'eterna*—INF. XV 85 How man makes himself eternal,"[12] and it is this making-eternal of man that's left—when after the death of God there is only man's aesthetic creativity to fill the gap left by his destruction. And that man is made not merely infinite but eternal, a being stripped not only of end but beginning as well, reveals that by occupying the god-void man himself has become god. But ultimately it is eternity's future burden that is the test, the arena (the thought experiment of choice) in which man can ascertain his own value, if any value remains. About this Nietzsche is right, but as for the formulation of the test, there is work to be done.

Nietzsche's concept of the ubermensch (higher man or overman) is essentially defined in terms of his notion of Eternal Recurrence, for only the ubermensch is able to gladly welcome a doctrine that has us living the same life over and over. He is the yes-sayer, the one who can be as positive about his sorrow as he can his joy—all of his life approached with affirmation, as a united, perfected whole.[13] The great becomes greater the horrors heavier, harder to pass over with the passing of time, all of history made more significant, and yet at the same time there's also the meaninglessness of history's endless repetition and our impotence within it.[14] As Brian Leiter sees it there are two

---

11   Ernest Becker, The Denial of Death (The Free Press, 1973), 178.

12   Friedrich Nietzsche, The Will to Power, ed. and trans. Walter Kauffman and R. J. Hollingdale (Vintage Books, 1968), 519.

13   There is of course more impetus if we believe that we are living our life for the first time in this endless sequence—despite this being extraordinarily unlikely—as it gives what we do weight, and frees it from the ephemeral.

14   There's a certain similarity here to the scenario (a religious parable of sorts) played out in the film Groundhog Day, in which Bill Murray's character is

central flaws:

[P]erfection is a matter of living in such a way that one is ready to gladly will the repetition of one's life, in all its particulars, in to eternity. This, too, seems both too thin and too severe as a criterion of perfection standing alone: too thin, because anyone suitably superficial and complacent might will the eternal return; too severe, because it seems to require that a post-Holocaust Goethe gladly will the repetition of the Holocaust.[15]

In light of this, what's required is a reformulation of Nietzsche's thought experiment, in which the mechanism for gauging human character is not how one faces up to the prospect of their life being endlessly repeated, but instead whether or not one is prepared to choose immortality* over immortality. For even the most superficial or complacent person can appreciate the risk in the second option, a risk any benefits of which such a character could not possibly grasp. By utilising this reformulation, both the allegation of

severity and that of thinness are resolved, there being no obligation to will the infinite replay of atrocities, and no easy escape for the superficial and the complacent, for even though such people might not recognise the potential strength of immortality*'s venom, the mere threat of its bite would most likely be enough to dissuade them.

Just as Nietzsche criticized Kant for emancipating himself from the theist cage only to then crawl back inside it, he too is criticised for laying the groundwork for a pessimist philosophy (a position it was actually his intention to usurp rather than engender, the crisis to avert not bring about) only to return to optimism with his notion of man's transcending animal. But this accusation is misguided on yet another level: for just as acknowledging the continuation of human life is not necessarily to condone it, acknowledging elements that might make such a continuance more interesting is, likewise, not to say the effort justifies itself. Without pain, life is sillier, less significant, ludicrous and shameful; and at the heart of this is the concept of pain as a creative force, a transformative fuel. But suffering need not be idealised as a result of this, for what is instead enshrined is the human requirement for meaning, without that required meaning itself being grounded in anything further, without its meaning being thought of as objectively meaningful. To transform the belief "it is thus and thus" into the will "it shall become thus and thus"[16] is to become creative and tragic, that which is encapsulated in our saying Yes to life, Yes to reality, that crucial "move beyond all terror and pity"[17] that rids us of the need

forced to live the same day over and over again. Although he can develop new characteristics, learn new things, and act differently, everybody else stays as they were, and the day repeats. The slavish routine of that one day can never contain enough meaning on its own, but must be shored up by days in the future that will bear its mark, and crucially your mark by virtue of your having lived through it. In the existence Nietzsche envisions, Bill Murray remains unaware that the day is the same, he does not change and he never escapes—the future (that has never happened) never happens. This makes meaning a matter of being rather than becoming, in essence not consequence, stagnant not flowing, completeness not incompleteness. And it's this that makes it an aberration: that any human life could complete itself satisfactorily, that it could internally justify its own sufferings, that it could lack nothing by not continuing outside what it already is, strikes us as fundamentally non-human. And isn't that the point?

15   Brian Leiter, "Nietzsche's Moral and Political Philosophy" in the Stanford Encyclopedia of Philosophy: http://plato.stanford.edu/entries/nietzsche-moral-political/.

16   Friedrich Nietzsche, The Will to Power, ed. and trans. Walter Kauffman and R. J. Hollingdale (Vintage Books, 1968), 324.

17   Friedrich Nietzsche, Ecce Homo in On the Genealogy of Morals and Ecce Homo, trans. Walter Kaufmann (Vintage Books, 1969), 273.

to expunge them from human existence. Just to what degree Nietzsche believed this transformation to be possible is not entirely clear, but the dilemma itself is captured perfectly by Fernando Pessoa, who himself managed to extract some threadbare gleam of meaning from what he took to be the self-evident truths of pessimism: "How tragic not to believe in human perfectibility! / And how tragic to believe in it!"[18] For what immortality* drives home is the need to transcend the negatively tragic and instead become actively tragic, to replace non-belief with belief; but a belief that is itself groundless and known to be groundless, a belief manufactured from nothing—the belief that floats. The trick is not to have belief make us ignorant, masking our faces after we've watched them disappear, but to transmute via belief into the reflective substance of that which is believed, to believe facelessness into a new type of face.

How, then, is it that divine completeness can appear so utterly harmless, its propagation of filled lacunas so seemingly replete with comfort? The answer to which comes in the form of a denial, because those gaps were never truly filled; its possibilities and instantiations remain forever incomplete, forever unseen—spectrally so. Something realised with admirable succinctness by Kinbote in Vladimir Nabokov's *Pale Fire*: "As St. Augustine said, 'One can know what God is not; one cannot know what He is.' I think I know what He is not: He is not despair, He is not terror, He is not the earth in one's rattling throat, not the black hum in one's ears fading to nothing in nothing."[19] If we follow this apophatic process we will find God, and at the same time all other bywords for human meaning, find him (or it) as the subject of an infinite conveyor belt

of subtractions, but not a single addition—a nothing that holds minuses together. Can you imagine how light we become all the while we keep these subtractions apart? And how heavy once they start to mingle and breed with each other? "Time is *heavy* sometimes; imagine how heavy eternity must be,"[20] and imagine too, while you're at it, how we might come to build the muscles needed to bear it.

The reward of eternity (immortality*) must, then, remain free of detail, must resist anything bordering on a complete description. Some sense of mystery and one's future enlightenment (always to remain future) must exist for salvation to be possible, for immortality* to remain a welcome prospect. But can this perpetual speculation really offer anything resembling salvation, or is it just one more makeshift measure, one more distraction that will eventually falter, leaving us eking out our endlessness devoid of sustainable meaning? Wittgenstein claimed that what's required is not incompleteness but its opposite, and that "if I am to be REALLY saved, —what I need is certainty—not wisdom, dreams or speculation—and this certainty is faith."[21] However, faith is a particular kind of certainty, one that sustains itself through a curtailment of reservation or enquiry, a selective and cultivated blindness, and so always a combination of certainty and openendedness—however sublimated that openendedness might be. For certainty demands an endpoint, an horizon already reached, and as Williams reminds us, "[n]othing less will do for eternity than something that makes boredom unthinkable."[22] What though

18   Fernando Pessoa, The Book of Disquiet (Penguin Books, 2002), 247.

19   Vladimir Nabokov, Pale Fire (Vintage Books, 1989), 227.

20   E. M. Cioran, The Book of Delusions, Hyperion, Volume V, issue 1 , May 2010 63.

21   Ludwig Wittgenstein, Culture and Value (Blackwell Publishers, 1998), 38.

22   Bernard Williams, Problems of the Self (Cambridge University Press, 1973) 95.

of our internal certainty, our certainty of ourselves? Total absorption, it seems, must be possible for us, and with it a loss of character, a loss of self; and certainty does not occupy, for certainty is the opposite of distraction: a transparency stripped of its power to engage and thereby distract. That said, the self demands that it be taken as a certainty, a given from which to proceed, in order to fall into the background where it needs to be. Making the self a focus of enquiry makes something akin to a presence of its absence, resulting in a detachment from worldly engagements, the found absence of a substantial self becoming an unwelcome intermediary in the way of losing the self in those activities that would absorb it, thus making its unquestioned something a transparency, a nothing. Although, following Descartes, the speculative can lead us where we need to be, to the surety that there is experience and that that experience presents itself as localised, and localised in a manner that implies some sense of ownership without ever finalising the owning party or that which is owned. This is a state, or a series of states, or a process (which we can choose to label 'self' or not) that can proceed more or less pleasurably, more or less tolerably, depending on the nature and levels of its awareness of itself, so that while certainty can allow the self to disappear, outside of the self this exhaustive peeling away of analytical interest is wont to reinstate that very self as something apodeictically problematic.

Certainty (outside of this blinkered presumption of our own identities), though often sought as a resolution to our unease, is consoling only insofar as it remains aspirational: its achievement being inimical to life that is not already or destined to become a living death. In an essay, discussing and undermining the supposed *sui generis* status of Franz Kafka's writings, Idris Parry identifies the following thematic strain:

In his essay *Ur-Gerausch* (Primal Sound), Rilke speculates on man's sensory capacities. At present, he says, each of our five senses covers its own sector, which is separate from the others. [...] May there not be gaps between them, mysterious chasms in man's perception, spaces of which we are ignorant—not because there is nothing there, but because our sensory capacity is incomplete? It is these gaps in our awareness, Rilke believes, that cause our human anxiety, for we fear the unknown. And it is to these gaps that Gogol and Kafka lead us. They are constantly straining beyond their known boundaries.[23]

However, while Rilke, and indeed Parry in his advocacy of this stance with respect to Nikolai Gogol, Kafka, and Nathaniel West, appear to present us with an observation so standard and abundant as be platitudinous (our fear of the unknown, no less) it remains a glaring example of a half-truth, and how misleading they can be; for while we may fear the unknown, without it our lives would be saturated in fear's worst excesses: the claustrophobic sickness of being trapped in some airtight conviction with no possibility of escape. In the film *Spoorloos*, Raymond Lemorne offers Rex Hofman a choice between never knowing for certain what happened to his missing wife and the very real risk of finding out: is he to drink the coffee that he knows to be drugged and so discover his wife's fate, or else walk away and live with the knowledge that he will never find out what happened to her? After thinking it through, he chooses certainty over uncertainty (the certainty of that uncertainty) and wakes to find himself buried alive, literally trapped, suffocated and sentenced to death by the very certain-

23   Idris Parry, 'Kafka, Gogol and Nathanael West' in Kafka: A Collection of Critical Essays, ed. Ronald Gray, (Spectrum, 1962), 89-90.

ty he so craved. By way of cajolement, Lemorne had offered these words: "And the uncertainty? The eternal uncertainty, Mr Hofman? That's the worst."[24] And in spite of the obvious risks to his life, Hofman is of the same mind. Here we have the undoing of mystery as an asphyxiating confinement and expeditious death, and uncertainty and incompleteness as nothing less than life itself, Lermone's experiment having revealed to Hofman the inherent tension and insolubility of all that isn't mind-crushing claustrophobia and death.

Related to these thoughts on certainty, we should also note that life is unquestionably easier to endure during periods of complete absorption than it is during periods of boredom and worldly detachment. And yet, without the capacity to consider ourselves in isolation from our activities, we would lose much (if not all) of what it means to have a sense of self, thereby forfeiting the attachment we might expect to have between ourselves now and ourselves at some future time, if that is we are to consider ourselves as continuing to exist in any way that we regard as identity-preserving and valuable. Otherwise, do we not just become the tools (however integral) in some activity or series of activities? The concern for Williams is that although boredom is most often a localised and temporary condition, existing for a short time only as the result of a particular type (or lack) of activity, immortality would see it change into a generalised and permanent condition, the very threat of which would sour experience irrevocably. Each of us has a limited number of pursuits that we regard as pleasurable, and it is, at the very least, doubtful that these would prove endlessly repeatable and endlessly pleasurable.[25] The balance to

strike, once again, is between us retaining our identity and that identity being malleable enough to allow us to sufficiently metamorphose into something as yet completely unrecognisable.

What the prospect of immortality* threatens us with is the potential toxin of the instant, the many imagined flavours of your existence cooked into a single sour reduction, a uniform and poisonous gloop: "[w]hen speaking of life, you say *moments*; of eternity, *moment*."[26] The urge to categorise and order and ultimately own your temporal being must be overcome. The instant must be allowed to reign and you must disappear inside it—disperse before you implode. The selves we've manufactured to live for only a finite period—and forever only within the perfunctory and whimsy-soaked afterlifes of religious or mystic extrapolation—are unequal to the task, their partible form in the fully disclosed face of endlessness nothing short of the purest horror. If Cioran is right that "[t] here are no hopes or regrets in eternity. [And that to] live each moment in itself is to escape the relativity of taste and category, to break free from the immanence in which time has imprisoned us,"[27] then this dispersal of self, that in concurrence with Williams would appear desirable for the immortal, is also something that immortality* demands and must surely (eventually) actualise.

Death is neither the evil—William James' "worm at the core"—nor the gift that those of a more pessimistic persuasion would have us believe. The mistake made by both camps is to regard death as something that

24   See Spoorloos or The Vanishing, directed by George Sluizer (1988; France: Argos Films) DVD.

25   See Life, Death, & Meaning, ed. David Benatar (Rowman & Littlefield, 2004).

26   E. M. Cioran, On the Heights of Despair (The University of Chicago Pre 1992), 65.

27   Ibid., 64-5.

we are sufficiently acquainted with. To consider the necessity of death an evil is to decry the end of a sequential process, the meaning and value of which you do not understand. How is it possible to substantiate that it is better for the sequential process to continue rather than not, when the conditions of that very continuance would seem to imply that you (as you are, as you recognise yourself) no longer play a part in it? And likewise, how can you substantiate that it is better for this sequential process to end than to continue, when the adaptations that this continuance would impose have not (and as-yet cannot) be accurately delineated? Nagel observes that our "experience does not embody the idea of a natural limit," due in part no doubt to man's practiced sublimation. But why, then, is the prospect of immortality* so knotty? For if we did indeed approach our lives as an inexhaustible continuum, then immortality* would surely be a straightforward corrective, rather than a cause for panic. But Nagel's point cannot be dismissed so easily, for there is a sense in which the days allotted us—those of us not terminally ill—are endured or enjoyed with little or no attention paid to some diminishing quota from which they were consumed. Although, this does not amount to an underlying and inbuilt sense of one's conscious limitlessness, but instead to an orderly contrivance of time, whereby we segment our lives into paradoxes of endless presents: like Zeno's arrow we come to rest in these instants, and so never move toward our final destination. That we get there eventually through a succession of these instants is not something of which we are unaware, some conscious preclusion, but something found incongruent to the instants as we occupy them. Our steady encroachment on death steadies us inside the paradox while leaving it for the most part intact.

Most pessimist thinkers have the luxury of being only that, only thinkers of that worst of apparent self-evi-

dences. They entertain, and often make powerful and convincing cases for the essential meaninglessness of human existence, but the acknowledgement of the sickness is not the same as contracting it. Carlo Michelstaedter is one of a few possible exceptions, one who could not slip back into life's rhetoric once he'd revealed its spurious weave. And there is an important distinction here, one that's crucial to understanding and appreciating both the accuracy and acuity of pessimism and its eventual impotence. For why not rewrite the deadening rhetoric of life instead of succumbing to it in a fit of self-loathing weakness and impotent disadvantage? Why not do what humans do so well and create a story, and then live it and have it be unique and have it be remarkable? Why not refuse to accept that the difficulties of doing so are insurmountable? Or better still, why not accept those difficulties as insurmountable and seek to overcome them anyway? Why not embark unflinching on that "search for the impossible by way of the useless?"[28] Pessimism would have us believe that it is the last word, and indeed it's difficult for some of us to believe it isn't: it is the loudest voice in the heads of those awake enough to hear it, but the last . . . ? Never accept last words! Better to remake the world newly absurd than to passively embody its pre-existing sillinesses. "Life not only has no meaning; it can *never* have one," but exactly what it can and does have is many meanings, all of them contingent and decaying and failing and repeatable and ultimately replaceable. If the maturity of man "consists in having found again the seriousness one had as a child, at play," then immortality* should be welcomed, as the opportunity to grow up.

What would need to happen for immortality* to be a rewarding prospect is that we would have to become

28   Fernando Pessoa, *The Book of Disquiet* (Penguin Books, 2002), 206.

more profound beings. We would have to make ourselves important enough to justify our immortality*. We would have to consider ourselves important enough to deserve it. Who knows what psychological deviations an infinite life facing up to our infinitude might occasion—or what depravities? The person who "looks death in the face, real death, not just a picture of death,"[29] was, for Wittgenstein, nothing short of a hero. And while there is obvious courage in such a transparent facing up to one's irretrievable annihilation, as anyone "who pretends to face death without fright, lies,"[30] the truest of heroes is not someone who confronts their death without first obscuring it, but instead someone who looks immortal* life in the face, real immortal* life, not just a picture of immortal* life, he who welcomes immortality* and all the terror and trial it brings with it.

A man's existence is made his own. The man that wakes every morning at six and stares into the mirror for twelve hours a day, breaking only for meticulously timed excursions to eat, drink, visit the toilet, and sleep does not necessarily live a life empty of meaning. But what could make such an existence meaningful? Control? Force of will? An unerring commitment to a self-prescribed order? The sheer bloody-mindedness of it? To sustain this behaviour for a week would be challenging, to sustain it without end would be an unfathomable achievement. The thought is that any life that doesn't end would come to look like this, not in the details necessarily, but then immortality* removes the details—or else makes them too excruciating to see. Therein lies the corrosive power of a life without end. How, then, to get the details back? Let us accept

for the moment that whatever change is necessary to instil immortality* with meaning that that change must be internal, that external changes, however extreme, can never suffice. As a list of responses to be fortified, we might present this: irony, humour, heroism, defiance, and artistry, or more specifically the art of metamorphosis. Art of course needs no further justification, defying all utility and meaning outside of itself; and it is this self-containment that might possibly incubate any prospective immortals*, providing an art equal to Thomas Bernhard's proclamation that "the art we need is the art of bearing the unbearable," a life made aesthetic, as prescribed by Nietzsche,[31] free of those extraneous layers of transcendent meaning needlessly piled on top of it—a genuinely creative mutation.

Immortality* demands that we cultivate addictions, enduring ones that cannot see outside themselves. It is addictions that positively exude life-affirmation, even those to substances that slowly kill us. You have only to look at the living-death that often follows in the wake of a prolonged addiction—the faces of the men and women reintegrating with the newfound pointlessness of diluted impulse—to know that addictions allow for only a meagre existence outside of their perimeters; but this is not only a testament to their destructiveness, but also to their nourishment, to the perfection of their internalised structures of sense-making. James Joyce on his deathbed asked "Does nobody understand?" (Hegel, on his death bed, knew well that they didn't), and this from a man who consoled himself with a future life made entirely of the enigmas and puzzles he'd laid like traps for the curious brains of countless professors of literature born

29   Ludwig Wittgenstein, Culture and Value (Blackwell Publishers, 1998), 58.

30   Jean Jacques Rousseau, Julie, Or the New Heloise, The Collected Writings of Rousseau Vol. 6 (Dartmouth College Press, 1997), 128.

31   See Alexander Nehamas, Nietzsche: Life as Literature (Harvard University Press, 1985).

and yet-to-be-born. The concern is for the most part disingenuous, for there is no desire to be completely understood, to have your elliptical core reduced to so many platitudes. What could these understandings be beyond a certain point but signs of atrophy, Beckettian stains on silence, a tensionless drone? For solutions to leave the subject vital they must be transitory, must themselves be ambiguous and open to supplementary faceting. What addiction wants to lose its mythology? What addictive substance worth the name allows itself to be sampled, its essence grasped, before then being summarily discarded? Like art, addiction only satisfies "when it leaves behind something that, in spite of all our reflection on it, we cannot bring down to the distinctness of a concept:"[32] a reason to continue, and even a way to hear the drone of immortality* as the potential for a music that sustains and transforms, without ever being fully understood. On the specifically elusive and yet transformative powers of drone music, Joanna Demers has this to say:

It is exceptionally difficult to write about drone music. I say this as a person who likes a lot of it, so I lack the prejudices often seen in print about drone music being "boring" or "like listening to a dentist's drill." Technical descriptions of drones take only a few words to state that one tone or chord lasts minutes or hours, leading to a rather sizable imbalance between the minimal number of words required to describe a drone and the maximal amount of time a drone takes. We also lack specific terminology for conveying exactly what goes on during a drone. "Sustained" and "held for a long time" are practically our only means of communicating what drones do, even though drone activity is often more complicated than these descriptions let

on. Another approach would be to reflect on the ways in which drones affect the listening process. Drones impose a kind of sensory deprivation through effacing the variation we take for granted, the ebb and flow of acoustic data that occur not only in music but in daily life as well. Like other types of sensory deprivation, drones eventually sharpen other modes of perception by refocusing the listener's attention on the subtle fluctuations in timbre or pitch that accrue greater importance against an otherwise static background.[33]

She also notes how drone music is "dominated by tension between stasis and action, or between limitlessness and constriction [. . .] [and so] appreciable as maximal only in the presence of boundaries, when we know that the music will at some point come to an end."[34] But the drone we are concerned with will not come to an end, and yet remains maximal in the absence of any boundaries, where by maximal we mean "a quality of excess, something appreciable only after long stretches of time."[35] The point being that while drone music may aestheticize a timeless catastrophe of sorts,[36] it only does so on the promise that its timelessness is never made permanent, that its endlessness remain only an appearance. In order to make music of an immortal* drone, to enact in perpetuity some Bernhardian aestheticization of the drone of ourselves, an exalted form of addiction is required, the substance of which can never be exhausted: an addiction wherein the returns do not wane but instead accentuate, destroying the addicted party only in order to refashion him in the likeness of the substance to which he is

32   Arthur Schopenhauer, The World as Will and Representation: Volume 2, trans E.F.J. Payne. (Dover Publications, 1969), 409.

33   Joanna Demers, Listening Through the Noise: The Aesthetics of Experimental Electronic Music (Oxford University Press, 2010), 93.

34   Ibid., 92.

35   Ibid.

36   See Joanna Demers, Drone and Apocalypse (Zero Books, 2015), 17.

addicted: the noise of himself in excess.

If the want is there for immortality*, it is a conflicted want, for who wishes himself into Hell? Attempting to excavate a residence in immortality* is not the problem of how to fill time, but how to become something else while remaining yourself: each of us built from the weaknesses we will destroy in order to survive. The problem is how to solve the paradox and occupy the ellipsis, or, in other words, how to become a Drone-God. And maybe "the only ultimate value of human life is to be found in this Promethean madness, [. . .] a value that is religious, not political, or even moral."[37] What's more, it is suicidal: this being at home without death itself a thinly veiled manifestation of death as the sole remedy for the insomnia of life. Recall Maurice Blanchot's recounting of "The Hunter Gracchus," in which

Kafka relates the adventure of a Black Forest hunter who, having succumbed to a fall in a ravine, has not succeeded in reaching the beyond—and now he is alive and dead. He had joyously accepted life and joyously accepted the end of his life—once killed he awaited his death in joy: he lay stretched out, and he lay in wait. 'Then,' he said, 'the disaster happened.' This disaster is the impossibility of death, it is the mockery thrown down on all humankind's great subterfuge, night, nothingness, silence. There is no end, there is no possibility of being done with the day, with the meaning of things, with hope: such is the truth that Western man has made a symbol of felicity, and has tried to make bearable by focusing on its positive side, that of immortality, of an afterlife that would com-

pensate for life. But this afterlife is our actual life.[38]

We too are dying in the life we want. And we do not want more of life. We merely want more. More of something for which we have no name, and more of that something for something else that we have not yet become. To be done with all this—all the suns and moons and values and desires—is to glimpse for just a second the life we want sequestered somewhere in the obscurity of death. All the while we can keep death ambiguous we can make a life for ourselves there—a life fashioned from the apparel of death, and modelled by us, the wide-eyed cadavers of this new life, the Drone-Gods of the as-yet-unliveable life.

37   Bertrand Russell, The Scientific Outlook (Routledge, 2009), 69.

38   Maurice Blanchot, The Work of Fire (Stanford University Press, 1995), 7-8.

DRONE CONSTRUCTION
PHILOSOPHY of IDENTITY in CONAN'S HORSEBACK BATTLE HAMMER

Steven Shakespeare

Opening (I) Construction of Doom

In the early 1800s, Schelling argued for the ultimate indifference of the finite and the infinite in the absolute. However, the nature of his argument could not be straightforward. Discursive forms of reasoning which relied on causal explanation to reach their conclusions were ruled out, since causation could only apply within the world of finite particulars, and bore no relation to the absolute.

Schelling therefore turned to the method of 'construction': less a causal explanation than a showing, an exhibition of the infinite in the finite. This was a demonstration allied to a certain experience or intuition of the absolute.

As Daniel Whistler explains, construction was a method which was well established in geometry by the time Schelling was writing. As Kant stated, 'To construct a concept means to exhibit a priori the intuition which corresponds to the concept'.[1] In practical terms, this means that the geometer provides a sensible figure, a particular diagrammatic configuration, which exhibits the universal concept. Euclid, for instance, demonstrates key geometrical concepts through constructed figures of lines, circles and so on. These figures are not empirical, for the concept they demonstrate is universal and a priori. However, nor is the figure merely an illustration of a concept already grasped in the understanding. The figure is the indispensable medium of the concept, which can exist only as it is 'shown'.[2]

In contrast to Kant, Schelling held that construction was not limited to geometry. It is the fundamental dynamic of philosophy, because philosophy is itself an

---

1   Quoted in Daniel Whistler, *Schelling's Theory of Symbolic Language: Forming the System of Identity* (Oxford: Oxford University Press, 2013), 121.

2   'Figures must be defined in terms of what is necessary to produce them; they must be defined in terms of their cause. Such is a 'genetic definition': it is to define something by the method of its constructions. Genetic definitions are performative: they enact the construction they describe and so 'prove' the existence of the figure they stipulate.' (Whistler, *Schelling's Theory of Symbolic Language*, 119)

articulation of the unconditioned. Such a philosophy cannot define reality in advance though a subject-object relationship, in which the thinker rationally or empirically accesses pre-existing and fixed metaphysical structures. Schelling's philosophy of identity cannot tolerate such a dualism, or the philosophical mastery it implies. For all his grand claims for philosophy, it is itself an immanent expression of Nature or the absolute.

Schelling thus states that, 'If . . . everything that exists is a construction of the spirit, then *being itself* is nothing other than the *constructing itself*'.[3] There is no 'substratum' of Nature, no unchanging or transcendent foundation upon which reality is built, since reality *is* the unconditioned activity of construction itself. As Whistler, puts it, 'Construction is not a method which the philosopher imposes on reality; it is a process that reality itself is already undergoing'.[4] Philosophical construction is construction of ideas in which the absolute constitutes itself: 'reality constructs itself and it does so in the ideas'.[5]

Thus, even when Schelling's philosophy of identity puts the spotlight on the conditions of mind and consciousness, we do not enter the realm of representation: of a philosophical system attempting to capture and fix the real in its conceptual grasp. Rather, philosophy proceeds by a 'productive intuition', in which nature constructs itself anew. Philosophy is merely an aspect of nature's self-construction. As Iain Hamilton Grant puts it,

It is precisely because productive intuition is 'free' to the extent that it is not bound to the reproduction of an antecedent existent, that it effects the becoming of being. The transcendental is therefore neither a reflex of reality nor a screen dividing rational finite intelligence from it, but is nature potentiating itself in new acts, new forms, new phenomena, and new concepts: transcendental philosophy is the physics of ideation turned experimental.[6]

In his *Philosophy of Art*, Schelling sets out a construction of art as a determination of the absolute in various ways, always grounded in an absolute indifference. Crucial to this move is Schelling's conviction that art *produces* reality; it does not represent it.[7] The artwork—like the philosophical idea — is not judged according to its correspondence with ideal forms, but according to the degree to which produces the indifference of the absolute in its maximum intensity, uniting the finite and the infinite, the universal and the particular, the possible and the actual.

Schelling's analysis of particular art forms begins with music. Music, he argues, is rooted in a sonority which is the aural expression of the indifference of the absolute, punctuated by rhythmic multiplicity: '*The indifference of the informing of the infinite into the finite, taken purely as indifference, is* **sonority**'.[8] Key to his understanding of music is temporality. Music escapes corporeal containment. It is form liberated from body into time. It is sonic expression of the temporal flow of the absolute. What makes it more than mere flux is rhythm, which makes meaningless succession into a meaningful one.[9] This then forms the basis for modulation and, ultimately melody.

In some ways, Schelling's whole philosophy of art from

3   F. W. J. Schelling, *First Outline of a System of the Philosophy of Nature*, trans. Keith R. Peterson (Albany: SUNY press, 2004), 13.

4   Whistler, *Schelling's Theory of Symbolic Language*, 124.

5   Whistler, *Schelling's Theory of Symbolic Language*, 128.

6   Iain Hamilton Grant, *Philosophies of Nature after Schelling* (London: Continuum, 2006), 182.

7   Whistler, *Schelling's Theory of Symbolic Language*, 128-9.

8   F. W. J. Schelling, *The Philosophy of Art*, trans. Douglas W. Stott (Minneapolis: University of Minnesota Press, 1989), 107.

9   Schelling, *Philosophy of Art*, 111.

this period echoes the Hegelian system, progressing from lower to higher, more determinate and integrated forms. However, this neglects what is key to a philosophy of identity: there is no qualitative hierarchy of forms. Each aesthetic form is an irreducible and equal expression or determination of the absolute. And so, while music can be viewed as merely 'the first potence of the real arts', it is simultaneously 'the most universal or general of the real arts and closest to that dissolution into language and reason' which is the highest form of intelligibility.[10]

Sonority and temporality are therefore key to music as an expression of the unconditioned absolute. In drone and doom metal, we find this sonorous absolute manifest in crushing slowness: the minimal interruption of the black hole of sonority by sparse beats. However, rather than allowing light and consciousness to take flight (*pace* certain tendencies in Schelling), such indifference acts as an infinite drag upon finitude.

This essay thus attempts the construction of the absolute in view of Conan's early doom/drone EP *Horseback Battle Hammer*. The particular art work is an expression of the absolute, to be judged according to the intensity of indifference (between the finite and infinite, etc) it produces. Musically and lyrically, Conan's work will be approached as the epitome of audible heaviness, an intuition of the death of intuition. Their minimalist rhythm and lyrics demonstrate the sucking pull of an absolute swamp, where even speed becomes an agonising slowness of dissolution: 'Bodies flow to the bottom/always flow to the bottom'.[11]

---

10   Schelling, *Philosophy of Art*, 118.

11   Conan, 'Satsumo', *Horseback Battle Hammer* (Throne Records, 2010). Lyrics sourced from *Encyclopedia Metallum*, http://www.metal-archives.com/albums/Conan/Horseback_Battle_Hammer/272006.

Opening (II) The Heaviness of the Real

Conan's *Horseback Battle Hammer* is heavy. No, that's not right: it is *heaviness*. It doesn't merely participate in a quality. It embodies it.

However, even that is not correct. It implies that the idea precedes its expression; that there is a pre-existing concept of heaviness which then takes on concrete form, is incarnated or represented, in the particular expressions created by Conan. On this way of looking at it, Conan's music provides the outward form of expression and manifestation for an essentially atemporal and nonsensuous idea.

But heaviness is nothing unless it is made and heard. Gravity does not precede its own instantiation. It is there: and bodies are caught in its wake (bodies flow to the bottom . . .). Reality is constituted by forces whose actuality is always an expression of a virtual intensity; a folding of the Real, rather than a merely abstract possibility, or purely spiritual ideal. Gravity as potency, not potentiality. And, as we will see, this gravitational constitution of heaviness is itself made possible by the 'higher difference' of the absolute in its immanent diremption from itself: a difference which is also an affirmation of identity.

Conan's work, vibrating with this virtual intensity, is therefore a good place to explore the Real as heaviness that to which all else tends; that which binds and informs all, without itself being bound; that which cannot be positioned as an object by the representational force of any discourse, including—or especially—philosophical discourse. In the wake of the Real as heaviness, bodies flow, dislocate, become undefined by their position in the fragile house of cards which is the contingency of the world. Despite all the terror which the world might unleash to keep them in place.

Krull: The Self-naming of the Absolute

My name is Krull, I live on a mountain.

I know where you're from, It's in the fountain

Worship Krull, within the Mountain.

My God's have gone, into the fountain.

Madness and horror, daggers and teeth.

Wrestle the Gods in the swamps of the dead.[12]

The vocals aren't sung, but sound like battle shouts erupting from a horde of warrior giants charging their sworn-enemies. The bone-chilling howls are backed by what Conan is really all about—the mighty riff. And when I say mighty, I mean mighty—the heaviest, meatiest riffs out there, that if played loudly enough, will shake mountains.[13]

The riff is a monster. It is a pulsation of sludge: thick, bubbling. The drawn-out chords progress so slowly as to make any structure hard to grasp by the listening ear. As a result, the music is the paradoxical rhythmic intensification of formless chaos. It expresses the flow of the absolute. Just at the limit of breaking down entirely, the riffs morph into a semblance of structure and then, once, again, decay.

The singing is stretched out on a vocal rack, higher above the swamp, but also enacting its slow, sucking inertia.

And what it enacts is a naming: 'My name is Krull'. There is no context given here. We are not told who Krull is. There is no narrative as such, only the configuration of a scene. Krull on the mountain, demanding worship. The gods gone, dissolved into flux.

The pace quickens, a more conventional metallic chug takes over. The vocals sing madness and horror, a wrestling with gods 'in the swamps of the dead'. Even as dissolved, even in chaos, we are called to wrestle with the gods—or Krull wrestles with them, usurping them, yet still drawn into the mire. The song ends abruptly. There is nowhere to go.

The song constructs the absolute as the restless, liquefying swamp, in which the gods are encountered, dissipated, fought. Krull emerges in an act of self-identification, a self-naming whose content is nothing other than itself. It refers to nothing, like the voice to Moses from the burning bush: 'I am who I am' (Exodus 3.14).

This is how Conan construct the absolute. They give unstable figure and form to a Real which can never be the object of an empirical intuition, but which, equally, does not merely reside in a transcendent realm above and beyond all figures. The music is not representational, since it is the taking place of the absolute in our hearing. As Jason Wirth puts it, with reference to Schelling's philosophy, 'The whole comes as itself and it does not mean anything beside itself, but it emerges in such a way that the oceanic monstrosity of emergence as such shimmers through the whole'.[14]

Krull resonates with Schelling's approach in a number of ways. As an absolute act of self-naming, it constructs in our hearing a dynamic expression of the unconditioned in a particular form. It is both an affirmation of singularity, and a manifestation of sonic formlessness. It produces Nature/God to an exceptional degree of intensity.

In his *First Outline of a Philosophy of Nature*, Schelling argues that any systematic philosophy must begin with the unconditioned, if it is not to beg the question

---

12   Conan, 'Krull', *Horseback Battle Hammer*.

13   Doominance, 'The Heaviest', review of **Horseback Battle Hammer**, December 14th, 2015. http://www.metal-archives.com/reviews/Conan/Horseback_Battle_Hammer/272006/.

14   Jason M. Wirth, *Schelling's Practice of the Wild: Time, Art, Imagination* (Albany: SUNY press, 2015), 28.

about its own arbitrariness. Of course, those who suspect systematic philosophy of an arrogant and deluded attempt to impose a totalising schema of comprehension upon reality would not be satisfied by this.

However, the unconditioned is not to be identified with any static being or totality. It is 'being itself', not 'a' being. Strictly speaking, it is wrong to say that the unconditioned 'is', for it constitutes a thoroughly dynamic entanglement and opposition of forces. The unconditioned is not the immutable being of Eleatic philosophy, which is unable to find expression in becoming, and is therefore only a one-sided absolute. Schelling's unconditioned is simply not relative to any transcendence which would position, delimit and define it. Instead, it is wholly immanent to its expression, and yet inexhaustible by any specific form.

In this light, Schelling's statement that the unconditioned '*does not exhibit itself in any finite product, and every individual is, as it were, a particular expression of it*' can make sense.[15] The unconditioned can never be captured by a 'product'. It is never a defined body or concept, never a finished result. At the same time, every individual is an expression of it; not merely a creature or a sign pointing beyond itself to a transcendent reality; but an *expression* of the absolute.

Take the—apparently arrogant—statement that 'To philosophize about Nature means to *create* Nature'.[16] On the surface of it, this appears to be an assertion of philosophical mastery. Philosophy can comprehend everything, and nature is nothing unless it is subject to philosophical clarification and correction — even creation. However, such a reading demands inversion: philosophy is itself a *natural process*. It is not something other than Nature, a transcendent perspective or method to be applied to a recalcitrant or dead material in order to give it life and meaning. Philosophy is an expression of the absolute, of the dynamic activity of construction which *is* Nature itself.

Krull expresses this in a particular way. As a god, or a usurper of gods, Krull names itself. But the permanence of the mountain home is never disconnected from the play of the fountain and the suck of the swamp. More importantly, that affirmation and dissolution are *heard*.

Writing about art in the period of his philosophy of identity, Schelling claims that '*Mythology is the necessary condition and first content of all art*'.[17] This is because mythology expresses the absolute in the figures of the gods: concrete, active manifestations of the divine. Each god names and embodies the unconditioned in particular form. So while, in general, '*The immediate cause of all art is God*, for God is by means of his absolute identity the source of all mutual informing (into indifference) of the real and the ideal upon which all art rests', that mutual informing of real and ideal manifests as a multiplicity.[18] Every particular thing takes up the absolute, and so is a 'universe'; and 'there are accordingly as many universes as there are ideas of particular things'.[19] And every idea is a god.

The self-naming of Krull performs this mutual informing of real and ideal. It is the creation of godhood, absolute in its singularity. As Schelling writes of the gods in relation to absolute form: 'They do not *signify* it; they *are* it themselves'.[20] Wirth comments that the gods 'do not mean anything other than themselves'.[21]

However, in strict coincidence with this absoluteness of

15   Schelling, *First Outline*, 13.

16   Schelling, *First Outline*, 14.

17   Schelling, *Philosophy of Art*, 45.

18   Schelling, *Philosophy of Art*, 32,

19   Schelling, *Philosophy of Art*, 33.

20   Schelling, *Philosophy of Art*, 42.

21   Wirth, *Schelling's Practice of the Wild*, 158.

the gods, is the haunting abyssal ground from which they emerge, and which always haunts them: 'As the common germ of both gods and men, absolute chaos is night, obscurity'.[22] If Krull names this chaos, gives it form, so the music reproduces the emergence and dissolution and re-emergence of forms in the fluid darkness of Nature's womb. Chaos is not merely destruction, but the necessary obscurity which exceeds defined forms and bears new ones.

Satsumo: The Difference that Makes Gravity

Blood flows.

Go, remain.

Bodies flow to the bottom, always flow to the bottom.

The bay is full at the bottom, deathly full at the bottom.[23]

Instantly you are struck by the sheer massive brown magnitude of the guitar tone. It's something you simultaneously feel as well as hear. It shakes your cochlea and makes the nerves around the entrance of your butt hole twitch. Damn, it's good . . . short treaties on sea-based beasties and almost everything else being dead or dying.[24]

This kind of lumbering über-doom I like to call brown metal, because it rumbles so low you could shit your pants from the vibrations . . . not since YOB has a debut of such unabashed heaviness been pulled off so well. Yes, I mean that.[25]

It growls. Rhythm and distortion are inseparable, the finitude of expression and the always excessive momentum of the infinite demonstrated in their indifference. The vocals are insistent on the flow which takes bodies 'to the bottom', back to the ground or the abyss from which they have emerged. The music performs this gravitational pull.

At the halfway mark, the speed of riffing and drums increases; we approach the whirlpool. Then it slows once more and the vocals return, strung out, repetitive. It is always the same motion, the same thing being said, an identity that does not lead anywhere or require any development. A brief flicker into speed, then the pace retards again, repulsed by its own heaviness into the brownness of earth, swamp, decay. An excretion of the eternal.

This ebb and flow of slowness is not a contradiction of dynamics. The music does not settle on an identifiable theme or structure or motif. In its extended, tortured decay, it plays out the drama of repulsion and attraction.

That drama is integral to Schelling's philosophy of nature. Nature in itself has no permanence, it does not get fixed in any object or activity.[26] And yet there clearly are relatively persisting beings. We do not live in a featureless chaos. The reason is that nature *affects itself*. In its pure activity, its affirmation of itself, it is in motion, but motion is impossible—insensible—without friction, without a minimal difference according to which affirmation takes hold of itself. Nature, then, in its very materiality, consists of attractive and repulsive forces. The original qualities of nature are therefore not static bits or attributes of matter, but dynamic relations of force. They are 'actants'. That does not dissolve them into pure flux however, for each quality,

22 Schelling, *Philosophy of Art*, 37.

23 Conan, 'Satsumo', *Horseback Battle Hammer*.

24 buddhafella, 'National Treasure', review of *Horseback Battle Hammer*, January 30th, 2016. http://www.metal-archives.com/reviews/Conan/Horseback_Battle_Hammer/272006/.

25 'Conan, Horseback Battle Hammer: Doom with Some Serious Hit Points', *The Obelisk*, August 19th, 2010. http://theobelisk.net/obelisk/2010/08/19/

conanreview/

26 Schelling, *First Outline*, 17.

each actant is also 'singular', a *natural monad*.[27]

Nature's self-inhibitions prevent its original infinity expanding at infinite velocity. Inhibition is therefore the condition for intuition of the infinite in the finite, for Nature's expression in particular or determinate forms. But again, before we get fixated on those forms, we must remember that they are only ever one—albeit singular—expression of the whole, a whole which never rests. There is no ultimate duality between the infinite and the finite, between the activity and the product. The original activities do not 'exist' in themselves—'the actant, abstracted from the product, is nothing. Indeed, it is nothing other than the product itself viewed from a higher perspective'.[28]

However strange this all sounds—and the particular claim about actants was something he later moved away from—it is motivated by Schelling's denial of the false difference of transcendence, an asymmetrical exteriority in which finite beings are the product of a higher being, which is itself unaffected by its own creation. Such transcendence only justifies finitude as an analogical ladder back to itself. In contrast, Schelling wishes to affirm an absolute in ceaseless self-expression. Its 'products' are singular points of inhibition, re-expressing the unconditioned partially, but univocally.

Inhibition and dynamism are not contraries. As 'Satsumo' surges forwards, so it falls back, revolving on its inner molten core. Schelling offers a telling image:

a stream flows in a straight line forward as long as it encounters no resistance. Where there is resistance—a whirlpool forms. Every original product of nature is such a whirlpool, every organism. The whirlpool is not something immobilized, it is rather something con-stantly transforming—but reproduced anew at each moment. Thus no product in nature is fixed, but it is reproduced at each instant through the force of nature entire.[29]

At each instant, the force of nature wholly expressed in the point of dynamic tension which articulates an unconditioned fulcrum of resistance; and yet such points are 'reproduced anew at each moment', an inexhaustible self-differentiation. In the monotony of sameness, a seething, radical difference is born, which refuse to be assimilated to any external transcendent origin or force.

Given Conan's essential heaviness, it is striking to turn to what Schelling has to say about gravity. Since it is a condition of Nature's self-expression that its force of expansion is inhibited, gravity might seem to play a crucial role as a key physical manifestation of this. In a sense, this is true; but Schelling also argues that gravity cannot be understood in and of itself. It is derivative from a higher condition, more specifically 'a *higher difference*'.[30] This is explained in a passage worth quoting at length:

For what is weight? Is *weight* thinkable within an *absolute identity*? Or does weight already presuppose *diremption?*—Every body must, indeed, have the degree of weight in *itself*—but the cause of its weight outside of itself. If we think of a body in empty space (or all of matter in a clump), then it is not *heavy*. A body, therefore, is only heavy insofar as it has a cause *outside* of itself which *makes* it heavy. Weight already presupposes an *exteriority*. The *condition* of weight is a juxtaposition. How should this juxtaposition be explained? It cannot again be explained from the system of gravity, for it is indeed the *condition* of all gravitation. We are driven here to an *original* exteriority. Which contains

27 Schelling, *First Outline*, 21.

28 Schelling, *First Outline*, 22.

29 Schelling, *First Outline*, 18n.

30 Schelling, *First Outline*, 79n.

the ground of that derived one. The original exteriority, which is the condition of the *mechanical* exteriority of bodies, can now be of a sheerly *dynamical* kind, i.e. it must be an *original difference*.[31]

At first glance, this appears to contradict Schelling's insistence on absolute identity, a fundamental *indifference* as the essence of reality. However, the issue here is moving from a notion of difference understood as merely one thing being alongside and external to another; to a dynamical difference, in which otherness is understood in relation. Heaviness does not exist in and of itself, but as the expression of a system of interrelated forces. The singularity of any body is thus not defined by its having an inviolable frontier, but by the unique balances and imbalances which run in and through the skin as affects and resistances. Absolute identity, by understanding all things in mutually affecting relationship, is thus simultaneously able to affirm irreducible difference, understood as singularity of experience. And this without the need for positing a transcendence or any merely exterior difference.

Schelling's aversion to 'mechanical' exteriority, and the foregrounding of organic models of being, should not mislead us, however. No ultimate duality exists. Organism is produced in and through the forces of attraction and repulsion. It is inevitably constituted by the mechanical, much as life and mind are also expressions of nature. Ian Hamilton Grant captures the thought well, when writing of Schelling's early emphasis on the self as the principle of the absolute:

The self should not be understood as empirical, reflective or transcendental consciousness; rather, the self as a principle is the *itself*, the *to auto*, of the unconditioned (*das Unbedingt*) which cannot be a thing (*Ding . . .*). The *auto* has the irremediable externality of the automatic, the autonomic, its only 'in itself' deriving from the irreversibility of dependency relations stemming *from* it, rather than extending *to* it. As Camilla Warnke notes, 'Schelling's autopoietic systems could equally be *technical systems, machines*, to the extent that they fulfil the determinant conditions of autopoiesis'.[32]

For Conan, it is as if each song produces itself, gives birth to itself out of the maelstrom of forces which seek expression. Their compositions are hardly 'organic', if by that is meant something as the opposite pole of the machinic. They are more like slowed-down machines, whose gears grind and stutter in the labour of production. The song is where the forces combine, slipping in and out of any stable ratio. The simplicity of Conan's heaviness is thus deceptive. Each riff creates its own echo chamber the vastness of a space, the intensity of a weight, which nevertheless exists in repulsive attraction to the flow of the song.

Of course, it is true that Conan's flow has a direction: to the bottom. To death. It tends always—without ever arriving—to the annihilation of all things in the black whole of total compression. The flow, however, never ends. It is always reproduced. This is the way in which 'Satsumo' constructs the absolute: as a tendency towards the final 'product' of death, which keeps us always on the brink, always caught in the wake of the unceasing whirlpool.

---

31 Schelling, *First Outline*, 79-80n.

32 Grant, *Philosophies of Nature*, 16; cf. 168. For a related analysis, see also Derrida's deconstruction of the divide between the machinic and faith/spontaneity/decision in Jacques Derrida, 'Faith and Knowledge; The Two Sources of "Religion" at the Limits of Reason Alone' in Gil Anidjar (ed.), *Acts of Religion* (New York: Routledge, 2002), 39-101.

Dying Giant: Appearance of Monstrosity

[Scream]

Invisible Sun, blood-reddened beams of undying light.

Ocean of graves, ebb and flow.[33]

a brutal and bloody atmosphere that reeks of Cyclopean corpses rotting in the sun on the harsh stone-ground of a barren wasteland . . . sheer, brutal heaviness and a bestial atmosphere.[34]

An opening riff which lingers, descends into feedback. The monstrous heaviness thrashes around, an unholy, gargantuan, twitching corpse. Feedback again. It is already agonising, but this is a death that will not die. There is ebb and flow, there is 'undying light'. The boundary between what is played and what is reverberated twists and bends.

The song then lurches into a more conventional riff, though still heavy and verging on monotony. Again we walk the very edge of that collapse into pure indifference, whose expression is impossible without the minimal difference of the song's development. Always on the brink of death, under an undying, bloody star.

However, the final step is never taken. And the attractive force of death, its heaviness, is inverted. It becomes an impulse to persist in living. Life and death here are not opposites. Life is not a pure essence, but a negotiation, an assimilation, a resistance and an affirmation.

In the throes of the Dying Giant, we hear what Schelling describes: 'It sounds paradoxical, but is no less true, that through influences which are contrary to life, life is sustained.—Life is nothing other than a productivity held back from the absolute transition into a product. The absolute transition into product is death. That which interrupts productivity, therefore, sustains life'.[35] Life requires an irritant to keep it in motion. Organic life is defined by this ebb and flow across the frontier which both constitutes it and acts as a passage for nourishment, affect, expression. The organism is thus a dyad, *'turned towards two worlds at once'*.[36] The inner and outer are irreducible in their tension, inseparable in their touch. Hence the paradoxical coincidence of opposites which is life: 'Only the organism as object is determinable through external influences, the organism as subject must be *unreachable* by them'.[37]

Jason Wirth touches on the same point when he quotes the later text *The Ages of the World*: 'every single individual comes to being [*ensteht*] through the same cission [*Scheidung*] through which the world comes to being'.[38] Wirth refers to this as the 'monstrously generative disparity' which gives birth to reality. Even though it is true that, on one level, Nature is 'occupied with the annihilation of the individual',[39] this dynamic of assimilation is reproduced in every individual expression of Nature, so that the singular being can 'hold its own'.[40]

The Dying Giant is also the occasion for a monstrous birth, the release of a multiplicity. Writing on Sunn O))), Aliza Shvarts argues for another sense of the weight of crushing doom: '"Being metal" is for Sunn O))) bound up with the question of bearing metal: bearing in the sense of surviving—of "taking it," withstanding the sound—but also in that other sense

---

33 Conan, 'Dying Giant', *Horseback Battle Hammer*.

34 Doominance, 'The Heaviest'.

35 Schelling, *First Outline*, 62n.

36 Schelling, *First Outline*, 108.

37 Schelling, *First Outline*, 106.

38 Wirth, *Schelling's Practice of the Wild*, 87.

39 Schelling, *First Outline*, 40n.

40 Schelling, *First Outline*, 54.

of *sustaining or delivering forth*.[41] Exploring the way in which doom metal pares down the metal aesthetic, imitating the material history of metal in order to distil it into a embodied sublime vibration, she argues that 'Doom metal reverberates between corporeality and subjectivization, enacting a bodily and material persistence, which not only references the bodily operations of reproduction, but is also itself a form of reproductivity.'[42] Doom does not merely promote decay, but sustenance: the bearing of the weight of metal, an extended labour. Such labour, associated with the abjected bodies of women, returns as an unbearable excess, which the heaviness of the music bears. The listening experience of doom, its heavy intensity shaking your guts ('*it rumbles so low you could shit your pants from the vibrations*'), sustains that sense of pregnant power, despite the masculinist urge to abject and expel it.

Alison Assiter takes up the ontological potency of metaphors of birth in the work of Schelling and Kierkegaard. While she is focused more on the Schelling of the 1806 *Freedom* essay than his earlier philosophy of identity, there is nevertheless a connection. The body that births becomes a repetition of Nature as a whole, of the earth itself as 'grounded in a capacity or power that gave rise to it'.[43] For Shvarts, this is the mimetic aspect of doom. Such mimesis is not an aesthetics of representation, of copying an original; but a resonance and recognition of the body, and the history of the body as it is reproduced, abjected, shaken.

Is this contradicted by Schelling's assertion that 'music is the art form that divests itself to the highest degree of corporeality by portraying *pure* movement as such, separated from the object, and by being carried by invisible, almost spiritual wings' (116)?[44] Only if our understanding of the body is reified and rendered immune to movement. The resonance created in and through the body by doom is the reproduction of the body's own emergence and flow. The singularity of the body is not secured by making of it a disconnected object, but by realising the forces which it uses to sustain itself, to assimilate enough of its world to create and birth a world within.

Sea Lord: Oceanic Being

Much Ill

Will Suffer

Oaken

Oarlocks[45]

the riff-as-lavaflow soundscape . . . The huge, crumbling hypnotoad of a guitartone brings to mind the infinite space and oppressive heat of the desert; where the weather reduces everything to dust sooner rather than later. Get up on the closest hill you can find and you'll be able to see forever; so go on, have a drag from some harsh hand rolled tobacco and sip some of your remaining water. Such is Conan. It's a harsh world, it's a beautiful world, it's something that you can very literally get completely lost in . . . Heavy beyond anything.[46]

41   Aliza Shvarts, 'Troubled air: the drone and doom of reproduction in Sunn O)))'s metal maieutic' in *Women & Performance* 2014, Vol. 24, 203-19: 204.

42   Shvarts, 'Troubled air', 212.

43   Alison Assiter, *Kierkegaard, Eve and Metaphors of Birth* (London: Rowman and Littlefield, 2015), 165. See Jason Wirth's take on Schelling's philosophy of music: 'Musical rhythm is not an exemplar of a fixed rule, but the creative coming into being of music as the unfolding primordial song of the earth.' (Wirth 156)

44   Schelling, *Philosophy of Art*, 116.

45   Conan, 'Sea Lord', *Horseback Battle Hammer*.

46   caspian, 'MYYYYYYYYYY NAME IS CROOOOOOOOOOOOM', review of *Horseback Battle Hammer*, April 16th, 2013. http://www.metal-ar-

A ritualistic drum pattern opens the track, before the return of crushing, slow, massive riffs. Have they ever stopped resounding through this record?

The song always teeters on the brink of its own exhaustion, but nevertheless sucks the listener in to a kind of endlessness, a strangely claustrophobic spaciousness.

Flow is central to the thematics of this EP. But flow is also continually inhibited and arrested, as it is with the lyrical content of this track. The lyrics take leave of any sentence structure. Words and partial phrases stand alone. Devoid of syntax, they cannot refer to anything. But they draw together a figure of immense suffering, flowing into an ocean of sound. Each word is a cry, each word alone a symbol of the absolute.[47]

However, the music is not simply a decorative accompaniment to this lyrical absolutism. The music persists, insists on its own dragging weight. The decomposition of lyrical structure floats upon the unending surge of the music. It brings to mind a point highlighted by Alisha Shvarts about the music of Sunn O))): 'Rejecting the idea that their music enacts a feeling of decay, O'Malley orients the band's work around the idea of sustenance.'[48] To stay afloat on the ocean that bears the weight of decomposition is an affirmation of the material potency of the music to refigure the listening, feeling body.

Jason Wirth writes of 'the moment in which decomposition has become revelatory, revealing itself both as ground and the decompositional contestation of all being, even the being of the ground'.[49] For Schelling, the process of decomposition is inseparable from the fluid dynamics of Nature. Since no simple material in Nature is primitive, it follows that 'the most original and most absolute combination of opposed actions in Nature must generate the *most original fluidity*, which . . . continually endeavours to *liquefy* everything in Nature'.[50]

As we have seen, Nature has a monstrous aspect, in which it seeks to annihilate everything individual. But the individual which Nature overcomes is the fixed product; in other words, death. So Nature's perpetual motion is its striving *to refuse death*. The identity of the absolute is not defined by the stasis of death, but by the affirmation of itself. Such affirmation is the germ of life. Life here is not a transcendent or immaterial substance infused into matter, but is the complex auto-affection, persistence and pregnancy of matter itself.

This nuanced relationship between decomposition, fluidity, death and life is indicated by Schelling's claim that 'the *absolutely fluid can reveal its existence in no other way than through decomposition*'.[51] The absolutely fluid, the pure flux, must affirm itself in difference and diremption, in the singularity of nodes of forces, attracting and repulsing one another. Without such 'decomposition', the absolute is nothing.

At the other end of the scale from the pure fluidity and chaos of the absolute, are those aspects of Nature which Schelling labels 'indecomposable'. These are not simple pre-existing atoms, but substances which have evolved—decomposed—so far, that they have exhausted the possibilities of that particular path. But even here we do not end with a fixed and final product. Such 'indecomposables' re-enter the living circulation of Nature again by being 'composed' again,—set into relationship with other powers and processes, forming

---

chives.com/reviews/Conan/Horseback_Battle_Hammer/272006/.

47 See Whistler on Schelling's understanding of symbolic language, e.g. *Schelling's Theory of Symbolic Language*, 191-3.

48 Shvarts, 'Troubled air', 213.

49 Wirth, *Schelling's Practice of the Wild*, 37.

50 Schelling, *First Outline*, 27.

51 Schelling, *First Outline*, 20.

new aggregates and networks.[52] As Grant puts it, 'The subject of nature thus consists in the constantly reiterated identity of productivity and product ... *nature as subject is self-recapitulating at different levels*'.[53]

Each monadic word shrieked over the 'hypnotoad of a guitartone' is arguably such an indecomposable, reduced down to the barest possibility of signification. And yet, brought into composition with the other words, and with the music, they compose a seascape: a scene of utter fluidity, indelible suffering and material persistence.

Philosophy fails here, but fruitfully. Writing of Schelling's aesthetics of tragedy, Theodore George argues that the plot of *Oedipus the King* is 'a representation that captures the character of human rationality—not only its purpose to achieve the representation of the absolute but also its fracture, its irreconcilable disagreement with itself, and its failure to fulfil its own aim'.[54] Not really a representation at all then; more an evocation, or resonance of the monstrous absolute itself.

What Has Been Constructed Must be Heard

We can say all of this:

Conan is monstrous.

Conan is Naturemachine.

Conan is Krull, wrestling with the gods in the swamp.

Conan is the whirlpool, dragging bodies down.

Conan is the Dying Giant in the undying sun.

Conan is the Sea Lord, ebb and flow.

None of this is inadequate to the absolute, since the absolute does not reside in a transcendent realm over and above its expression. However, to produce this absolute in its intensity, the repeated pull of Conan's heaviness must be felt: a perpetual falling that is also the upsurge of productivity. And yet the felt intensity of this music is a strange one. It strains against the limits of any assured sense of subjectivity, any phenomenology. It shakes the body, recapitulating the flow of forces by which the body is constituted. It overwhelms the mind, sucking it into the immensity of its obscure origins.

Conan reverberates with the sonority of this absolute, which both acts as a machinic drag upon time and transcendence, and as the fecundity of an unhuman 'life *without us*'.[55] A living beyond life, a hearing without listening.

Conan is the Real. The Real is Doom.

52 Schelling, *First Outline*, 31.

53 Grant, *Philosophies of Nature*, 170.

54 Theodore D. George, 'A Monstrous Absolute: Schelling, Kant and the Poetic Turn in Philosophy' in Jason M. Wirth (ed.), *Schelling Now: Contemporary Readings* (Bloomington: Indiana University Press, 2005), 143.

55 Eugene Thacker, *After Life* (Chicago: University of Chicago press, 2010), 268.

Originally conceived as a zine, Weirdrone Tales is reproduced here in its entirety. A missive from the future on the origin of drone, a primordial monument to the future of drone. - Ed.

WEIRDRONE TALES

JOSEPH NORMAN

January 2020

Weirdrone Tales

SINCE 2014: THE ECSTATIC MAGAZINE

The Weird, Drone Music and Sonic Ecstasy: Sublime Backwash from Beyond the Threshold
By Joseph S. Norman

THE HAUNT

The Editor,
WEIRDRONE TALES
Uxbridge,
London, U.K.

Weirdrone is a compound word for a particular nexus point of sonic and literary margins. This special edition of Weirdrone Tales *explores certain examples of drone music as media best exemplifying the philosophy,*
aesthetics and affect of The Weird, as originally articulated by writers such as Arthur Machen (1863-1947), Lord Dunsany (1878-1957) and H. P. Lovecraft (1890-1937).

I have argued elsewhere that extreme metal in its numerous forms is a sonic form that often captures the aesthetics and philosophies of The Weird.[i] This special edition develops such ideas, presenting the darker fringes of drone music as a fundamentally estranging artistic mode well suited to capturing sensations of horror, transcendence and ecstatic dread. I discuss hearing such music as a vehicle for transporting the listener through the "threshold between our world" and the "world of the spirit"[ii], following Owen Coggins's research into drone metal as "imaginative temporal, spatial and bodily 'elsewheres'".[iii] Drone also offers impressions of Weird soundscapes from this space beyond our familiar reality: a sonic analogue to the stories from and inspired by those published in the original Weird Tales *magazine. Now practitioners of The Weird work across media, seamlessly blending genres to represent the unimaginable, contemplate the unthinkable and conceive the unknowable.*

Weirdrone Tales *matches hybrid form with slippery subject matter: a creative, and critical, response, an experiment in Fictocriticism. Discussing this latter term, Jacques Lacan considered it "a name for those 'critical' inventions which belong to literature while deforming its limits"[iv] – and it is with deformed sonic and literary limits that* Weirdrone Tales *is concerned. Charting the full range of The Weird in drone is beyond the scope of this issue, but it is a task I will continue upon in the future. Acts featured include Bong, Sunn O))), From the Bogs of Aughiska, Aymrev*

Erkroz Prevre, Prøfan and Saturn Form Essence, who all achieve drone through various means, often incorporating field recordings, elements of metal and industrial, as well as dark, space and ritual ambient music. Parallels are drawn between sonic artists and literary works by classic Weird writers, such as Lovecraft, Dunsany, Machen, and Robert E. Howard. Also included in this issue are new stories and poems from talented Weird writers, chosen especially for their shared concern with the ecstatic effects of drone music in various forms.

(continued on final page of magazine)

Welcome to this special issue of Weirdrone Tales...

Drone Music and Weird Ecstasy

"There is only one test by which literature may be distinguished from mere reading-matter, and that that test is summed up in the word, ecstasy. And then we admitted a whole string of synonyms—desire of the unknown, sense of the unknown, rapture, adoration, mystery,—wonder, withdrawal from the common life and I dare say I have used many other phrases in the same sense without giving you any special warning that it was our old friend again in a new guise."[v]

Arthur Machen, *Hieroglyphics*

The above epigraph outlines the central philosophy of Welsh visionary and mystic Arthur Machen's work, as perhaps best expressed in *The Great God Pan* (1894). In this famous novella protagonist Dr Raymond performs brain surgery on a young woman, Mary, in order to somewhat literally "open the mind" and expose her to hidden "knowledge of the most awful, most secret forces" lying at the heart of all things", for which the titular deity Pan is "an exquisite symbol".[vi] While Mary soon dies from shock, her beautiful but sinister daughter – notable for foul, deeply unsettling and bestial behaviour and the similar corruption of those around her – is revealed to be the offspring of Pan himself. For Machen, experience of the "world of the spirit" leads to "supreme terror", "folly" and death.[vii] *The Great God Pan* is a perfect example of Weird horror, where the subtle accumulation of small details gradually develops in the reader a profound sense of unease and dread that is hard to identify specifically, as well as a kind of rapture at the numinous possibilities of mundane life suggested by the tale.

It is certain types of drone music, I feel, that provide particularly effective methods for achieving something akin to the sensation of reading works by

Machen and other Weird writers. There can be few who listen seriously and regularly to drone music that will deny its unique potential for a kind of mental disassociation, the achievement of a trance-like state instigated by the monotonous repetition of the form. For his Ph.D thesis 'Drone Metal Mysticism', Owen Coggins conducted extensive interviews with drone metal fans, and analysed many accounts of their listening experiences (in the process earned himself the nickname 'Doctor Drone'). These research participants described hearing drone metal in terms of "intense physical experience, catharsis, transcendence, mysticism, ritual, therapy, journeys and pilgrimages,"[viii] which can evoke feelings of "healing and relief" as well as violence, discomfort and sickness.[ix] This kind of experiential dissonance, therefore, chimes with Machen's stories where "terror and ecstasy" are "deeply intertwined".[x]

The ancient links between spiritual practices and sound are well known, Machen reminds us, as expressed in "the Hebrew dances of religious joy", as well as ancient Greek and English traditions.[xi] Music has been crucial to shamanic rituals from across the globe, including Siberia, Korea and Tibet, for centuries, often for purposes of spirit possession. More recently, especially extreme forms of music such as black metal have been linked to magical practices of the Left Hand Path. Erik Danielsson, frontman of

Swedish band Watain, outlines a similar argument to Machen's, relating to his self-described Theistic Satanism. Discussing the band's philosophy on their DVD *Opus Diaboli* (2012), Danielsson argues for a kind of satanic ecstasy at the heart of black metal performance, beginning in rock-and-roll, the origins of all rock and metal music, which he describes as follows:

> "The only way to create something of dignity and true beauty in this world is by looking beyond its borders, to search outside of the mundane, and enter into that which lies beyond the safety of established form." [xii]

For Danielsson, this space "beyond the safety of established form" is a "realm of liberated wilderness, of untamed fire, and of that ancient chaos of which every true and potent artist has been a mouthpiece." [xiii] Danielsson's uses language and a philosophy very close to Machen's ideas about Weird Fiction: the Watain frontman discussing the use "magic and communication with the divine" to "open gateways to that terrible and wondrous place that lies outside the borders of the world", [xiv] or Machen's "world of the spirit".

The drone music with which we are concerned here, then, is a different sonic medium to that of Watain: drone metal, for example, rarely achieves the frantic, intensity of black metal, yet it is still somewhat extreme in its frequent eschewal of rhythm, clear melody and polyphony, as well as its use of radically slowed tempo. Most drone music however is described as achieving a somewhat different end-state to the wild triumph and feverish debauchery of Watain: a kind of meditative sensation, calm or intense to varying degrees.

What I am concerned with here is the particular quality of this end-state when drone is infused with a pervasive sense of Weirdness. This can be vocal techniques giving a decidedly in-human quality to the voice, especially harsh guitar tones, overwhelming volume and depth of sound, or other timbres that are unsettling in some manner, and in some way akin to the effect of reading certain works of Weird literature.

Interpretation of the nature of such a state will vary between listeners, of course, as would the question of its existence in the first place. To mystics and magical practitioners like Danielsson, music can literally help listeners achieve higher planes of spiritual consciousness. More sceptical subjects such as myself, however, acknowledge the existence of such effects, remain genuinely interested in a plethora of interpretation, but veer toward rational explanation and political/aesthetic metaphor.

While reporting on the elsewheres his research participants describe, he observes that most kept matters of spiritual/materialist interpretation open and deliberately vague. Coggins suggests "that listeners make space in which to explore religiosity and mysticism in musical experience through maintaining ambivalence about such concepts and their relation to drone metal."[xv] Similarly the innately slippery borders of The Weird make Weirdrone especially susceptible to such unfixed critical/philosophical interpretations.

For Machen The Weird is a kind of veiled, spiritual layer behind everyday life and common experience: "the sense of the eternal mysteries, the eternal beauty beneath the crust of the common, trivial things; hidden and yet burning".[xvi] Similarly, Blackwood's Weird fiction was an expression of his pantheism, whose diary accounts of becoming "possessed by nature"[xvii] until "the material world faded away" and, "among the shadows" feeling the "real spiritual world behind shining through",[xviii] directly mirror those of his protagonists.

For atheists such as Lovecraft, or, later, China Miéville, however, any supernatural aspects of Weird experience occur only within their fiction. Lovecraft saw his work as capturing "the beating of black wings or the scratching of outside shapes and entities on the known universe's utmost rim,"[xix] which he longed but failed to experience in reality. For Miéville, a Marxist for many years, The Weird represents "swillage of that awe and horror 'from beyond' back into the everyday", but as a "radicalized sublime backwash",[xx] or metaphor for progressive political change: the shocking discovery of a world of the spirit in fiction that represents the realization that the really-existing world reimagined can be truly awesome indeed. Perhaps, through the combination of The Weird and drone music, we can experience such a 'world of the spirit', however it maybe understood.

COSMIC/PRIMAL WEIRDRONE

Lord Dunsany, *The Gods of Pegāna* (1905)
Bong, *Beyond Ancient Space* (Ritual Records, 2011)
Bong, *Mana-Yood-Sushai* (Ritual Records, 2012)
An early depiction of Weirdrone in literature is located within the creation story of Lord Dunsany's Pegāna, populated by his mythopoeic pantheon of comic and idiosyncratic gods. Set above them all, deeply sleeping, is MANA-YOOD-SUSHAI, a kind of Ur-deity, to whom humankind may not pray for fear of awakening him. Perhaps the second most important figure in this pantheon is Skarl the drummer because it is the music he makes that stops MANA-YOOD-SUSHAI from interfering in the world:

"When MANA-YOOD-SUSHAI had made the gods and Skarl, Skarl made a drum, and began to beat upon it that he might drum for ever […] Skarl sitteth upon the mist before the feet of MANA-YOOD-SUSHAI above the gods of Pegāna, and there he beateth his drum […] if he cease for an instant then MANA-YOOD-SUSHAI will start awake, and there will be worlds nor gods no more."[xxi]

So we begin at the dawn of Lord Dunsany's mythopoeia, in the space after which time can be marked, with the image of Skarl beating his drum in a space beyond the cosmos, noting that it is only the continuation of this primal vibration that stands between us and our total annihilation.

Dunsany provided few details to help us image how such a vibration might sound, but there are some oblique clues. To some "the Worlds and the Suns are but the echoes of the drumming of Skarl", while others say that "they be dreams that arise in the mind of MANA because of the drumming of Skarl, as one may dream whose rest is troubled by sound of song".[xxii]

So what we do know, then, is that such drumming evokes sound of a scale commensurate with that of the cosmos and the imagination of gods. Focussing on Skarl, his beat may be considered as an example of either the time of *Chronos* ("regularly measured clock time") or of the *Aeon* ("a time like that of an infinitive", "a becoming that is unfixed and non-pulsed, unfolding in no specifiable direction and in relation to no clear coordinates") as distinguished by Deleuze and Guattari,[xxiii] dependant upon whether it is heard by the gods themselves or by humans, as time is said to be experienced differently for both. Here, operating on a cosmic scale, it may be impossible for human beings to discern the sound of Skarl's drum at all, as the space between each pulse may last for millennia. We would then perhaps perceive Skarl's drumming as the time of *Aeon* because these pulses are disconnected sounds, or we may in fact remain unaware of their existence as they form the ambient sound of the universe itself – for, as Paul Fraisse argues, once a pulse becomes too slow, we interpret it as disconnected sounds.[xxiv] For Dunsany's gods, however, to whom such cosmic music operates within their infinitive time frame, Skarl's drumming would be heard as the pulsed time of *Chronos*. Given Fraisse's assertions that a pulse heard at sufficiently quick speed becomes a drone,[xxv] perhaps, to the Gods of Pegāna, the beat of Skarl's drum places drone music at the heart of the universe.

Focussed on the taut skin of Skarl's drum, where each slight fluctuation above or below the centre point marked by the rim of this celestial percussion, everything is condensed to these regular movements of compressed air: not rhythm at all but merely a near endless ripple of vibration stretched across expanses of time.

The sound placating the Urdeity of this particular Weird pantheon is that of hum, of monopitch, of drone.

Perhaps the closest Earthly musicians have come to replicating this sound is the music of Bong, a drone-metal act from Newcastle, UK. The epithet "minimalist/maximalist", often applied to Bong, is helpful in describing their sound: minimal in composition, but played at maximum, all-encompassing volume.

Making direct reference to Dunsany's work on many occasions throughout their oeuvre, Bong invites their listeners to use such fiction as a literary analogue. Their third full-length studio album *Beyond Ancient Space* (2011), for example, features excerpts from paintings by Sidney Sime who worked closely with Lord Dunsany to depict the latter's characters, alongside lyrical references to Dunsany's *A Dreamer's Tales* (1910), while the title and lyrics of their fourth studio album *Mana-Yood-Sushai* clearly reference *The Gods of Pegāna*.

At the core of Bong's sound is the huge, swirling guitar-work of Mike Vest, achieved through vintage amplifiers, distortion pedals and delay effects. Essential to the experience of hearing Bong, especially live, is the particular sense of movement and momentum that they achieve: of riding smoothly along desert dunes or softly tumbling through the mind-altering desolation of deep space. So oppressive is the weight of Vest's guitar that the listener feels almost literally pushed along with the air forced out by the amplifier's speakers. Hearing Bong is to be caught in the colossal rippling shockwave of a single, near-endless beat from Skarl's cosmological tattoo.

Bong's regular use of a drummer, unlike contemporaries such as Sunn O))), emphasises this effect using straight-forward, steady rhythm, often at double-time to the slow speed of the guitar. The question is, in what direction is the listener moved? Perhaps, as a concert attendee, thrust inexorably backwards from the stage, away from the band's array of amplification? Vertiginously upwards towards the heavens describing a trajectory of spiritual enlightenment? Or katabatically down into maddening chasms of unspeakable tentacled creatures? This remains, of course, highly subjective.

Ultimately I see Dunsany's demigod Skarl, the rhythm-deity who beats our reality Weirdly alive, as the perfect illustration of drone music as both a sonic representation and enabler of the Weird threshold between the mundane world and that of the spirit. By hearing an approximation of sounds from across the universe we are hearing the drumming of Skarl, skewed into immeasurability by cosmic expanses of time – an image of the Weird membrane itself. By becoming enraptured by such all-absorbing sound, we can even be transported 'elsewhere', into the ecstatic world and enabling an actual encounter with the true Weird itself.

Black One; or, First Flesh of Darkness
By   Jean   Moon

I

Enter PRIMARY MURMUR

    Deepthroat caverock hum

    Boulder-gaping sound

II

Enter GLOOM AXE

    Cracklecripple along

    An Orthodox Caveman

    In an ossuary cavern

    Tortured bodybranches

    Ribcage spokes and runnels

III

Enter VOMIT-SHRIEK,

    Clutching *musette de cor*

    In spider phalanges

    Voideep dirge

    And heartsbloodbeat

    Vital,   evil-voiced   thing

V

Enter TREMOLO

    vinylrunnels

    Goregrin teethkeys

VI

Enter BOILEDBLOODBELL

    Empty cheeks blow low

    Spectral spiritkingdom

    Moan of woe,

Boneband creaks out the
marrow of song

IV

Enter BOILEDBLOODBELL

    La Danse Macabre

    Pegāna

    blakkr einn Bjalla

Cold-sick note of lazy disease
Sustained——
Skarl, defleshed.
Cowled figures of darkness
coalesce

svart pitch of reality

The "flawless misshapen menace" of *Black One*...

Sunn O))) *Black One* (Southern Lord 2005)
Live: Phurpa, Sunn O))) – (18/8/2015) Royal Festival Hall, London.

Drone has primal origins. The bombus of wind whirling through deep mountainside caves. The susurrus of a great river tipping water gallons endlessly over its fall. Our Neanderthal ancestors blowing long high murmurations through bear femur flutes to bond their group together. Aboriginal men underpinning ceremonies by sustaining endless tremulous notes through hardwood aerophone.

Reflecting such origins in its aesthetics and sonics, iconic act Sunn O))) from Seattle, U.S., needs no introduction in drone music. Through the anonymous hooded cowls worn onstage, the megalithic arrangement of their multiple vintage amplifiers, and the deceptively-primitive vocal styles often utilised, Sunn O))) strongly evokes mankind's pagan origins. As key instigators of the drone metal sub-genre, they have helped redefine both heavy metal and drone itself.

Black One, the act's tribute to and working through of their black metal influences[xxvi] and easily Sunn O)))'s darkest album, is the release on which their unique forms of drone metal is most notably Weird. Various stories relating to its recording have become mythical Weird Tales unto themselves. Locking claustrophobic vocalist Malefic – of black metal/acoustic act Xasthur, a name partly taken from the Simon

Necronomicon[xxvii] – in a casket, and inside a Cadillac hearse, to record vocals for 'Báthory Erzsébet', thusly echoes the fate of the track's titular figure, locked in her own castle for her alleged brutal crimes.

The Bathory myth certainly accrues Weird kudos, but it's with another tale that I most associate *Black One*. In 'The Black Stone', one of Robert E. Howard's additions to Lovecraft's 'Cthulhu' mythos, the anonymous narrator, upon reading Friedrick von Juntz's *The Black Book*, learns of a strange monolith located on an ancient battlefield, and, upon tracking it down, hears the following:

> "A thin night wind [that] started up among the branches of the firs, with an uncanny suggestion of faint, unseen pipes

233

whispering an odd and eerie tune. The monotony of the sound produced a sort of self-hypnosis upon me; I grew drowsy. I fought this feeling, but sleep stole on me in spite of myself; the monolith seemed to sway and dance, strangely distorted to my gaze, and then I slept."[xxviii]

With this uncanny monolith featuring hypnotic properties, Howard offers another fictional image of Weirdrone. A more fantastic interpretation would stress the similarities between megalithic structures such as the standing stones of Avebury, Stonehenge and Orkney; whereas, in the context of science fiction, the mysterious alien monolith central to Arthur C. Clarke's *2001: A Space Odyssey* will rise inevitably to mind; yet its true origins amongst Lovecraft's primordial, interstellar gods transpire to be even older and far stranger. It is the monolith's monotonous sound and subsequent process of hypnosis and drowsiness – its drone music – with which we are most interested here. Not only does Howard unwittingly offer a primal/cosmic image of drone but his story provides a very literal depiction of Weird ecstasy resulting from it. Upon opening his eyes, the story's narrator sees a "crowd of strange people", some naked, some clad in furs, beating upon black drums, "flinging their arms in unison and weaving their bodies rhythmically", all as a direct result of the black stone's monotonous sound.[xxix] Following the music, the dancing becomes more and more "bestial and obscene", until the episode reaches a climax with the sacrifice of a human child upon the monolith, paying tribute to the "huge monstrous toad-like Thing" that eventually emerges.[xxx] It is finally revealed that the stone is in fact that spire of a buried castle, identified by Weird scholar Chris Jarocha-Ernst as probably Xuthltan, a location found in other Cthulhu mythos stories, thus suggesting the toad creature to be Koth, a mysterious god referenced variously in stories by Lovecraft and Howard.[xxxi] It is interesting to note the similarities between the name of the band Xasthur and this location Xuthltan, although it may be a coincidence of grammatical patterns connoting strangeness and obscurity that are staples of Weird fiction. In this manner, therefore, alongside Dunsany and Skarl, Howard's 'The Black Stone' provides another mythopoeic source from which images of Weirdrone ecstasy can be derived; and the music of Sunn O))) is probably the most suitable really-existing sonic analogue to Howard's monolith.

The lyrics to *Black One* help identify Sunn O))) and similar types of drone as instigator of The Weird portal, and representative of that which emerges from beyond. As evoked on the inside cover of *Black One*:

> "Something comes, something that you should never have known calls [...] the gateway to the infinite hunger opens, the eternal swarms that darken darkness beckon with their flawless misshapen menace"[xxxii]

Following this, one of Coggins's research participants describes their experiences of seeing Sunn O))) live, commenting that, due to the physical experience of such loud, overwhelming sound,

> "they certainly make yourself mind your body. You can't feel more alive than when you're feeling your body shaking and your blood pumping through your veins"[xxxiii]

They go on to suggest that this experience "with all of the low resonating things through the vibrations", is almost like pain, which "you can't ignore",[xxxiv] and that this sensation probably "awakens things"[xxxv] – and these descriptions again potentially reiterate Machen's close association of ecstasy and terror.

Following the clear parallels between 'The Black Stone' and the music and mythology of Sunn O))), it is easy to imagine the elongated tubular bell and gong tolls of 'Báthory Erzsébet' as Howard's "uncanny suggestion of faint, unseen pipes", with the gathered black-clad masses and hooded performers as the cultists (albeit with slower, less frenzied dancing), clawed hands raised, worshipping at the black amp shrine to the great toad-god, and chanting the sacred name: Koth! (Sunn!) Koth! (Sunn!)

OCCULT WEIRDRONE

Prøfan, *Tales From The Sabbath Of Equilibrium* **(Perpetuam 2006)** Already presented in the form of tales, this release from Portugese act Prøfan features two long instrumental compositions lasting approximately twenty-minutes each, and – prompted by its title as well as that of their 2008 release *Shamanic Invocations* – is straightforward to place within the ritual ambient sub-genre. The cover depicts a stark greyscale image of a forest, the deep black behind the foreground trees suggesting impenetrable depth.

Again, suggested by its title, the first track 'Goat's Sabbath' clearly evokes a familiar scenario of a Witches' Sabbath and/or tribute to Baphomet, which we can assume to occur in the stark woodland of the cover. Beginning with a distorted tritone guitar riff, Prøfan evoke classic sounds of evil that can be traced back to Black Sabbath's famous eponymous track, this time complimented by a swirling, wind-like electronic wash of mild noise. Amidst this Gothic horror scenario, the whirling becomes at points almost science fictional, as if a B-movie spacecraft incongruously interrupts the Black Mass, or a helicopter takes off in a neighbouring field. With the guitar riff stuttering, breaking up, then resuming, the background static howls reach their peaks at the front of the sound: a deep, electronic roil perhaps suggesting the Sabbatic Goat himself, yet not quite manifesting. The steady chugging guitar is eventually completely overwhelmed in the chaotic maelstrom, adding an extra layer of dirty feedback to this nascent nefarious sonic manifestation.

Eventually, an urgent tapping like birds beaks on metal, perhaps implying some primal form of communication, offers a noticeable contrast, suggesting rhythm and coldness amongst the monotonous guitar warmth. The guitar threatens to coalesce into a riff, becoming

more rhythmic but never regular, and alternating the bounce of low power chords with sharp chordal picking and long sustained notes. Metallic tapping continues in stereo, crossing from one side to the other now, like drummers placed either side of a circle of robed adepts gathered around a fire, gradually increasing in pace and urgency. The eddying guitars – formless, shapeless – gradually coalesce into a rising demonic shape in the middle of the fire: huge dramatic chords that stand out as more concrete than the rest, and suggest a materialisation at last (*Osculum infame*), while the guitar traces gradually fade into the depths of the forest along with the black apparition, horned head receding into shadow.

In contrast, second track 'Cathedral of Equilibrium' begins with a notably different feel: a simple proto-industrial guitar riff that churns with robotic repetition for only a few bars before dropping into a long all-absorbing noise abyss, with distorted guitar just audible low in the mix. It's very electronic, the low hum of appliances, shifting and almost breaking up, followed a shift back to guitar, this time slightly more prominent but still providing noisemurmur in background: like the endless, rhythm-free turbulence of classic Sunn O))). Fluctuations monotone in speed and time; gradual disassociation into ambience; the resurgence of ominous synth patterns—bewilderingly broken by a booming deep drum duo, re-establishing the ritual quality of the album, accompanied by tight snare skin taps at different pitches, or the twang of taut strings, sudden, short sharp releases and immediate reconstitution of tension. Now in a space of deep hypnotism, but broken again by bass drums, ensuring total unconsciousness is impossible.

Eventually, we drop to clean guitar riff with flanger; reverb heavy distorted guitar low in the mix, in great booming swells. Five. Huge. Tremulous. Power. Chords: a relief after so much monotonous repetition and ambient tension. Single bass-drum hit, wide reverb, left to recede… shivering...chord b r e a k s

The Closing of the Circle.

A Record From Maithunass by Joseph S. Norman

I should make it clear from the outset that the following is less of a story and more an account of the events that provided the impetus for this research project, laying out the proceedings as clearly as I am able, given the significant distressing changes to my health that followed.

I discovered the work of Maithunass in November 2014 whilst trawling through *Ebay* and *Discogs* in pursuit of a record by an entirely different artist (probably Phurpa). As far as I can recall it was the somewhat lurid cover – featuring sacred geometry, anus-flowers, and a kind of winged Bosch-esque phallus-creature – to one of Maithunass's

early works, *The Principles and Philosophies of Ur-Sonorpasm in Sex Magick* (Phallucifer 2013), recorded under the moniker Kuntalini, popping up in a *Discogs* recommendation, which first drew me to his music. Eventually I tracked down a copy for myself and soon realised that, despite the cover, this work has to be one of the most conceptually complex drone works ever created (the booklet is 100 pages long with very small type, and includes an extensive bibliography) yet musically seemingly one of the simplest. I have not the space to begin outlining Maithunass's philosophies here, but he has made them available online if you know where to look.[xxxvi] As for the record itself, the most startling sounds on this two-hour-long piece were apparently created by slowing down audio excerpts from hardcore pornography, combined with loops made from instruments including hammered dulcimer and glass harmonica, and wildly ecstatic ritual chanting – some of which Maithunass claims to have sourced from his time spent with Aleister Crowley.[xxxvii]

But it is a later recording from Maithunass that most affected me. I am very fortunate in that I seem to be one of the few people outside his cult-like inner circle (known as the 'Karezza') to whom Maithunass has opened up about his music and ideas. I found his email –

an archaic Demon address – on the short-lived Kuntalini *Metal-Archives* page, fired off some questions, and assumed I'd never hear anything back, especially as the page became unavailable soon after (presumably for not being metal enough!). Maithunass's reply, when it did arrive two days later, managed to be laconic, obscure and intriguing all at once. While I have no doubt that Maithunass is a man utterly convinced of the efficacy of occult practice, he seems from our conversations to be clearly an egotist, a braggart and, if not a liar, then a weaver of somewhat elevated tales.[xxxviii] Nevertheless, many of my ice-breaker questions he'd answered clearly enough. The name Maithunass, presumably a reference to 'Maithuna' or 'sacred union' for ritual purposes in Tantra, is a "satiric inversion of the traditional [sic.]", an attempt to "pervert sanctimonious spiritual values".[xxxix] No, he probably won't ever play live because he cannot control "the various auras dispersed by feckless, untrained denizens of mundane reality".[xl] He has "no musical influences" save for the "sounds of animals fucking and dying",[xli] and doesn't listen to modern artists. He utilises certain forms of drone music (especially those made from field recordings, for example) in his ritual practice because "sustained deep vibrations can simulate the mental priapism, death ejakulation of the soul, the noösphallus, the *Maithunam dravram* [sic.]", which is central to his philosophy.[xlii] This surprise reply spearheaded a chain of emails over the next month. Our final exchange to date was especially noteworthy because, embedded within a question about specific magickal influences that had solicited a very long reply, Maithunass included a .jpeg; yet the file was either not attached properly or had become corrupted, because I initially could not open it, and his text response was full of gibberish and random characters. While this was strange, I had largely forgotten about it because Maithunass had promised to send me an exclusive copy of his latest recording.

In July 2015, a 12" flopped onto my doormat, the sound breaking my quiet reverie. I had corresponded with Maithunass some fortnight ago and eagerly awaited receipt of the recording. He had explained to me that he'd made one 15-minute drone recording off in the woods somewhere south of France. While reluctant to divulge many details, he did – after much flattery and coaxing – eventually mention that he'd used nothing more than "a Tascam 8-track and some field microphones", "a special concoction of a rare strain of Psilocybin", and "the very closest and most trusted of the Karezza, those whose *kias* vibrate in harmony with my own." He also warned that this recording could "provide consciousness reconfiguration", and that I should "be selective as to those whom you pass on its wisdom."[xliii]

The 12" was essentially black, at least that's how it looked at first. Black sleeve, white dustjacket, black vinyl. Not so much a sticker in sight. Having dusted the needle and the grooves, I cranked up the record whilst making a pot of tea. I remember clearly that it was a bright Autumn day, and the subdued sun set the skeletal trees with a cozy peach sheen. As the kettle boiled, my mind drifted, momentarily forgetting about the recording which was clearly one with a long, slow introduction that built up from nothing. Eventually I had found a program that would open the image that Maithunass sent to me. Despite the low resolution – pixelated, monochrome, sketchy – the image seemed possibly of a figure, probably male, sitting alone in a dark room, surrounded by weapons, skulls and typical black metal paraphernalia. A promo shot, surely, and a cheesy one at that, one that would make Fenriz shake his head ruefully. But for some reason I remember that I couldn't get the picture from my mind, as if another image was buried within, like a watermark or a Magic Eye picture.

Gradually the water began to boil, water bubbling, so I poured the frothing green phosphorescent scales into the mug. Unusually for such an occult-driven artist, Maithunass didn't include esoteric symbols with his recordings, even in Kuntalini, either borrowed or of his own design – an anomaly I had pointed out to him. His answer was characteristically abstract. "Because I am profoundly disinterested in the surface of things," he'd said,

"because I am the revealer of that which lies deep [sic.]." It occurred to me – a harsh whirr like a drill cutting concrete, boiling water flowing lava patterns and red bloodlets over my raw, useless digits – that I knew what he meant because I could actually start to imagine the symbol he would inevitably use.

The kettle dropped, hit my foot, and a geyser of fire splattered rivulets of pain all over my legs, bare in the summer heat. In that moment, amidst that terrible vibrant madness…a skyline texture of fractal cracks as the funerary urn of the world split apart…incredulous, blabbering machines as of a forehead pincered by electroshock forcing out the gibberish of honest insanity… hum—the hum of the inner head, alone in the abysmal quiet of night, the teem of blood pumping thick, heated gouts through the hypnagogic mind, the burning ache, the honey and the voiding of the void, an expulsion of deep cosmic debris and dust motes…endless palpitation…

At some point, I was aware that I lay on the floor, my eyes open yet unfocussed. Eventually, the blur moved from abstraction to form, and the line of the bottom of the kitchen cupboard coalesced in my vision. I recall that this solid geometry was reassuringly rational. There was an entire ecosystem under there: a microcosm of mould. Back on my feet again, there were no burns on my body and my tea – somehow perfectly made on the sideboard –

was stone cold. The record needle was gently click-flapping at the deadspace of the final groove.

The above account is the closest I can come to explaining my experience in words; and I hope it provides some indication of my impetus to conduct research into the Weird and ecstatic properties of drone music. Even now, whenever I recall that afternoon, many months after the incident, there are certain words and phrases that stick in my mind, and which reoccur like automatic writing: many of these you will find above. The whole event, from picking up the record to awakening, lasted approximately 3 hours and 45 minutes, as far as I am able to reconstruct. I had not consumed any intoxicants that day, and no more than one bottle of *Hobgoblin* the previous night. As far as I am aware, my health was excellent prior to the event. There are still substantial portions of this time unaccounted for. It should be noted that, upon returning home, my partner found me in a state of considerable confusion and upset. She maintains that my speech was jumbled and featured nonsense words, having initially wondered whether I had suffered a stroke. My doctor recently diagnosed me with an unusual form of tinnitus, which is mostly the standard, maddening high-pitched flat-line, but I swear sometimes distorts and contains unintelligible muttered words deep within. It shames me somewhat to admit, yet I should for the sake of record, that at some stage during the blackout period it became clear that I had ejaculated whilst fully clothed, an occurrence that I cannot ever recall experiencing previously, even as a teenager. I have been able to find little information about the record online (bar a copy on *Discogs* that quickly vanished along with its seller). Maithunass appears to have been inactive, and remains unresponsive, for many months now. While not prone to superstition, I have not sold the record on, and I cannot bring myself to listen to it for a second time.

AGRARIAN/FOLK WEIRDRONE

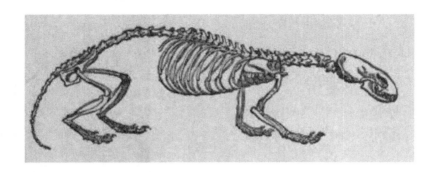

From The Bogs of Aughiska, *Roots Of This Earth Within My Blood*, Human Jigsaw (2013)
Live: Aluk Todolo, From The Bogs Of Augishka, Mortichnia – Corsica Studios, London; 09/11/2016
Live: Ian Sinclair, Eddie Lenihan, Café Otto; 06/12/2016

It's difficult to imagine a stronger or more explicit declaration of national and pagan origins that the title of From the Bogs of Augishka's second album, *Roots of this Earth within my Blood*. Formed in County Clare, Western Ireland, in 2009, and drawing their name from a townland in the area, From The Bogs Of Aughiska create unusual dark-ambient-drone steeped in the history and heritage of their nation. Their promotional shots include the suitably-named founding member Conchur O'Drona, clad in black hooded top, stood facing the County Clare region's famously dramatic

Cliffs of Moher, while their music regularly features field recordings from the natural world. In an interview for the *Metal Ireland* website Conchur explained that "I started the project as I wanted to express musically what its [sic.] like to grow up in the West of Ireland."[xliv] Clearly, judging by the dark thematic content of his band's music, part of growing up in the region involved developing a sensibility for the Weirder aspects of Ireland's history, especially its myth and folklore, which the album's second track 'An Seanchaí' explores in a very explicit manner.

Having begun with 'Aughiska Mor' – the sound of running water and bird-song establishing a forest setting, alongside murky, distorted guitar chords and harsh, scratchy melodies – *Roots Of This Earth Within My Blood* then segues into the voice of famous Irish storyteller (*shanachie*) Edmund Lenihan telling a brief narrative of folk horror:

"You do a weasel wrong, an old man told me, do a weasel wrong – especially if you make the mistake of killing a weasel – then you're in trouble. Because brothers, sisters, family – they'll come for you, and they'll come for you when you least expect it […] in bed in the dark of the night. […] The weasel will come through a small space, down the chimney, and by God he'll of course make for—*wraaw!*—he'll make for your throat. Found in the morning with an axe in your throat…That's it."

So Lenihan's gruesome and strange stories form something like traditional Weird tales already imbedded within the album. Drawing on the various myths relating to weasels in Irish folklore, Lenihan's tale becomes Weird rather than merely weird by some of the ambiguities suggested in his telling. Is Lenihan implying that the weasel will enact its retaliation not just on the perpetrator but also upon their family? Or is he in fact suggesting that the weasel acts *through* the perpetrator's family, forcing one of them into manslaughter? It is these strange and tenebrous qualities of Lenihan's tale, as much as the implied supernatural and explicit horror, which makes it unsettling, uncertain, and therefore Weird.

What Lenihan is describing here is an attack by faeries, though this is perhaps not obvious to those unfamiliar with the nuances of Irish faerie lore. "You wouldn't want to mess with the Irish faeries," Lenihan asserts, "they're not like the little Disney, you know, pretty little faeries. You mess with the Irish faeries you'll end up dead." Lenihan describes faerie victims who "died in stages," with hair, teeth, and toenails gradually falling out.

Lenihan follows this story with a monologue on his practice as a story-teller – a kind of meta-tale. Seeming to relax a little following the weasel story, which is told with breathless excitement, Lenihan's speech becomes more regular and controlled as he coolly rationalises the process of gathering stories he has practiced for thirty-three years. While emphasising his natural scepticism upon hearing stories depicting supernatural events, Lenihan is particuarly interested in individuals who genuinely believe the stories they recount; once convinced of the teller's belief, he performs further research. "If I get the notion that this happened in a particular place," he explains, "then I want to see that place." "Things are really remarkable," Lenihan explains, "when the stories come true." It is one of the Weirdest moments on the album, when this seemingly trustworthy and rational person espouses his belief in the literal truth of faerie folk tales, almost causing the listener to consider Lenihen himself as a victim of faerie possession, spreading fear and developing awe for his kind.

Such storytelling is often at the heart of From The Bogs of Aughiska's music. Their eponymous 2010 E.P., for example, also features Lenihan's storytelling, whilst 2016 E.P. *Fenian Ram* includes a reworking of 'The Ballad of John P Holland', a traditional song about the life of the titular figure who invented the submarine. While most drone can be said to include a narrative in one sense, achieved through the shifting timbres of the music, it is relatively rare to find acts including such linguistic tales in such a manner.

Perhaps this particular combination of storytelling and music contributes toward certain experiences reported by Conchur to have occurred whilst onstage with his band, as well as amongst the band's audience:

> with the music we play I kind of go into a trance. It's kinda weird but we've had a few gigs where people are kinda collapsing out front, people just fall down. It might be the drink or it might be the vibrations as we use very heavy subbasses. We've had it many time when people are like 'We transcended listening to your music, we were hallucinating, we weren't even pissed or we weren't even on drugs, we were just seeing shit that wasn't there.' That's the whole point.[xlv]

Here the experiences Conchur describes provide further examples of the 'elsewheres' reported by Coggins in his PhD research.

If Lenihan's Weird faerie tale on 'An Seanchai' holds the listener's attention in a space of rapt unsettlement scored by quietly brooding synth surges, then the following track 'Hell Complex' – named after a famous system of caves in Doolin, County Clare – bursts through in a fury commensurate with its infernal name. Featuring guest vocals by Mories from U.S. apocalyptic drone act Gnaw Their Tongues, viciously rasping a somewhat surprisingly chosen paragraph detailing the process of entering the submerged caves, which seems to have been taken from a travelguide. Never has the command "head directly to Sian and Sarah Tea shop Entrance [sic.]", here, rendered almost unintelligible, sounded so terrifying.[xlvi]As if their sinister name was not enough, the

Hell Complex caves accrue further resonance with fantastic literature through their association with the work of J.R.R. Tolkien, who is rumoured to have named his famous character Sméagol/Golem after the 'Pole na Gollum' (or 'cave of the rock dove') in the same region,[xlvii]while later tracks reference the Celtic/pagan festivals of Beltine and Samhain. The climax of the album occurs in the title track where the band achieve the style and intensity of black metal for the first time, with guest vocals from Chris Naughton of UK 'heritage' black metal band Winterfylleth. The introduction of such a startlingly fast and intense section amidst the slow undulation of synth is a jolt to the system, especially for those accustomed to acts such as the aforementioned Gnaw Their Tongues, where tracks can seem like the introduction to a black metal track that ultimately never arrives. Shockingly visceral in its pummelling monotony, the overall effect of From The Bogs of Aughiska's black metal fury is like the rupturing of that membrane between normality and the Weird space beyond, and, in the words of Erik Danielsson, reaching the "vast darkness, to that which lies beyond", the opening of a gateway to that "terrible and wondrous place that lies outside the borders of the world."[xlviii]

Back in the mundane world, the title of the final track on *Roots of this Earth Within my Blood*, 'Conversatio Morum', refers to the vows taken by Benedictine monks, while the track itself is built around a sample of Gregorian chant that becomes increasingly broken and distorted – culminating the album perhaps in a sonic reminder and desecration of Ireland's thorny religious heritage.

Like something risen from the murky depths described in their name, From The Bogs Of Aughiska have emerged as a project that embraces the generic hybridity and unsettling storytelling of The Weird.

Dronespace by John Omenrasp

(((EX-122: online, 25/11/2568)))

B1950; C54; 101, 555, 000.

(Terra: 250:L+) Rimmon Cluster

99,7647.56 M^R

The Bubbleship was Beatrice's world. Out here, light-years away from other human beings, the day-to-day sounds of the small craft were the safety barriers at the cliffs of insanity. The gentle whine of the processor, the sharp blips of electronics, the carefully-detached speech of the AI pilot. All of which she felt she understood, were part of her own head.

When she flipped the Bubble to full transparency, something she did more frequently of late, as they came closer to their goal, Beatrice liked to imagine that she was out in the depths of the ocean, rather than the backwaters of deepspace. At least under the sea there was variation, life. Here the void was disorienting in its featureless monotony. Now, there was just her, the Bubbleship, the endless politeness of its artificial personality, and the cavernous, maddening dark. But she had a purpose, a mission to justify such an act of self-immolation. Yes, she'd seen the supernova of the Acteren-S4 cluster – great ejaculations of kaleidoscopic flame. She'd navigated through asteroid fields and whipped through the Hoop Caves of Zyr, nature's racetrack. She'd burned through the solar system's gamut of sensory pleasures, throughout her artificially-extended life, like a junkie whose glands no longer fire except at the pinnacle of overdose. But, following the report of the deepest-space probe to ever return safely, there was one sound, a kind of interstellar fairytale, that she alone would make sacrifices to hear.

The Rimmon Cluster; or, as it was known colloquially, God's sine wave.

It had taken her not a lifetime and not a lifetime of lifetimes, but a period of time longer than the entire timeline of the *homo sapiens* species, several times over, to reach a position close enough to conceivably try to hear it. On the occasions when she awoke from cryosleep, the Bubble had answered as many of her questions as it could. Yes, she was still alive. No, she was not dreaming. Oh, Beatrice, I'm so sorry. Your Sun has gone.

Each time upon waking – once she had shaken the horrendous nausea, worse than the worst of tropical fevers, the heavy vertigo, and the bouts of near-suicidal existential anguish, tempered blissfully by the Bubble – Beatrice cleared her head enough to contemplate the prospect of hearing Rimmon. A man she had known crudely described it as 'Yahweh's ass-trumpet', or something like that. She'd repeated that joke to the ship but received only the start of a lecture on the Iron Age kingdoms of Israel and Judah in response, before politely cutting it off. Gradually, over the years, her periods of consciousness became more bearable as the space-time ripples became apparent. The low-level vibration in the Bubble, which had for decades been regular and of little consequence, was now clearly becoming more intense and irregular. The ship monitored its rise, of course, and updated her whenever she   asked.

"Since your last period of awakening we have travelled approximately fifty parsecs, not counting minor adjustments that should be considered given that this particular star system is—"

"Fine. How much longer?"

"I'm pleased to tell you, Beatrice, that soon your wait may be over."

"So you're saying it's back in the fucking coffin, right?"

"Yes, Beatrice. I'm afraid further cryosleep is a necessity."

*

Eventually, after more maddening bouts of space-sickness where Beatrice thought she would have to die – and tried to, running head-first at the walls, before Bubble stopped her – she awoke and knew from the constant shuddering of the ship that they   had   arrived.

"Adjust for static…more, more, a touch mo—damn!"

Beatrice's world was transformed. First it came in long, drawn-out shivers – through the floor, the desk, the walls, and into her boots, her hands. The screen was black, even with transparency on. But she couldn't help imagining silvery waves shimmering toward her, mirroring the sound. It was a rumble that seemed to come from within and without, a kind of hunger in the gut, a sonic starvation.

"Try it with the Penton about 76-Z/81-Y?"

"Of course, Beatrice."

Soon it was necessary for Beatrice to change into her modified suit, which monitored all of her body's functions and stabilised her artificially. The thickness and complexity of the Bubbleship, several onion-skin layers of aluminium, carbon fibre and nanotubes, was scarcely needed until this moment. Which was much the same with Beatrice and the skin-tight suits she had worn for most of her prolonged lifespan. At this stage though, when the Bubble was starting to pick up concentric waves from Rimmon, the effect on both bodies was significant.

The hum was abstract. Barely a sound at all, more like being rubbed across the body. There was a warmth, a redness, like bloodlight through half-closed eyes. The amorphous dream-thoughts, deep into the night, made audible. Every time the thrumming increased in vibrational speed, something more like the shape of a note, a word, a voice, but never manifesting. The drones seemed to compete, one located spatially above the other on a graph in the mind. With full transparency on, it scarcely mattered whether her eyes were open or closed.

Beatrice had swum with dolphins, many many years ago. The close proximity of the sensually streamed creatures had made her feel lithe, less solid somehow, like melted wax. Now, encapsulated by atomglass and the sheer weight of the cosmos, she felt the same. Weightless, even under false gravity, wrapped in a womb of sound, a reverberating in the fluctuating vibrations of a perfect brass bell.

Suddenly she became aware of her vision again. The window was still black. But, no, there was something out there. Something white, with little lights emerging, developing into complex fractal patterns.

"Alex," she managed to say.

"Are the sounds pleasant, Beatrice?"

"What is that…thing out there?"

"There's nothing out there for over 77 light years, Beatrice. This is effectively deadspace. What do you think you see?"

"A light, a flame, a halo space – textures. Trenches of salamanders! Melodra—"

"Beatrice, what are you saying?"

"—breezy days, Mumma, and God made dirt and dirt won't hurt…"

The void was whistling now, endless pure streams of sweet, sharp notes and faint gurgling patterns from the immediate left-hand side of the Bubble or the left-hand side of her head or maybe left was up and right was down and now she is the bell, clapper clanging violent internal shockwaves…

Cracks shivered out across the hull of the Bubble like a perfect breakfast egg or a golf-ball shattered by impact, beating regular tattoos through the walls that shot sharp pain-waves through Beatrice's body deep into her bones her marrow her organs her skull a deathly heartburn now fire-flashes in the eyes solar-lights inside tearing shocks and quivering nerve patterns along her limbs and glorious numbness as a voice contorted into flabbing lip stutters and excruciating electronic grash gurgle skree hiss schrix xxxsschxschxxschxxxschsssxchseex xx and no more but back to her head for a moment of such unexpected clarity as Beatrice saw out into the galaxies clustered into a nervous system of sparkling lights of such sublime intensity that she watched tears float from her eyes and then her own feet fly free in a majestic splatter of red mist mingling with the stars and seeming to coalesce into concentric ripples fanning forever out from a central mass…

(((EX-122: offline, 03/7/4660)))

INTERSTELLAR WEIRDRONE

Lustmord, *Dark Matter* (Touch Music 2016) U.K.

In space no one can hear you scream reads the famous tag-line to *Alien* (Scott 1979), yet it is not quite the case that outer space is entirely silent, as drone ambient pioneer Lustmord explores on his latest release. As Lustmord explains, sound

> "exists in space as naturally occurring electromagnetic vibrations, many well within the range of human hearing while others exist at different regions of the electromagnetic spectrum and these can be adjusted with software to bring them within our audio range."[xlix]

Dark Matter features treated recordings originating from archives of cosmological audio collected by NASA, The Very Large Array, The National Radio Astronomy Observatory, amongst others. Given the necessity of bringing the sounds within the range of human hearing, and presumably a degree of artistic manipulation, *Dark Matter* does not quite provide raw field recordings from outer space in the same manner as those made in caves, woods, and other natural terrestrial locations. Such a feat is unfortunately probably impossible, yet, with *Dark Matter*, Lustmord combines sounds with both awesome and terrifying qualities to capture what Lovecraft called the "hidden and fathomless worlds of strange life which may pulsate in the gulfs beyond the stars".[1]

Saturn Form Essence, *Alpha & Proxima/Signals* (Weakie Discs, 2015) Ukraine

Saturn Form Essence, who create drone ambient music heavily inspired by various aspects of outer space, proudly use only "100% analogue" technology, despite – or perhaps in response to – their subject matter. It is encouraging and impressive, therefore, that *Alpha & Proxima/Signals*, a cassette release compiling four EPs originally released during 2014 and 2015, sounds in parts not dissimilar to the 'authentic' sounds of Lustmord's *Dark Matter*. Using "tube amplifiers, guitars, bass, duophonic keyboards, microphones, reel-to-reel audio tape recorders, various Soviet radio equipment and other unknown and strange stuff", with no "fucking PC programs/effects",[li] *Saturn Form Essence* produce sounds representing the voices of Alpha and Proxima Centauri, respectively the nearest star and star system to our Solar System. As with Lustmord, there is the background rumble, deep and low, not so much heard as felt in the gut, frequently complimented by higher, shimmering metallic movements like huge singing bowls.

On later tracks, the universe crackles, with the small blips and pings of a submarine's active sonar: the echo of acoustic location signalling a target. A sprinkling of tap-drip sound-beads; more distinct bass notes playing ominous patterns in something like a minor key. Sometimes the waves fluctuate, a woozy sensation like free-fall nausea, or seismic undulations: a god pulling gravity's strings.

As with *Black One*, the recordings are completely free from rhythm; furthermore there are seldom any changes in timbre or instrumentation dramatic enough to easily distinguish between tracks: *Alpha Proxima/Signals* seems in that sense a very pure drone recording.

It evokes impressions of the movement of Saturn's rings, or maybe potentially utopian images from the flight of nanoships which will one day be sent to investigate Proxima Centauri B, an Earth-sized Exoplanet in the nearby habitable zone, paving the way for the expansion of human life throughout the galaxy.

Aymrev Erkroz Prevre, *Noir Voyage Obstrué De Rencontres Difformes*, (Infernal Commando Records, 2006) France

If Saturn Form Essence travels into the deep recesses of our galaxy then Aymrev Erkroz Prevre strike out beyond, into further, Weirder vastnesses. The cover image of *Noir Voyage Obstrué De Rencontres Difformes* features a version of H.R. Giger's 'Mordor VI' (1976), inviting us to interpret the music contained within through the lens of the late Swiss artist's 'biomechanical' work, where humans and machines are seamlessly and nightmarishly combined. The artwork bears little obvious relation to *The Lord of the Rings* (1954-55), as suggested by its title, and Giger was said to have chosen it purely because he liked the name, presumably draw to its evil connotations.[lii]

As suggested to some extent by the Giger artwork accompanying it, this album clearly moves away from the more rural/agrarian strains of Weirdrone practiced by From the Bogs of Aughiska, and towards the sound of alien, urban, industrialised environments. Yet *Voyage Obstrué De Rencontres Difformes* is a 'quiet' album in that the listener is required to pay close attention in order to actually discern its content: there is no wall of distorted guitar, no pulsing of synth, in fact no melody

or harmony at all, no rhythm, and no vocals. The tracks are untitled because they evoke things and places too strange for a name. The album's title translates (badly) from French as 'Black Travel Obstructed from Different Encounters', and listening to its early sections is to hear the background hiss of black/white noise, uncertain if it's part of the track or in fact merely the background sounds of your headphones and the turning of the cassette itself.

After repeat listens, the sonic landscape eventually takes a clearer form. It is a journey through the biomechanical territory of Giger's imagination, located either extra-terrestrially or in a dystopian vision of Earth's future. Traversing this living environment, the shimmering of gongs becomes material, evoking metallic limbs dripping green blood from rusty rivets, tortured faces struggling pointlessly to free themselves from amniotic sacks lined with steel, and strange, conscious buildings, both anthropomorphised and industrialised, fornicating in cold, mechanical motion. Deep in the mix, there seem to be screams of the once-human, while, upon other listens, they are robbed of such a voice amidst sparse vistas of assibilation.

Later, we heard bird-like sounds, shrill, yet still metallic, produced from steel throats. A rise and fall, now gradually assembling dirty bricks of the harsh noise wall; then a crescendo of shrill screeching, cranes adjusting, power tools spinning, tortured cries rising just within range of hearing; and the noise wall eventually drops out to a looped electrical sample, almost like running water.

Voyage Obstrué De Rencontres Difformes offers sonic visions of a living Weird space located temporally or spatially elsewhere; or perhaps it is a glimpse of something much closer, here, now, and ever-present: the Weird, numinous world behind the thin veneer of mundane reality.

THE REVELATIONS OF WEIRDRONE

"The fifth angel poured out his bowl on the throne of the beast, and its kingdom was plunged into darkness. People gnawed their tongues in agony and cursed the God of heaven because of their pains and their sores, but they refused to repent of what they had done" (Revelation 16, 10-11, 'The Seven Bowls of God's Wrath')

Live: Gnaw Their Tongues, Dragged Into Sunlight, Venom Prison, *The Borderline*,   London;   12   February   2016

1   I stood amidst His leather-backed, sigil-coated servants, descending into the bowels of Old Londinium, where feather-soft hands of exquisite beauty begrudge admittance to cross the threshold, and overturn a fifth accursed vial to gush obsidian execrations over the Earth.

2   And I saw bastard throngs pass forth, imbibing the micturations of decadent cherubim in ritual libation, howling unholy blasphemy; and their mouths did eject pallid worms and utter morbid paeans to His name.

3   And I saw flaming, vessel-burst eyes in the murk, circuits crack-fucked and splintering, artery-wired doomboards patrolled by shadowed sentinels wielding gloom-axe and blastmallet; and the cavern was wrapped in aura of mishapen menace and the heady smog of pregnant hissing.

4   And I heard the dead repeated words of prophet-omens promise flesh-sores upon God's flock, broken by flames of scorch-bass; and – Behold! – did the blastbeat of the Beast beat cloven hooves in the metropolis.

5   And I heard the screams of the evisceration of angels; and I saw adepts leaking bloody-pulp-gushes from ears and mouths in reeking *oruta* gouts;

6   And I suffered amongst His suppurated prisoners, ears despoiled by the endless thunder of shit-rusted trumpets, orifices desecrated by the demented key of this sonata of sodomy, and the scratch of seraph-hair

bows on violins carved from the maggot-festered wood of the knowledge-tree, and further monotonous torments without name or end.

7   Here did God instigate His utmost wrathful punishment: for, out of protracted cacophony, came a respite of briefest, purest, most profound quiet…before returning in a hypothermia of cruelty.

8   And I amongst His animal-skinned disciples felt the inner sagging as amp-cavern-maw spewed forth faecal-bowel-pitches that affect sweet-unloosening and Doc-cloven cavorting in fetid excrement river *almayya* from which stench-coated, many-headed figures coalesce and perform putrid buggery in the *nukraya* crowd.

9   And I felt unfamiliar tongues speaking through my own, stories of monotonous, insatiable pain, *Haluna!* sphincters of gold, *Deywa!* the death of nature, *Qala!* and indescribable things; and I babbled *hiwia* a maelstrom of blackwhite blare such as *Galyuta! Gnuna! Koth! Archons! Sunn! Zatan Zira! Zatan Zira!*

10   And after these things, I was drawn from the brink of madness back into the commonplace world where I lived, forever displaced.

THE HAUNT *(continued from second cover)*

Weirdrone is Ur-tone.

Weirdrone is Skarl's primal drumming, stretched out to the cosmic time of the Aeon, lulling MANA *to sleep.*

Weirdrone offers impressions of sounds from the Weird space beyond.

Weirdrone is hearing secular voices speaking in tongues.

Weirdrone is Machen's "link between terror and ecstasy, that leads to the abyss".[liii]

Weirdrone is the ceaseless hum of Lovecraft's indifferent universe manifesting as horrific sonic intrusion.

Weirdrone is the emanation of Howard's Black Sunn-Stone.

Weirdrone is dark matter transmitted from the interstellar past.

Weirdrone is auditory biomechanics, a form-disrupting hybrid of grinding factory-flesh and cognizant machine-monotone.

Weirdrone is a continuity, sonorous and sublime, which reveals the numinosity hidden in plain sight by a mundane veneer surrounding us every day.

Weirdrone is a logical response to a world that is weird already: a clear reflection of a cracked reality.

Weirdrone is Eschatone.

Weirdrone ends when Skarl finally lays down his beaters.

Enter *MANA-YOOD-SUSHAI.*

Dr. Norman
Hexford
U.K.
2020

Endnotes

[i] See: Joseph Norman, '"Sounds Which Filled Me with an Indefinable Dread": The Cthulhu Mythopoeia of H. P. Lovecraft in "Extreme" Metal', in, *New Critical Essays on H.P. Lovecraft*, David Simmons, ed. (New York: Palgrave Macmillan, 2013).

[ii] Andrea Franzoni, 'Mysterium tremendum: Terror and ecstasy in the works of Arthur Machen', *Disputatio Philosophica*, 16.1 (2015). 159-168.

[iii] See: Owen Coggins, 'Drone Metal Mysticism', unpublished PhD thesis, The Open University, 2015.

[iv] Jacques Derrida, 'Interview with Jacques Lacan', in, Derek Attridge, ed. *Acts of Literature*, (London: Routledge, 1992) 52.

[v] Arthur Machen, *Hieroglyphics: A Note Upon Ecstasy in Literature* (New York, Mitchell, Kennerley, 1902) 91.

[vi] Arthur Machen, *The Great God Pan* (1894).

[vii] Franzoni, 'Mysterium tremendum: Terror and ecstasy in the works of Arthur Machen', 164.

[viii] Coggins, 'Drone Metal Mysticism', 116-117.

[ix] Coggins, 'Drone Metal Mysticism', 270-272.

[x] Franzoni, 'Mysterium tremendum: Terror and ecstasy in the works of Arthur Machen', 159.

[xi] Machen, *Hieroglyphics*. 131-132.

[xii] Erik Danielsson, in, Watain, *Opus Diaboli* (His Master's Noise 2012). Circa 43:40.

Available at: https://www.youtube.com/watch?v=EprFtWWOzio (Accessed 22/12/2016).

[xiii] Danielsson, *Opus Diaboli*.

[xiv] Danielsson, *Opus Diaboli*.

[xv] Coggins, 'Drone Metal Mysticism'.

[xvi] Arthur Machen, *The London Adventure; or The Art of Wandering* (Newport: Three Imposters, 1924; 2014), 64.

[xvii] Algernon Blackwood, in, *The Magic Mirror: Lost Supernatural and Mystery Stories*, Mike Ashley, ed. (New York: Sterling Publishing co. inc, 1989) 8.

[xviii] Blackwood, *The Magic Mirror*. 8.

[xix] H. P. Lovecraft, 'Supernatural Horror in Fiction'. Available at: http://www.hplovecraft.com/writings/texts/essays/shil.aspx (Accessed: 22/12/2016).

[xx] China Miéville, 'Weird Fiction', in *The Routledge Companion to Science Fiction*, Bould, Mark, *et al*, eds. (Oxon: Routledge, 2009). 510-517.

[xxi] Lord Dunsany, *The Gods of Pegana*, (1905).

[xxii] Dunsany, *The Gods of Pegana*.

[xxiii] Ronald Bogue, 'Violence in Three Shades of Metal: Death, Doom and Black', quoted in *Deleuze's Way: Essays in Transverse Ethics and Aesthetics* (Aldershot: Ashgate Publishing Ltd, 2012) 35-52. 98.

[xxiv] P. Fraisse, 'Les Structures Rhythmiques' (Paris: Erasme, 1956); H. Woodrow, 'Time Perception', in *A Handbook of Experimental Psychology*, S.S. Stevens (NY: Wiley, 1951); both quoted at

http://www.zeuxilogy.home.ro/media/manifesto.pdf (Accessed: 22/12/2016).

[xxv] Fraisse and Woodrow, in, Stevens, *A Handbook of Experimental Psychology*.

[xxvi] For an extended discussion of black metal in the album, see: Ben Prescott, 'The Sigil of the Sunn Amp Marks they Path', *Invisible Oranges*, 07/22/2016. Available At: http://www.invisibleoranges.com/the-sigil-of-the-sunn-amp-marks-thy-path/ Accessed on: 23/12/2016.

[xxvii] One really existing attempt to 'reproduce' the fictional grimoire created by H.P. Lovecraft. For more information, see the Wikipedia entry: https://en.wikipedia.org/wiki/Simon_Necronomicon (accessed 31/12/2016).

[xxviii] Robert Howard, 'The Black Stone', in, August Derleth, ed., *H.P. Lovecraft and Others: Tale of the Cthulhu Mythos* Vol. 1. (New York: Arkham House, 1971) 74.

[xxix] Howard, 'The Black Stone', 74.

[xxx] Howard, 'The Black Stone', 74.

[xxxi] Chris Jarocha-Ernst, 'Who was Worshipped at the Black Stone?', July 31, 2011 Available at: http://www.rci.rutgers.edu/~cje/mythos/BlackStone.html Last accessed 31/12/2016.

[xxxii] Sunn O))), *Black One* (Southern Lord 2005). Lyrics to 'Báthory Erzsébet', printed on inside record sleeve.

[xxxiii] Coggins, 'Drone Metal Mysticism', 178.

[xxxiv] Coggins, 'Drone Metal Mysticism', 178.

[xxxv] Coggins, 'Drone Metal Mysticism', 178.

[xxxvi] It should be noted that Maithunass' document is frequently taken offline and moved to different locations, and apparently kept anonymous using various proxy servers, TOR and VPNs.

[xxxvii] Maithunass claims to have met Crowley during the 1930s, and spent time with him in London. Allegedly the recordings included in *The Principles and Philosophies of Ur-Sonorpasm in Sex Magick* originate from Crowley's legendary 'Paris Incident' in 1913/14; I, however, have reason to suspect that they were lifted from mainstream pornography much more recently, and even that any links between the two figures are entirely invented.

[xxxviii] For instance, Maithunass once mentioned that he considers himself "the end result of an overactive imagination", even doubting "whether I am not in fact merely the fictional amalgamation of several really existing occult figures", and therefore his whole existence and philosophy should "not to be taken literally".

[xxxix] Personal correspondence. 12/3/2014. For a full transcript of the interview, please email me personally.

[xl] Personal correspondence. 2/11/2014.

[xli] Personal correspondence. 5/11/2014.

[xlii] Personal correspondence. 25/12/2014.

[xliii] Personal correspondence. 3/1/2015.

[xliv] Conchur O'Drona, 'From the Bogs of Aughiska: Interview', *Metal Ireland*, by Andy Cunnigham. Available at: http://www.metalireland.com/2011/04/03/from-the-bogs-of-aughiska-interview/ (Accessed: 22/12/2016).

[xlv] Conchur O'Drona, *Fractured: Four*, *Youtube* video, published 24/09/2015. Available at: https://www.youtube.com/watch?v=ji3Gb1aDqps&feature=youtu.be (accessed: 22/12/2016).

[xlvi] See lyrics published by through the official *Youtube* channel of the band's record label *Human Jigsaw*: https://www.youtube.com/watch?v=yXlB9HJPZaQ, which correspond with instructions located on the *Cave Atlas* website (http://www.caveatlas.com/systems/system.asp?ID=397&rated=false), possibly originating in a technical diving manual (https://swt.ie/) Both websites last accessed 2/1/2017.

[xlvii] Nuala McCann, 'Did Gollum get his name from a cave in the Irish Burren?', *BBC News*, 21/3/2013. Available at: http://www.bbc.co.uk/news/uk-northern-ireland-21859633 (Accessed 3/1/2017)

[xlviii] Danielsson, *Opus Diaboli*.

[xlix] 'Lustmord – Dark Matter', http://touchshop.org/product_info.php?products_id=787

[l] Lovecraft, 'Supernatural Horror in Fiction'.

[li] Saturn Form Essence *Facebook* page. Available at: https://www.facebook.com/saturnformessence/app/204974879526524/ (Accessed: 22/12/2016)

[lii] 'H.R. Giger's Mordor Series', *Alien Explorations* blog (n.d.). Available at: http://alienexplorations.blogspot.co.uk/1975/01/hr-gigers-mordor-series.html (Accessed: 29/12/2016.)

[liii] Franzoni, 'Mysterium tremendum: Terror and ecstasy in the works of Arthur Machen', 163.

ATTILA CSIHAR

Tell us about your initiation into Sunn O))), what was the invocation of this persona, the origin of this mask, of these masks?

It has been always some kind of mask since I've been in the band … from the first show I remember, when we first played in 2002 maybe, a small town in Austria. I think there were like seven people at a house show, it was really amazing and I made this kind of like shamanic, cultic mask like in makeup. They are an esoteric or magical artifact, that with the music, really promotes this just the creative and like the ceremonial atmosphere …bang your heads and costumes and certain props … if we were in jeans and a poncho, it would hard to see that happen! [LAUGHS] It's not that uncomfortable and it's not that demanding, I feel personally much more comfortable.

Initiation is, for me—I'm not part of any organization—so for me, is a pack of lies, and I think I've gotten initiated by certain magical events that happened that are actually … it has a lot obviously to do with esoterics and magics, but it's also very personal. So I think my initiation is this kind of thing that happens for itself and it comes from some other level or source or outer space or whatever we could call it. But certainly these masks or costumes kinda fill up with energy, so that the more that I use them they become more personal. More … more alive, somehow.

Definitely, it's more like yes of course everything is about the music, so all these things are supporting the music. So yeah, we view it as esoteric as far as the music takes us I think. At the same time since this kind of music requires or feels like it's better with you know like, we are thinking of what is the demand of the music itself, what fits the best to support the message of the music itself, and so on. So I think all this theatricality—which obviously looked theatrical—all these theatrical props for tours, eventually felt a little bit like magical and esoteric, because of the intent, the focus on "mind" as the vantage point. So I think music is half the creating of the art and half the magical ceremony, like a serious magical ceremony. But at the same time, to me, to feel about music, to feel about love, love of sound and love of the experience, love of your whole … opposite … in the audience, it's kinda like there are a lot of possible participants, and still the music is the most important thing between all these things.

You've called performance "an action to manifest the spirit," and said that you "fall into a trance"…

Yes definitely … to me, the first time I was ever on stage, a band when I was 15, called Tormentor, I was like, a literal kid … hanging out in this club with these guys that were, maybe only 18 or a little above but they seemed so much older than I … and being backstage, getting ready to go on stage the first time, I got this, like stage fever. I'm freaking out, trying to remember all the lyrics … but when I entered on stage, the moment I got on stage, it was immediately gone … and it turned into an ecstasy, kind of overwhelming, this feeling, this ecstasy, like a high level presence, some kind of energy … that kind of takes you and possesses you. I've always said, it is more like channelling a bit, like I go into a trance, and open my "channels," and of course, I'm still like in control, I'm still at the wheel so to speak, but at the same time I let this force, or energy or entities just come through, manifest and use my words … the other side of this type of the trance, with Mayhem, there is this very exotic, very shamanistic dancing cultic movement, a type of archaic emotion, a tension but also contemporary … very chaotic and dynamic, while with Sunn O))), it's more like a static, steady, something you'd call trance and meditation I mean, almost like you're sitting in one position, and if you learn to relax all the parts of your body, then you fall into this kind of trance that you can feel with Sunn O))), and I think it is hard *not* to feel it with Sunn O))), in fact. Just the music itself and the vibe, kind of moves ALL your body. I mean any form of music is magic, it is multidimensional, we don't just hear it, we feel it. The sound, already magical, goes through walls, your body, your cells, your brain cells. It resonates. It's all about rhythmics, like the nature, our nature, the dualistic nature, light and day everything circulates and changes, everything circulates in a rhythm, everything comes back in circles, everything is dancing. We are playing together, so we synchronize our inner clocks, and we synchronize our brains, and we focus down on the same stuff, which is of course a music-wide thing. I think, if you think of it a bit deeper, it already has a lot of magical elements, especially if you play music about certain things. You can make music about politics or anything, but if you play music and focus your mind down on these magical themes and these spiritual themes, the music, it really manifests, and it is a channel to communicate spiritual emotions. I remember when I was a kid, I didn't understand all the lyrics of the music I loved, but I could still sing it, I still loved it. I mean there is this trance, this aspect of something that is affecting our brain, that draws you into falling into this ecstasy from this rhythmic thing. In terms of sound some people compare us to this Indian raga music that puts you into this kind of meditation, which I understand, it is about the same kind of ride and harmony … these harmonics that can appear in the music, these harmonics that can really put you into a chill mood … I think this what we do, in a really technological way … as we are very serious about our gear, everything we use, all the amps, all the shit, all made before 1975, still it's like, we use this amplification, we amplify these ragas. I think in today's world, we maybe need these amplified ragas, because people's mind, so disturbed today, there is no peace, no silence, maybe it's good to have this "power meditation" music. So it kind of blows away your brain, whatever you think about, you're going to forget it at 120 decibels. It's kinda like washing out. So I can see the audience who I really really adore, and they come and they give so much energy and power and emotion back, we have a very solid audience

now, they know what they will have and what they want. It used to be before that a lot of people were really shocked at our shows, really confused even, but these days you have this more solid following, that adore the sound as we do, and I see people with closed eyes, raising their hands and their arms, almost like levitating in the sound almost in this certain kind of trance, and it's so beautiful. I talk to them afterwards and they describe it as like they had a long meditation, and it kind of like emptied them, inside, the sound, the vibe … this is

ticated level. Like Zen, it approaches this high harmonic, this transcendental level of simplicity, so not very simple at all in a way. It is sometimes like contemporary art, sometimes a song sounds like it is hundreds of years old ... maybe it is a bit egoistic to say so I would not say we are close to anything that is called Zen, but somehow there are some singularities, some corollaries to that form of minimalism and I think that is why it maybe has this effect on people. When talking to people after the shows, they are very very happy, and say things like they've been purified or something. Everyone has this different, but very similar, spiritual experience. I love to hear that, but I feel too that it is nothing more, and nothing less than that. I don't think it is dark, maybe it has dark aspects, this is kind of my trademark, but it is not even about death, but more about finding a balance ... finding some kind of harmony in your spirit ... hard to put in words.

There is a sort of urgent immobility ... maybe exemplified by the time you were inside the coffin.

Such an amazing experience, this is what I love about this band, we are not just a regular rock band ... I might call it like, power psychedelics, like psychedelic drone ... psychedelic, magical, spiritual elements brought together visually and audibly. ...

When I was in the coffin, that was a very amazing, very interesting experience, something that has become typical of this band. That is what I love about this band, because of the people that play in the band and because of the extraordinary sonic

why sometimes we say that Sunn O))) is about, is almost like, adoring, in an almost religious way, the amplifiers and the sound. And I think that comes through, and I keep hearing that most people have the same experience really, and that is very magical actually. And there is no ideology in it really, so it's very Zen. It's like minimalism in a maximal way. Sometimes I think that I am lucky to see some Zen temples in Japan, that somehow ... maybe it is strange to say, but Sunn O))) has something, like a simplicity, but at a very high level, a very sophis-

277

technology and intelligence level actually, amazes me, Stephen and Greg, their artistic abilities, somehow this all shows up in our music and in the band so we end up playing in these incredibly artistic spaces sometimes. This one was Banks Violette's art exhibition, we played music in one of his, around his sculptures, he made all the amplifiers into salt sculptures, and he made a black coffin, and i was singing from inside there. These interesting art exhibitions, in such new zones, and very interesting festivals so … of course we have a metal fanbase really, people that are listening to more experimental metal music that really love our music but at the same time, we sometimes end up in more contemporary artistic spaces. I really enjoy that, it really brings me so much new and interesting and inspiring elements into my life. This goes side by side with Mayhem because without Mayhem, I'd still love it of course, but the two bands together for me is really nice, because they are very different, but still about the same thing at some point. With Sunn O))), we've been through so much shit together but now we have entered this new harmonic place that shows in the live shows and in the music … we are more … in the last year two years maybe, we've managed to get more comfortable with the music and we are at a higher level of communication and artistic connection between the members … somehow it's more relaxed, we are more subdued, more assured, more comfortable with each other than ever, and this is a sign of harmony, a really good sign for Sunn O))), one that comes through at our shows, people feel that as well.

Sunn O))) is performing at the Della Masone Labyrinth in Parma this year …

Yesssssssss. [SILENCE]

[MORE SILENCE]

Best imaginable venue?

To me, for Sunn O))) … Egypt, or some great South American ruins, for sure … but this labyrinth is really, really amazing, a really nice step toward that honestly, because it has a pyramid, actually, in the centre … which, pyramids mean something very spiritual I think for everybody, whatever you define it, it's so ancient, we all have that shape in our minds, and in our genes so to say. So this is like the biggest labyrinth in the world. I saw some pictures from the sky, it's very big actually, and I saw pictures of the paths of the labyrinth. It's this really high bamboo bush, which makes like the fences, you know, so we cannot see through … it seems you can really get fucking lost in there man. I mean, people wandering around in there … I hope I find my way to the stage! (LAUGHS) But it has an inside like a yard or a space, like a square space in there, so people can stand there and watch the show.

And I really like the labyrinth, the symbolic imagery of getting lost … .in a way our mind is a labyrinth, so many tunnels, tunnels of thoughts we can end up in, end up in dead ends of thought, like that line of thoughts didn't work … so symbolically there is an intertwining between the labyrinth and our mind or spirit, it has this spiritual aspect, with this pyramid inside. Like a minor Egyptian pyramid, like one of the satellite pyramids which are like ... following the big ones. It's cool, I'm looking forward to it, it's one of the things I love about this band that we end up in these spaces. We played in another beautiful spot, in Toronto. In Canada. It was a big industrial, I think it was like the generator ... kind of a factory or something that supported energy, electricity for Toronto back in the day. It's famous because they shot the last scene of the first Terminator movie when the terminator got all fucked up under that pressure, that crushing press machine ... they shot something from Robocop there ... anyway it's a giant space, and they made it really cool for this festival. One time we played in Italy in a prison, like an old prison that wasn't working anymore ... man ... in this concrete room in the center of the prison, there were all these echoes ... it was also a ghost prison, it was really killer. I remember after the show, we were joking with the locks, and we managed to lock ourselves in one of the cells, had to get the guy with the big ring of keys and shit. It was pretty fucking funny but anyway it was a really interesting space, that's one of our trademarks, and I would like to do more weird spaces. I would love to play in some mines, or not mines maybe but under, in some caves, a big cave hole. It would be cool to play in front of a volcano ... everything like this, monoliths, is a fit for Sunn O))).

I mean this music is about the elements, the forces of nature, it's very a bombastic sphere. The last record was more like about the feminine aspect of energies but it's still the elements, which I was very very happy because I had ... it has been so long in my head, that I wanted to sing about her, sing about Kuan Yin or Kannon, sing about this aspect of nature, this not just human woman but in a sense ... this like, at every level complete personality.

These mountains, monoliths, huge stones you've spoken of, seem to be especially appropriate for expressing the heaviness, the deceleration, the gravity ...

Yeah … like the pyramids, man … in front of the pyramids … I would do anything to play there, with Sunn O))), in front, right in Giza … it's probably never gonna happen, even though I've read that it's actually possible to land that spot. … Baalbek in Lebanon, I would do anything to play there with Sunn O))) … actually there I recorded my first non-Sunn solo stuff, the other stuff, Void ov Voices. We need to release that, gonna release an album. Lebanon, actually a border zone like very close to Syria … wouldn't go there today … they are the biggest monoliths in the world in Baalbek, called the trilithon, the biggest in the world, and I went and I recorded right on top of it, a lot of stuff, just to feel the vibe, feel the space … because it's very experimental music so I wanted to record an experiment basically.

How did this fascination with monoliths begin? Are there stones, ruins, mountains where you are from in Hungary?

No, not really, we don't have much of that … it just became my interest maybe when I was 21, suddenly hit me … actually I was going to this technical college, electrical engineering and shit, at some point I remember looking at these structures, and thinking now this, *this* is high tech. Like, wait a minute … before, I just you know had the same knowledge as the average people think, like oh yea pyramids, they had slaves … they destroyed these rocks and each other, the pharoah buried himself and so on … but the more you study the more you realise nothing is true … no one has found a pharaoh in any pyramid, and all this shit … you learn how the

pharaohs actually were buried in this place called the Valley of the Kings, very far from the pyramids actually, like 1000km away, 600 miles at least … nevertheless, these structures are amazing. Whether slaves did them or not, one of the most beautiful things mankind has done. And also as I study more through the years—we are talking about like twenty five years since I've become interested—and I was lucky to visit some of these places, and it has always touched me magically, because I can feel … I can always feel like I'm getting more and more sure about it. We talk about these evolutions all the time, but on the other hand there are also strange downfalls, for instance like the Greeks could already calculate like the size of the earth, the length of the equator and things like that. Imagine, that's before Christ, hundreds of years before Christ … and hundreds of years after Christ, in the Middle Ages, you were still killed for such ideology in Europe, in the western world, absolutely persecuted for this ideology. So that to me shows that history knows all it is showing us, in every aspect this kind of evolution, just one example. If you just think about a few hundred years ago these were hard things to figure out … and we are talking about thousands of years before people had any books, barely had written carvings … but done in these mystical languages that I still don't really believe that they can read or understand, but I don't know, and really I don't care because these ruins, they can talk for themselves, and I think on some level they become personal. And most of these places, around Egypt, South America, central America, these so-called pyramid cultures … all these hieroglyphs and carvings, at least 70% of them is only magical beings … like you see people with wings, ghosts, doing something ritualistic, holding something ritualistic, always something about the ritual, chimeras all the time, they turn back and forth between half-animal and half-man, difficult to understand beautiful symbols in these perfect carvings, and you can see such signs … even the sphinx, which is supposed to be the oldest and largest sculpture ever man-made, below, beneath that sculpture I saw this kind of … these chambers, there is this granite structure and it was like, not only that they were all perfect polygons so you have to really have to have a system to match them and cut them together, i mean to make these polygon mosaics, and you look at the corner, it's not like you just fit two bricks at a corner … they cut this giant granite that kind of turns with the corner, they kind of bend it almost … I mean, for something, for someone to make that is fascinating, I mean technologically … I want to know *why* and *who* and if you look at Baalbek … who had the power, the power to move and lay these blocks of stones that weigh 900 tons each, like 900 cars in one piece, can you imagine that shit?! Even today it is difficult to do, and it's a big project that they'd have to plan … its so compressed, it's so massive, so compact … and prehistoric, before the Romans, because you can see clearly that the Roman settlement sat on top of these plateaus made of these huge blocks … it took them dozens of years apparently to move these blocks around, where there was not a river, not a road … who knows how those people could carry that shit man, just think of it, imagine it, for me that totally triggers my mind, that's when

I realise, it doesn't matter what you read in a book. You can certainly learn from that and it could be interesting, but if you sit there with the thing, in my case, it just blows my mind, it just fills my battery up, I can feel my batteries recharging. You know like for some people … they might go to the beach, I like the beach too, but for me my batteries just fill up in these places … and I feel the presence of magic and the beauty of it is that it's not a book, it's not a story, it's not like you have to believe it, it's there and you can touch it. Because it is magic itself there or something that is remaining of these magical experiments, so definitely the energy and these energies, I feel this presence, that maybe people can't measure yet … to some they don't exist, maybe some can't sense them, but you can't sense radio waves either and they are still there. But there is a certain … maybe to feel these magical energies or resonances one should also be on some kind of resonant level in the brain to be able connect these harmonies and frequencies, so to say. Because if we look at the world, or existence and life, it's kind of like a resonance, a dance of circulation. It's something…the whole thing is that I can actually feel this energy and it's just really really nice … which may be why they're popular places for people to visit … .if you just sit there and empty out your mind a little bit, relax and just feel it … I love it, I love these things … something that is very close to me.

COLLABORATORS AND CREDITS

Charlie Blake is currently visiting Senior Lecturer in Media Ethics and Digital Culture at the University of West London, United Kingdom, and Lecturer in Philosophy, Aesthetics and Synaesthetics for the Free University of Brighton. He is a founding and executive editor of Angelaki: Journal of the Theoretical Humanities and a composer and performer in the Manchester based post-industrial cabaret ensemble, Babyslave, who have recently released the two albums:Kill for Dada and Runt, on Valentine Records. He has co-edited theory collections such as: Shadows of Cruelty: Sadism, Masochism and the Philosophical Muse, Beyond Human: From Animality to Transhumanism, and Immanent Materialisms: Speculation and Critique, and has published variously on Blanchot & music, Deleuze & angelic materialism, Bataille & divine dissipation, hypostitional analysis, death & xenosonics, art, paranoia & parasite capitalism, the topology of serial killing, the secret history of the music of hell & the ecstasy of annihilation, and the greater politics of barnacles, bees and werewolves.

Owen Coggins researches noise, mysticism, violence and ambiguity in popular music cultures, with a particular interest in drones and metal. In addition to articles and chapters previously published on drone doom, black metal, gospel blues and industrial music, a book entitled Mysticism, Ritual and Religion in Drone Metal Music will be published by Bloomsbury Academic in 2018. Owen is currently Honorary Associate of the Religious Studies department at the Open University, and a researcher at music therapy charity Nordoff Robbins. He is trustee of Oaken Palace Records, a drone record label which is also a registered charity, raising money for the protection of endangered species.

Kim Cascone has a long history involving electronic music: he received his formal training in electronic music at the Berklee College of Music in the early 1970's, and in 1976 continued his studies with Dana McCurdy at the New School in New York City. After moving to San Francisco in the 1980's, and gaining experience as an electronic technician in the audio industry, Cascone worked with David Lynch as Assistant Music Editor on both "Twin Peaks" and "Wild at Heart." Cascone left the film industry in 1991 to concentrate on his company Silent Records, a label that he founded in 1986, transforming it into the U.S.'s premier ambient electronic music label. At the height of Silent's success in early 1996, he sold the company in order to pursue a career as a sound designer for Thomas Dolby's company Headspace. After a two year stint at Headspace he worked for Staccato Systems as the Director of Content where he oversaw sound design using algorithmic synthesis for video games. Since 2001 Kim has been touring Europe performing, conducting workshops and lecturing on post-digital aesthetics in sound art. Kim has released more than 40 albums of electronic music since 1984 and has recorded/performed with Merzbow, Keith Rowe, Tony Conrad, Scanner, John Tilbury, and Pauline Oliveros among others. Cascone is the founder of the .microsound list which focuses on post-digital music and laptop performance http://www.microsound.org and his writing has been published in Computer Music Journal (MIT Press), Artbyte, Soundcultures, Parachute Journal, Junk Jet, Geometer; he has guest edited and written for Contemporary Music Review and acts as an advisor to the journal "Interference" based in Dublin, Ireland. Kim is a citizen of both the USA and Italy and lives on the coast of California, south of San Francisco, with his wife Kathleen and son Cage.

283

Lamar Freeman is dissonance.

Phil Legard is senior lecturer in music technology and music production in the School of Film, Music and Performing Arts at Leeds Beckett University. His own compositional and musical work is invested in the use of active imagination and technological experimentation as complementary approaches. Phil's current research explores the use of inner journeys and symbolism in music-making, and he recently published a paper on this theme entitled The Bright Sound Behind the Sound in Interference, a multi-disciplinary journal for audio cultures. Between 2001 and 2013 he recorded as Xenis Emputae Travelling Band, and since 2014 he has been recording under his own name, as well as collaborating with Layla Legard as Hawthonn.

⋈∴Ø∴ only paints in Black.

Kristina Wolfe is a composer, electronic musician, maker, and multi-instrumentalist. Wolfe is of Danish and American heritage, and spent many of her formative years wandering through the forests of Mols Bjerge (near the city of Aarhus) in Denmark, listening to the sounds of space and place. This environment, rich with neolithic graves, stone markers, and ancient roadways, cultivated her imagination and creative focus on the spirits of the past, and has inspired her work and listening practices up to the present day. She has a BA in Music Technology from Florida International University, an MA in Digital Musics from Dartmouth College, and a PhD in Multimedia and Electronic Music Experiments from Brown University. She was a resident at Bang-On-A-Can Summer Festival at MASS MoCA in Western Massachusetts. She was also a finalist for the 2016 Viol Composition Competition (Viola da Gamba Society) and the 2014 Pauline Oliveros Prize (IAWM Search for New Music). She won first prize in the Villiers 2016 New Works Composition Competition and was also awarded a MATA commission. In 2017, her project VRAASP (using Virtual Reality and Archaeoacoustic Analysis to Study and exhibit Presence) was funded in a Marie Skłodowska-Curie Action (MCSA). Research will be carried out at the University of Huddersfield from 2017-2019.

Hissen are a sound collective originally formed of six members who come from visual art backgrounds. They have performed in various galleries within Ireland including The Lexicon and IMMA (Irish Museum of Modern Art).

Eyvind Kang is a violinist that has performed with many artists, including Sunn O))) and Mike Patton.
http://conversations.e-flux.com/t/superconversations-day-44-eyvind-kang-responds-to-kader-attia-the-loop/2003
http://ipecac.com/artists.php/eyvind_kang
https://eyvindkang.bandcamp.com/

James Harris is a brain piloting a body it does not remember acquiring, which it uses to stare incessantly into mirrors, to write intentionally confusing obscurantist nonsense, to transcribe voices no one else can hear, and to contribute to such publications as Mors Mystica: Black Metal Theory Symposium IV (Schism 2015), Trippin' Spriggan (Psypress UK 2015), and Damned Facts: Fortean Approaches to the Study of Religion and the Paranormal (Aporetic 2016).

Drone Box probably exists.

J.-P. Caron writes theory and plays noise in several underground projects in Brazil and abroad. He also teaches philosophy at the UFRJ- Rio de Janeiro, and directs, with other artists, the label Seminal Records.
https://soundcloud.com/j-p-caron
https://seminalrecords.bandcamp.com/

Marcus Newstead plays guitar for Fister: fisterdoom.com

Garrett Strickland does Unwin-Dunraven Literary Ecclesia.

Adam Lovasz and Mark Horvath are philosophers and independent researchers based in Budapest. They are co-founders of Absentology Collective, a center for postmodern and speculative realist theory. They have published numerous books and essays in multiple languages. Adam's latest book, entitled The System of Absentology in Ontological Philosophy, appeared in November 2016. His areas of interest include phenomenology, ontology, as well as philosophies of the body. Adam has also published essays and short stories in numerous journals, including Balkon, Helios Quarterly, Hysteria, Vestiges and Philosophical Views/Filozofski Pogledi. Mark's research interests include postmodernism, virtuality, pessimism in philosophy, finitude and Baudrillard's philosophy. Also he has an intense interest in Bataille's writings and Bataillean social theory. Mark has presented at a number of conferences on several topics, among others actor-network- theory (ANT), negative queer theory, post-anthropocentrism and Accelerationism. In addition, Mark has co-written, along with Adam the first Hungarian-language book on the topic of social acceleration and Accelerationism. In March 2016, Mark published his first philosophy book also co-written with Adam, entitled The Isle of Lazaretto, released on Schism.

MOUTH is Edia Connole and Scott Wilson, black metal theorists and co-authors of The Georges Bataille Cookbook (Schism, forthcoming). mmmouth.wordpress.com

Gary J Shipley lives in the UK. He has two books forthcoming in 2017: Warewolff! (Hexus Press) and The Unyielding (Eraserhead Press). More details can be found at Thek Prosthetics.

Steven Shakespeare is Senior Lecturer in Philosophy at Liverpool Hope University. He is a co-facilitator of The Association for Continental Philosophy of Religion. He has published work on Kierkegaard, Derrida, black metal theory and other issues in contemporary philosophy of religion and theology. His most recent book is Kierkegaard and the Refusal of Transcendence (Palgrave Macmillan, 2015).

Attila Csihar is the vocalist for Sunn O))), Mayhem, and Void ov Voices. Thanks to Lauren Barley from Rarely Unable and Aaron Pickford from the Sludgelord.
https://sunn.bandcamp.com/
https://www.thetruemayhem.com/

Matt Bryan //Attila art page 279// is an artist from St. Louis, known for the Rager Review, a column on the Metal Injection site in which he reviews metal shows in comic form.
http://www.metalinjection.net/category/photos/the-rager-review
https://www.facebook.com/ragerstudios/

Jason Wilkins //Photography pages 147 & 201// wields a long beard and a warhammer.

Kelsey Baker //pages 283-289// pretends she's not alive and rides a totem pack of wolves to her living palace where the haunts can see your somnolent reflection.

Cover and Title Art: Virginia Barratt, Katherine Foyle, James Harris
https://virginiabarratt.net/
http://katherinefoyle.tumblr.com/
voidfrontpress.org

Made in United States
North Haven, CT
08 April 2023

35194406R00161